475
L14a   64962

DATE DUE			
Mar 9 '81			

GAYLORD M-2   PRINTED IN U.S.A.

ABSTRACT
SYNTAX
AND
LATIN
COMPLEMENTATION

ABSTRACT
SYNTAX
AND
LATIN
COMPLEMENTATION

ROBIN T. LAKOFF

RESEARCH MONOGRAPH NO. 49
THE M.I.T. PRESS
CAMBRIDGE, MASSACHUSETTS,
AND LONDON, ENGLAND

Foreword

This is the forty-ninth volume in the M.I.T. Research Monograph Series published by The M.I.T. Press. The objective of this series is to contribute to the professional literature a number of significant pieces of research, larger in scope than journal articles but normally less ambitious than finished books. We believe that such studies deserve a wider circulation than can be accomplished by informal channels, and we hope that this form of publication will make them readily accessible to research organizations, libraries, and independent workers.

HOWARD W. JOHNSON

Acknowledgment

I should like to express my gratitude for the financial and moral support given me in the preparation of this thesis by the American Association of University Women, under the Ellen C. Sabin Fellowship for the year 1966–1967.

In the course of thinking about and writing about Latin grammar, over several years, I have benefited greatly from discussion with a number of people and from their criticism of earlier drafts of this thesis, as a whole or in part. I should particularly like to thank Dwight Bolinger, Morris Halle, Paul Kiparsky, and John R. Ross for their advice and comments.

My deepest gratitude is due my thesis advisor, Susumu Kuno. His patience with unreadable earlier drafts of this work has been heroic, and his suggestions have been invaluable to me. Every page of this thesis has been shaped by his criticisms. All errors remaining are, of course, my own.

I should also like to thank my husband, George Lakoff, for aid and comfort above and beyond the vows of matrimony. His suggestions and comments have directly shaped this thesis; his development of transformational theory is what makes such a work possible. He has lived for a year on hamburgers and TV dinners, suffering along with me the day-to-day crises of thesis writing. To him, a double portion of Peking Duck.

ROBIN T. LAKOFF

Cambridge, Massachusetts
February 1968

Abbreviations of Latin Authors and Texts Cited in This Work

Caes. = C. Julius Caesar
    B. C. = *Bellum Civile*
    B. G. = *Bellum Gallicum*

Cat. = C. Valerius Catullus

Cato = M. Porcius Cato (Maior)
    R. R. = *de Re Rustica*

Cic. = M. Tullius Cicero

Ac.	= *Academica*
Att.	= *ad Atticum*
Brut.	= *Brutus de Claris Oratoribus*
in Caec.	= *Divinatio in Caecilium*
Cael.	= *pro Caelio*
Cat.	= *in Catilinam*
Clu.	= *pro Cluentio*
Deiot.	= *pro Deiotaro*
Div.	= *de Divinatione*
Fam.	= *ad Familiares*
Fin.	= *de Finibus*
Flacc.	= *pro Flacco*

Lael.	= *Laelius de Amicitia*
de Leg. Ag.	= *de lege Agraria*
Manil.	= *pro lege Manilia*
Mil.	= *pro Milone*
Mur.	= *pro Murena*
N. D.	= *de Natura Deorum*
Off.	= *de Officiis*
de Or.	= *de Oratore*
Phil.	= *Philippicae*
Planc.	= *pro Plancio*
Quinct.	= *pro Quinctio*
Q. Fr.	= *ad Quintum Fratrem*
Rab. Post.	= *pro Rabirio Postumo*
Rep.	= *de Re Publica*
Rosc. Am.	= *pro Roscio Amerino*
Sen.	= *Cato Maior de Senectute*
Sest.	= *pto Sestio*
Sull.	= *pro Sulla*
Tusc.	= *Tusculanae Disputationes*
Verr.	= *in Verrem*

Hor. = Q. Horatius Flaccus
    Ep. = *Epistles*
    Od. = *Odes*
    S.   = *Satires*

Mart. = M. Valerius Martialis

Ov. = P. Ovidius Naso
    A. A. = *Ars Amatoria*
    F.   = *Fasti*
    Met. = *Metamorphoses*
    Trist. = *Tristia*

Petr. = T. Petronius (Arbiter)

Pl. = T. Maccius Plautus
    Am.   = *Amphitruo*
    Asin. = *Asinaria*
    Aul.   = *Aulularia*
    Bacch. = *Bacchides*
    Capt. = *Captivi*
    Cas.   = *Casina*
    Men.   = *Menaechmi*
    Merc. = *Mercator*
    Mil.   = *Miles Gloriosus*

Poen. = *Poenulus*
Ps.   = *Pseudolus*
Rud.   = *Rudens*
Trin. = *Trinummus*
Truc. = *Truculentus*

Plin. = C. Plinius Secundus (Maior)
   H. N. = *Historia Naturalis*

Quint. = M. Fabius Quintilianus

Sal. = C. Sallustius Crispus
   Cat. = *Catilina*

Suet. = C. Suetonius Tranquillus
   Aug. = *Augustus*

Tac. = Cornelius Tacitus
   H. = *Historiae*

Ter. = P. Terentius Afer
   And. = *Andria*
   Eun. = *Eunuchus*
   Hec. = *Hecyra*
   H. T. = *Heauton Timorumenos*

Verg. = P. Vergilius Maro
   Aen. = *Aeneid*

Contents

xi

1. Introduction

The Latin language has been studied probably for a longer uninterrupted period of time, and by more people, than has any other language. Because of its dominance of the intellectual and religious life of Europe over a long period even after it had ceased to be spoken, its grammar has aroused more curiosity than that of any other language. During the Middle Ages, virtually all of the grammatical work done in the West —including work on the nature of language in general—was based on Latin. For this reason an examination of the syntax of Latin will answer some of the questions that have intrigued scholars most.

Moreover, Latin is in a unique position with regard to relationships among languages. As one of the oldest attested Indo-European languages it displays traits present in Greek and Sanskrit but absent from the modern languages of the same family. This makes it especially valuable in studies of various complex grammatical phenomena— cases, moods, and the like—that we find important in the ancient languages but subordinate or altogether missing in more modern ones. More than this, however, Latin is valuable because of its descendants, the Romance languages. These languages superficially resemble English more than they do Latin, leaving aside vocabulary and morphological details. But Romance is directly descended from Latin. This apparent contradiction has puzzled all scholars who have sought to deal with the relationship between Latin, the Romance languages, and other related modern Indo-European languages. A close study of certain

1

syntactic features of Latin may provide us with clues as to the extent of the disparity between Latin and Romance and as to how this disparity arose. None of the languages as old as Latin has such a body of daughter languages, nor has any of them descendants whose written history goes back as far as does that of Romance. We have a very rich supply of data from classical Latin itself—richer than that of any other ancient language—and plentiful material covering most of the intervening stages between Latin and the modern Romance languages. A large and continuing supply of data is vital both for synchronic study of a language at one point in time—as, for example, a study of Ciceronian Latin—and for diachronic work attempting to account for the changes observed in a language over a period of time—such as a study of the differences between Ciceronian Latin and modern Spanish. In the case of Latin we must also constantly bear in mind that classical Latin was, in fact, probably never a spoken language. The plays of Plautus, written about 200 B.C., are written in a language that is demonstrably closer to the language of Petronius, who wrote about A.D. 50, and also to modern Romance languages than it is to the language of Cicero and Caesar. In our work on Latin we are fortunate that there is preserved a small and inadequate, but nonetheless extant, body of this spoken language, Vulgar Latin—from Plautus through the beginnings of Romance—side by side with writings in the classical language.

For these reasons, a study of Latin syntax can yield valuable information in a number of areas that we could not hope to touch in a study of a modern language, or, for that matter, of any other ancient language.

In his work on English, the linguist can always ask himself, as a native speaker, whether a certain sentence is grammatical or not. If he asks several speakers of English, he can generally expect to find reasonable agreement. But for work in Latin there are no native speakers to test sentences on. Yet the linguist is constantly faced with the need to determine the grammaticality of sentences that have never been used before. The reason for this is that in any language there is a potentially infinite number of sentences. In the majority of cases, a native speaker can accurately distinguish between those that are grammatical and those that are not, though they are all new to him. For example, it is reasonable to suppose that the reader of this page has never before seen any of the sentences on it. Yet he will accept all of them as grammatical sentences of English. But he will reject another sentence, equally new to him, as ungrammatical: *John ate that the apple was red.* (An asterisk [*] will be used throughout this work to indicate an ungrammatical sentence [as opposed to the philological use of * to designate an unattested form].) Also, most native speakers can pinpoint the source of the difficulty in this ungrammatical sentence; it concerns the way *ate* is used rather than, for example, the fact that the subject of *ate* is *John*. We need these judgments and will have more to say later about their significance. It is, of course, a handicap not to have available native speakers to make such distinctions, often more delicate than this. But in many cases, even nonnative speakers can judge the grammaticality of a sentence in a language they know well. For example, hardly anyone with a good knowledge of Latin would doubt that (1a) is a grammatical sentence of Latin and that (1b) is not.

(1a) Puto Ciceronem Catilinam amare. 'I think that Cicero likes Cataline.'

(1b) *Puto ut Cicero Catilinam amet.

He can make this judgment, although neither of these sentences appears anywhere in the corpus of attested Latin sentences. Therefore we do not need attestation to certify that a sentence is grammatical.

In making the claim that the Latinist may rely on his own judgment rather than solely on attestation, we are rather sharply in opposition to the traditional view of philologists. But we should point out that even these philologists must contradict themselves in teaching Latin composition. They must, in their capacity as composition teachers, correct sentences they have never seen before. They must rely on their own knowledge of Latin, similar in some respects to that which the native speaker of Latin had. The traditional view stems from the fact that the Indo-Europeanists and philologists of the last two centuries, along with the Bloomfieldian descriptive linguists, viewed language as a finite organism. They felt that the way to analyze a language was to proceed from the smallest elements to the largest. The smallest elements are the sounds of a language, the individual phonemes. These are, of course, finite in number and easy to describe by simply cataloging. The next-smallest units were the roots and grammatical suffixes and the like—the morphemes. These, too, were finite in number and theoretically at least catalogable. The cataloging of these elements—called phonology, etymology, and morphology—was as far as any of the nineteenth- and early twentieth-century linguists got. They never attempted seriously to work on the sentence; they were kept busy with the smaller elements. Of course, they could never have adequately described the syntax of a language; they could never catalog all the possible sentences. Therefore, traditional works called "Syntax" (we might consider Hirt's work on Indo-European and the Ernout-Thomas *Syntaxe Latine* as examples) did not discuss the composition of the sentences, which is the subject of syntax, except as a collection of morphemes. But, as we shall see, such an approach left much to be desired.

The scholar who thinks of sentences as collections of discrete morphemes cannot account for a wide variety of facts, and he must distort others. For one thing, this method of dealing with the older Indo-European languages led to a preoccupation with the search for the origin of specific sentence types. There has been, for example, a great deal of debate on the origin of the indirect-statement type seen in *dico eum venire*. No Indo-Europeanist has asked how this is related to other structures in which sentences occur inside other sentences (*accidit quod venit, impero ei ut veniat*); their question is rather: How is this occurrence of the infinitive ending related to other occurrences of the infinitive ending?[1] What (they are then led to ask) was the function of the infinitive per se, in the proto-language, from which this complex use in conjunction with an accusative noun evolved? These grammarians view the infinitive as the noun of the verb, and their examinations of indirect statement phenomena start from this assumption. Therefore the main questions they ask are: What is the case of the infinitive—accusative, dative, or locative? How does it combine with the other noun in the accusative? Ernout and Thomas, in their *Syntaxe Latine* (1953, pp. 271f.), present a typical set of arguments:

> La proposition infinitive a été tout d'abord un cas de double accusatif du type *doceo pueros grammaticam*. La phrase *sentio eum venire* s'est analysée, d'une part, en *sentio eum*, "je l'aperçois," et, d'autre part, en *sentio venire*, "j'aperçois venir." Le nom à l'accusatif parut ensuite faire groupe avec l'infinitif: *sentio eum // venire* est alors *sentio // eum venire*. Et les latins d'époque historique, oubliant l'origine de cet accusatif, le considérent comme un veritable "sujet." La proposition infinitive est constituée des les premières textes. . . . Cependant, la langue parlée s'en détournait. Elle préférait la complétive avec *quod: gaudeo quod, dico quod* qui, en maintenant le sujet au nominatif et le verbe à un mode personnel, évitait toute ambiguité.

Ernout and Thomas, like most traditonal ph'lologists, say that an original structure in which accusative and infinitive were separate constituents—or, rather, found in separate sentences—was reinterpreted by later speakers as a structure in which accusative and infinitive were considered as a unit, that is, as parts of one constituent. Originally, according to Ernout and Thomas, such a sentence as *Sentio eum venire* was felt to be composed of two sentences. *Sentio eum* and *Sentio venire*. This would have been the case in the proto-language syn-chronically. Thus, for the hypothetical speaker of the hypothetical proto-language, the deep structure of *Sentio eum venire* (or rather, its proto-form) would consist of two sentences: the first containing a verb of perception with a human noun or pronoun as its direct object, 'I feel him,' and the second containing the same verb of perception (probably understood) and an infinitive, interpreted by Indo-European-ists generally as the "noun of the verb," an abstract noun equivalent in use to *beauty* or *arrival*: *I feel the coming*. It is highly questionable whether these sentences, *Sentio eum* and *Sentio venire*, were any more grammatical in Latin or proto-Indo-European (PIE) than are their translations in English. Moreover, if *Sentio eum venire* originally had the structure suggested and *Sentio quod venit* had a different structure (in the quotation given earlier, apparently assumed to be a single constituent), it is difficult to explain how one could be completely equivalent to the other in the vocabulary of speakers of Vulgar Latin; for such a speaker, *Dico quod venit* was identical in meaning to *Dico eum venire*. The claim the transformational linguist makes is quite different: he interprets both as single constituents of the larger sentence, both dominated by S and that S dominated by a noun phrase. Hence, the deep structures are identical, and the substitution of one for the other in one speaker's vocabulary can be readily explained. But the traditional view is still harder to understand in its assumption that in the proto-language one could not have complex sentences.[2] This feeling, either expressed or tacit, lies behind a great many of the ex-planations of complex sentences by parataxis, that is, the placing of two simple sentences side by side. Thus, traditionally, the sentence *Impero ut facias*, 'I order you to do it,' is derived (as by Bennett) from *Impero*: *Ut* (='just') *facias*. Also, *Gaudeo quod venit*, 'I'm glad that (='because') he is coming,' is derived from *Gaudeo quod* (where *quod* = 'it's that') *venit*, and as we have seen before, *Sentio eum venire* is derived from *Sentio eum* and *Sentio venire*, neither being a case of one sentence inside another. If this assumption were realistic and the proto-language actually could not embed sentences inside others, it could easily be shown that this proto-language had only a finite number of sentences, unlike any natural language known to linguistics. In no known language, no matter how primitive, is it impossible for a speaker to form complex sentences by some means or other, and it is incon-ceivable that, if PIE was a real language, as it clearly must have been (or, at least, as something relatively close to what we call PIE must have been), a speaker could not form complex sentences and therefore was unable to form an infinite number of sentences. To say otherwise is to say that PIE differed in the most fundamental way from any other natural language that we know, including Hittite and Homeric Greek. The tacit assumption of Ernout and Thomas, and of all other grammarians who explain complex sentences in terms of parataxis, is that PIE differs from its daughter languages, not in the way that Latin differs from English or English from Chinese, but in the way that a language whose sentences have a finite expressive power differs from one with sentences of indefinitely great expressive power. What would be required is a radical change between the two periods, PIE and the attested languages, in the nature of language itself, in the metatheory that dictates how a language differs, say, from animal noises, and what the rules of a language look like. That the nature of language should have changed is inconceivable.

When the word "inconceivable" is applied to a linguistic hypothesis, it is not being used loosely. The naïve speaker of a language may assume that nothing is inconceivable—that, for example, there are languages in which passive sentences are formed by reversing the order of all the words in the corresponding active sentence, in which the translation of the English nonsentence

(2a) *I devoured for John to do it

is grammatical, or in which the translation of

(2b) *The rock wanted to hit the farmer

is grammatical. If, in fact, such things were found in languages, we would be unjustified in calling anything of this kind "inconceivable." But, in fact, this is not the case. We know of no language in which sentence types are related through reversal of words alone. For example, where the translation of the sentence *John ate the salami sandwich* is passivized by being reversed, as *sandwich salami the ate John*. The ungrammatical sentences we gave before appear to be ungrammatical in any language into which one attempts to translate them. On the other hand, sentence (1b) *Puto ut Cicero Catilinam amet* is not inconceivable. In classical Latin it happened to be ungrammatical for *ut*-subjunctive to be used in a sentence with a verb of thinking. But this could have changed, and perhaps there were speakers of Latin who were able to say (1b). If we asked Cicero why he could not say (1b), he would answer, perhaps, "Educated people don't say *ut* after *puto*." On the other hand,

(3) Devoravi Marcum hoc facere

would be dealt with differently. Cicero might laugh or might say, "I don't know what that means." His reaction to the Latin sentence would be identical to our reaction to its English translation. Traditional pedagogical grammars recognize the distinction between conceivable bad sentences like (1b) and inconceivable ones like the sentences of (2). Sometimes they recognize it tacitly, by not discussing the second kind (since one would never find such a sentence in one's native language, one would never need to know how to translate it into the other language, and vice versa; hence, there is no need to teach people not to use it); or they mention the distinction briefly in passing, as do Allen and Greenough (p. 456):

> The peculiarity of the complementary infinitive construction is that no subject accusative is in general admissible or conceivable.

By "complementary infinitive" they mean infinitives occurring after words like *possum*, 'be able,' *debeo*, 'ought,' and the like. In their statement, they observe that *Possum Marcum hoc facere* is ungrammatical and inconceivable in Latin. This is like an English grammar pointing out that *I am able for John to go* is ungrammatical and inconceivable in English. Both the English and the Latin sentences are inconceivable because the concept of one person being capable of performing another person's actions makes no sense in any language. It might be possible to find a language where a word-for-word translation of such a sentence would be grammatical—but it would not express that impossible concept. Such a sentence might mean 'I am able to make John go' or 'I am able to allow John to go,' where the verb meaning 'make' or 'allow' is understood but not overtly expressed. This would be an exceptional situation, worthy of comment by a descriptive grammar. But the Latin or English situations are what one would expect. It is for this reason that most descriptive grammars do not mention that *I am able for John to go* is impossible in English and that *Possum Marcum hoc facere* is inconceivable in Latin.

We assume, then, that in order to know how to speak a language, one does not depend only on the grammar of that language; he also depends on an implicit, inborn knowledge of the nature of language, present in all human beings, a knowledge of what is conceivable in language and what is not. This general framework on which the specific grammars of languages is based is as much a part of the human baby's internal knowledge as is the instinct that causes him to cry when hungry. The English-speaking child must be taught that *I know for John to go* is ungrammatical. But if he learns Latin, he learns that the word-for-word translation of this sentence is grammatical. On the other hand, he knows because of his inborn knowledge of language that *I *devoured for John to go* is ungrammatical and, in fact, inconceivable in English. When he learns Latin, no one need tell him that the translation of this sentence is equally impossible in that language. The distinction between the two grammars, the one for all languages and the other for a specific language, is the difference between *universal*, or *general*, grammar and *particular* grammar. Allen and Greenough describe the distinction nicely (p. 163):

> ... fixed customs arose of combining words into what we now call Sentences. These customs are in part the result of general laws or modes of thought (logic), resulting from our habits of mind (*General Grammar*); and in part are what may be called By-laws, established by custom in a given language (*Particular Grammar*) and making what is called the Syntax of that language.

Allen and Greenough in this quotation express our distinction perfectly. The general grammar results from what is inborn, or "habits of mind," and here "mind" means "the human mind" rather than the mind of one national group or individual. The particular grammar consists of bylaws, aptly so called since laws are arbitrary and changeable, as are these rules. (Needless to say, only the rules of the particular grammar may change in time. We assume that the nature of general grammar, like the nature of the mind, does not change.) And finally, they rightly state that the grammar of a specific language, the syntactic portion in particular, contains only the language-specific rules, and not the rules of the general grammar. Thus, in a grammar of Latin it is stated that sentence (1a) is not grammatical; we need never state that **Marcus devoravit Publium hoc facere* is ungrammatical.

The native speaker can tell that certain types of sentences that are morphologically quite dissimilar are identical in meaning and are grammatically related. Conversely, he can tell that, although two sentences may be morphologically the same, they are different in meaning, are brought about by different grammatical rules, and are not interchangeable. As examples, we can look at the following Latin sentences:

(4a) Licet abeas.
(4b) Licet te abire. } 'You may go away.'

These two sentences are identical in meaning. There is no environment in which one can be found and the other cannot. Yet the first has a subordinate clause with a finite verb in the subjunctive, its subject, understood, in the nominative (*tu*). The second has a non-finite verb, and its subject (*te*) in the accusative. If we were analyzing these sentences morpheme by morpheme, we could say they were quite different grammatically. Yet, the native speaker knows they are grammatically related.

On the other hand, the sentence *Venias* may mean 'You may (perhaps) come,' 'You should come,' or 'May you come!' Morphologically, in Latin these three sentences are indistinguishable. An analysis using morphology could only consider them all variants of one type. Yet the native speaker knows they are distinct. We know he knows, because he can distinguish the first meaning from the other two in the negative: the negation of the first, 'You may (perhaps) not come,' is always *Non venias*; that of the other two, *Ne venias*. If the speaker can distinguish them in the negative, he knows they are of different origins.

Moreover, a strictly morphological approach is relatively unenlightening in studies of syntactic change in time. Thus, if the following sentences are assumed to be unrelated in Latin (the second certainly occurs in colloquial Latin in, or soon after, Cicero's time, and its existence is explained by bizarre circumlocutions by all modern grammarians), we have no way of explaining how the second developed into the usual Spanish construction (5c):

(5a) Dico Marcum venire.

(5b) Dico quod Marcus venit.

(5c) Digo que Marcos viene.

Nor can we explain the development of the imperative in Spanish from the subjunctive of Latin or the relationship in Spanish illustrated by these sentences:

(6a) Quiero ir. 'I want to go.'

(6b) Juan quiere ir. 'John wants to go.'

(6c) Quiero que Juan vaya. 'I want John to go.'

Traditional grammarians usually assume that (5a) and (5b) are unrelated sentence types, that (5c) developed from (5b), and that infinitival constructions comparable in some ways to (5a) continued to exist only marginally, as in

(7) Digo haber venido, 'I say that I went.'

They assume that the subjunctive and the imperative, like the indicative, are all coequal moods, each independent of the other, and that infinitival sentences are unrelated to sentences with subjunctives, just as they are unrelated to sentences with indicatives. If one follows this method of viewing syntax as a collection of unrelated parts of sentences and assumes further that sentence types are related if and only if they are morphologically similar, syntactic change becomes inexplicable. We cannot explain why change took place in one direction and not in another—why, that is, *Dico Marcum venire* became *Digo que Marcos viene* rather than *Digo que Marcos venga* (with the same meaning); these facts must be viewed as arbitrary. In (6a), (6b), and (6c) we find the infinitive occurring when the subjects of *querer* and *ir* are the same, and the subjunctive otherwise. We do not find such an alternation in Latin. If older methods of analysis were used, all that could be said is that a new grammatical construction arose in Spanish. We could not point to anything in Latin where it might have arisen. There would be no way of relating the constructions to one another or to their Latin ancestors. A theory of grammar that does not show the relationships among sentence types cannot give us a clue as to what may change, in what direction it may change, and precisely what the nature of a given change is. An adequate synchronic grammar of a language will provide us a basis from which to approach diachronic developments.

We want a grammatical theory that tells us how sentences are grammatically related to other sentences when they are and informs us that they are not grammatically related when they are not. Since we are dealing with sentences, we need a grammar that can describe an infinite set; sentences can, as was noted earlier, be embedded in other sentences, forming new ones. Theoretically, this can be done a very large number of times (in actual practice, because of limitations on understanding, we seldom find sentences produced by a very large number of embeddings). Thus we cannot point to any one sentence and call this the "longest sentence of English (or any language)." It follows from this that there are an infinite number of possible sentences in any language. If we want a grammar to describe all the sentences of a language, we require that the grammar account for an infinite number of sentences.

But the grammar itself must be finite in length. It is learned by a child in a short space of time and is stored in his brain, which has, presumably, a finite memory capacity.

A generative grammar, while consisting of a finite number of rules, is able to form an indefinite set of sentences. A transformational generative grammar is one that also shows what relationships hold in a language between the sentences so generated. It will relate an active sentence to its corresponding passive and will indicate the relationship between a sentence containing a subjunctive and one containing an infinitive. This study assumes knowledge of such grammars. If the reader is not familiar with this field, he is advised to consult one or several of the following references, in the order listed, which will probably provide an adequate introduction to transformational grammar: Postal (*1965*); Rosenbaum and Jacobs (1967); Chomsky (*1957*), (1962), (1965a), (*1965b*), (1966); and Lakoff and Ross (*forthcoming*). The references italicized are particularly valuable for the uninitiated or provide vital information.

Notes

1. The insistence of the Indo-Europeanists on asking this question has led them to some rather curious answers. Thus, it is generally believed, for morphological reasons, that the Latin active infinitive (*amare* < *-se*) is in origin an accusative, the passive (*amari* < *-sei*) a dative-locative. But it is very difficult to account for the difference between the active and the passive as a result of a case change, particularly a change between these two cases, which are both directional and the two closest cases in meaning. It is also hard to explain why the accusative infinitive and the dative-locative infinitive always appear in parallel positions in a sentence:

   Dico Marcum amare. 'I say that Marcus is in love.'
   Dico Marcum amari. 'I say that Marcus is loved.'

   The subject of the infinitive is in the accusative case in both sentences.

2. For example, it is generally assumed that all subordinate clauses are derived from separate sentences in the proto-language. This is true not only of sentential complements but of relative and adverbial clauses as well. The latter were interpreted as a type of relative clause: 'I left *when John came*' is interpreted, mainly for morphological reasons, as being derived from 'I left at some time, at which time John came.' While there is considerable syntactic justification for something close to this analysis, the use made of it by Indo-Europeanists, as well as their interpretation of the relative itself, is questionable. A clear example of this type of thinking is found in Woodcock (p. 98):

   When clauses became subordinate, it was felt that some connecting word was required to link them to the main clause. Such connecting words are the *subordinate conjunctions*. New words were not invented for this purpose, but old indefinite pronouns and adverbs were pressed into use. Their new function made them *relative*. Thus, *qui*, instead of meaning 'someone' (cf. *quis*, *qui*, in *si quis*, *si qui*), now meant '(someone) who'; *uti* and *ut*, instead of meaning 'somehow,' 'in some way,' now meant 'in *which* way,' or 'as.' Interrogative pronouns, adjectives and adverbs could perform their new function without any change of meaning.

   It was tacitly assumed that in the proto-language such clauses had not been subordinate (cf. Woodcock's first sentence quoted). They developed into subordinate clauses rather the way sentential complements did: from complete sentences in their own right. It is also never made clear just how the indefinite pronouns could have been pressed into use to become relatives. In a sentence like *I saw the boy who has green eyes*, the antecedent of *who* is not an indefinite *someone* at all; it is rather *boy*, and, in' fact, it is evident that *boy* is present in the underlying structure of the relative clause. There is probably some syntactic relationship between relatives and indefinites, to account for the frequent morphological similarities between the two. But what that is is not clear, and certainly it is not that the relative is derived from the indefinite.

2. The Structure of the Complement

2.1 Recursive Processes

In the previous chapter we stated that the number of sentences in a language was potentially infinite. This is so because sentences may be produced with other sentences inside them. This property of language, which enables sentences to be formed inside other sentences, is called *recursion*. By this device the phrase structure rules that produced the first sentence may be employed again to produce an embedded sentence, and so on.

The three recursive processes in language are conjunction, relativization, and complementation. All of these have been discussed at length in the literature of transformational grammar. The remainder of this work presumes a familiarity with the third of these processes; the other two play a subordinate role, if any, in our discussion. Therefore complementation will be discussed at some length in the following sections.

2.2 Sentential Complements

The result of the operation of complementation may be any one of several possibilities. To illustrate, all the italicized words in the sentences[1] (1a)–(1f) are complements of the main sentences:

(1a) It is possible *that John ate the egg foo yong.*

(1b)   I liked *for John to eat the egg foo yong.*

(1c)   I said *that the egg foo yong was cold.*

(1d)   I wanted *John to eat the egg foo yong,* but he ate the spareribs instead.

(1e)   I wanted *John to eat the egg foo yong but not the spareribs.*

(1f)   I said *that if John ate the egg foo yong, he would be sorry.*

Complements are sentences embedded in other sentences, as are relative clauses; but complements are embedded differently, under different conditions, and function differently both grammatically and semantically. For example, we can list the two sentences that underlie (1a):

(2a)   It is possible.

(2b)   John ate the egg foo yong.

And likewise, we can set up two sentences that underlie (1c):

(3a)   I said it.

(3b)   The egg foo yong was cold.

In neither of these cases is there any constraint on which nouns may occur in the embedded sentences. In both cases, however, the pronoun *it* is present in the higher sentence. This *it* appears in the surface structure of (1a) but not of (1c). We postulate its presence in all complement sentences, however. Its underlying presence in (1c) is suggested by various facts. For example, when (1c) is passivized, we get:

(4)   It was said by me that the egg foo yong was cold.

Although, as we said before, there are no identity constraints on the noun in complements, there are restrictions on the nature of the verb of the higher sentence. Thus, while (1a) is grammatical, (5a), with the same superficial structure of adjective-copulative verb in the higher sentence, is not:

(5a)   *It is magenta that John ate the egg foo yong.

And while (1c) is grammatical, a sentence containing one of many other verbs is not:

(5b)   *I ate that the egg foo yong was cold.

The verb must be one that can take an abstract noun as either its subject (for verbs that behave like *possible: be good, be mandatory, interest, concern, follow, entail,* and many others) or its object (for verbs like *say, think, imply, order, ask, want,* and many others). Embedded complement sentences function as noun phrases in sentences, either as subjects or direct objects of verbs. They may also function as subjects or objects of nouns that are nominalizations of verbs that take abstract subjects or objects. Thus, we find both of the following:

(6a)   I believed that John was a werewolf.

(6b)   My belief that John was a werewolf.

This is true also in the case of certain abstract nouns for which there are no corresponding actual verbs in the lexicon, such as

(7a)   My idea that Harry is the werewolf you are looking for is unable to be substantiated at this time

where there is no corresponding

(7b)   *I idea that Harry is the werewolf you are looking for ...

and in

(8a)   The fact that Ferdinand was wrong

where there is no

(8b)   *It facts that Ferdinand was wrong.

In the sentences of (6), (7), and (8), these complements may superficially appear identical to relative clauses formed on these nouns, as in these sentences:

(9a)   The belief that I have held for thirty years will never change.

(9b)   The idea that I formed about Mao's political beliefs is clearly right.

(9c)   The fact that I pointed out to Einstein in 1939 was important.

Although these appear identical in structure to the complements, they are not. This can easily be shown; similar structures can be conjoined:

(10a)   The fact that Ferdinand was wrong and Antoine was misguided.

But (8a) cannot be conjoined with (9c):

(10b)   *The fact that Ferdinand was wrong and I pointed out to Einstein ...

We have said that the complement in (1a) functioned as the subject of the main verb, and that of (1c) as the direct object, both alongside of the abstract pronoun *it*. We shall discuss and justify these assumptions further in the next section; but on the basis of them we can draw trees to represent the deep structures of the sentences (1a) and (1c), shown in diagrams (11a) and (11b).

(11a)   It is possible that John ate the egg foo yong.

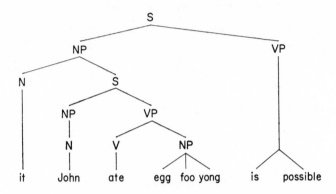

(11b)   I said that the egg foo yong was cold.

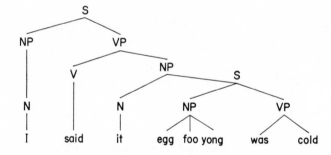

In these sentences the main sentence dominates the lower sentence; hence, complementation is a form of subordination. It is clear that the structure of a complement differs from that of a relative: the noun phrase, which in a relative sentence dominates itself, does not do so in a complement, in which noun phrase dominates a noun, always abstract, and a sentence.[2]

The word *that*, present in the surface structures (1a) and (1c), is not present in the deep structures represented by the trees (11a) and (11b). Likewise, if we were to draw the trees underlying (1b), (1d), and (1e), *to* would not be present. These words are introduced in the transformational component by rules that will be discussed in the next section. The remainder of this chapter will deal with the structure of the complement: restrictions in the deep structure as to which verbs can introduce a complement; the rules that change the deep structures like those of (11) into surface structures like those seen in the sentences of (1); the possible kinds of complements. In this chapter we shall be discussing the general theory of complementation, as developed by Rosenbaum and refined by Lakoff and Ross. In subsequent chapters we shall apply the general theory of complementation to structures we find in Latin.

2.3 Deep Structures

A sentence containing a complement is generated by using the same phrase structure rules necessary for generating any other kind of sentence, with one addition. The complement is an expansion of some noun phrase, either subject or object. Thus, the following set of rules will generate structures such as (11a) and (11b):

(12) 1. S → NP VP

    2. VP → V (NP)

and, to produce these structures, the one additional possible expansion:

    3. NP → N (S)

This rule is to be distinguished from another possible expansion of NP, the one that produces relative clauses (NP → NP S).

It is evident that not any verb can co-occur in a sentence with any noun. Some verbs occur only with animate noun subjects; others, with only abstract direct objects, and so on. Selectional restrictions such as these apply to complements as well. (For a discussion of selectional restrictions between nouns and verbs, see Chomsky, 1965a.) These selectional restrictions are part of the meaning of a verb; they will not change in time. If the verb *believe* changed so that it could take as direct object a concrete noun, it would no longer express the meaning it now expresses. Hence, it is likely that the selectional restrictions that determine whether a verb can occur with a complement subject or object are universal, since a meaning is universal.[3] Otherwise, translation from one language to another would be impossible. Therefore it appears likely that a verb which must take a subject complement in one language must also do so in any other language, and the same is true of verbs taking object complements.[4] Verbs taking subject complements seem to be intransitive, with one or two possible exceptions, such as *entail* (*John's having insulted Ludwig entailed Anita's divorcing Murgatroyd*). A transitive verb is marked as occurring in the environment before a NP (—— NP). If this environment is not present among the selectional restrictions, the verb is intransitive. In addition, the subject noun phrase after which a verb occurs is also indicated as NP ——. In both these cases NP is further specified as to what features it may contain. In this way we can represent the selectional restrictions of four verbs with respect to selection of NP subject and object as follows:

(13a) eat   (13b) magenta   (13c) believe   (13d) possible

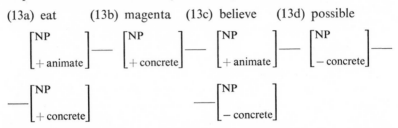

(If a noun has the feature [+ animate], it is necessarily also [+ concrete].) Examples (13c) and (13d) illustrate, respectively, a verb that must take an abstract noun phrase as direct object and a verb that must take an abstract noun phrase as subject. There are only two possibilities for these noun phrases. The noun may be abstract (*explosion, belief, idea*), or it may be followed by a sentence, that is, a complement. Hence, all the following are possible:

(14a)   I believed the report.

(14b)   Complete understanding of English grammar will be possible in twenty minutes.

(14c)   I believed that he had reported the truth.

(14d)   It is possible that you will eventually understand what I have just said.

But neither of the following, where the noun subject or object is concrete, is possible:

(15a)   *I believe the Empire State Building.[5]

(15b)   *The aardvark is possible on Mondays, Wednesdays, and alternate Fridays.

Nor is the following possible where the restriction that the subject or object NP must be concrete had not been met.

(16a) *I chewed his understanding.

(16b) *The conception Freud had of the world is undoubtedly magenta.

(16c) *I always chew it that John loved his mother.

(16d) *That General Blarf has won the battle is magenta.

We shall later discuss all of the following transformational rules that operate on deep structures of the correct form to produce complement-containing sentences:

Rule (1) Complementizer-Placement

Rule (2) Complementizer-Change

Rule (3) Equi-NP-Deletion

Rule (4) *It*-Substitution

Rule (5) Flip

Rule (6) Passivization

Rule (7) Extraposition

Rule (8) *It*-Deletion

Rule (9) Preposition-Deletion

Rule (10) *That*-Deletion

Rule (11) $\left.\begin{array}{l} For \\ Poss \end{array}\right\}$—Deletion

2.4 Complementizing Morphemes

If we know a verb is marked so that a complement can occur as its subject or object, we still do not know enough about this verb to use it correctly. For example, the following sentences all contain verbs that take complements as their direct objects, and all the following sentences contain complements as direct objects of the verbs. Yet not all these sentences are grammatical.

(17a) I said that John was a fool.

(17b) I want John to do that.

(17c) *I said for John to be a fool.

(17d) *I want that John does that.

A complementizer is a marker added to an embedded sentence indicating that this sentence was produced by the operation of Phrase Structure Rule (12) 3, given earlier. Only when that rule has applied are complementizers attached to the lower sentence. The sentences just given are examples of the use and distribution of two of the complementizers of English.

A complementizer has no meaning of its own. It is not generated in the deep structure but rather inserted by a transformational rule. As the preceding example sentences indicate, there are various complementizers in English, and different ones are grammatical in different sentences. Which complementizer is found in a particular sentence is governed by the verb of the main sentence. Most verbs can occur with only one complementizer. Some apparently occur with more than one. In certain cases, a verb can take any of two or more complementizers, usually with some difference in meaning. In this case the deep structure of the verb with one complementizer will probably be different from that of the same verb with another. For example, the meaning of *say* is different in the following two sentences; in the first, it means *tell, declare*, in the second, *order*:

(18a)   I said that you were coming.

(18b)   I said for you to come.

That *say* in (18b) is, in fact, a separate verb from *say* in (18a) can be shown from the fact that the latter behaves like a verb of mental state (*think, believe, declare*, etc.), while the second behaves like a verb of ordering. This is true both in regard to the complementizers possible (*say that, think that, declare that, order to, command to*) but also in certain restrictions that are found between the subjects of the higher and lower sentences in some verb classes. Verbs of ordering cannot have the subjects of the higher and lower sentences identical: **I order me to go.* But verbs of mental state can: *I said that I went.* Facts like these suggest that sentence (18a) is different in deep structure from (18b) and hence the verb *say* in (18a) differs from *say* in (18b) both in selectional restrictions (e.g., limitation of subjects) and in transformational rules which it undergoes (different complementizers). But for a few verbs, the deep structures of the verbs appear to be the same, and the meaning is not different, nor are the selectional restrictions:

(19a)   I believe that Millard Fillmore was President in 1732.

(19b)   I believe Millard Fillmore to have been President in 1732.

In this case, the verb *believe* can undergo one of the complementizer rules optionally. Since complementizers are attached to sentences by transformational rules, to be discussed later, the subcategorization features determining which complementizer is attached can be viewed as instructions indicating which rule or rules apply to the structure in question. Such rule features have been discussed by Lakoff (1965). They differ in a number of ways from selectional restrictions. These are language-particular, just as the transformational rules they refer to are language-specific. They can change in time: a verb that takes one complementizer in Latin may take another one in Spanish. In fact, the subcategorization features may differ from person to person synchronically within one language. For example, for some speakers of English both of the following sentences are grammatical; for others only one or the other.

(20a)   I like their eating ice cream with their fingers.

(20b)   I like for them to eat ice cream with their fingers.

This difference is governed by the fact that, for some people, *like* is subcategorized in one way; that is, it has among its features one specifying that it is to undergo that complementizer-placement rule which attaches possessive-*ing* to the lower sentence; for the other group of people, the only possible complementizer-placement rule for this verb is *for-to* placement. For a third group, either is acceptable; both features are present in the verb's complex symbol.

There are a number of different complementizers in English. A few of these are quite common. Others are found very seldom, often in just a few verbs or classes of verbs. This sort of distribution is not extraordinary: a similar situation exists in Latin, but the distribution of common and uncommon complementizers is not identical to that of English. For example, the one in Latin corresponding to *that* plus the finite verb, very common in English, is comparatively rare in Latin. More will be said about Latin complementizers in the next chapter.

We have given examples of a complementizer that changes the underlying lower sentence merely by attaching *that* before it. It does not change the form of the verb, and if sequence-of-tense rules have operated to give a past tense in the verb of the lower sentence, this complementizer does not interfere with the process. Because this complementizer appears to have the least effect of all the complementizers on the structure of the embedded sentence, it is tentatively suggested that it should be considered basic.[6] That is, if we adopt this suggestion, if the structure N S has been generated in the phrase structure, the rule that inserts *that* before S will automatically apply. This rule would then be called complementizer-placement, or *that*-attachment. This yields intermediate structures like the following:

(21a)   I want that John goes + future.

(21b)   I say that Harry be + present a dirty fighter.

(21c)   I instructed that Elizabeth bring + past me the gooseberry tart.

If no other rules applied to this output, the lower verbs of the three preceding sentences would, in the morphological component, be changed to *goes, is, brought*. But in the first and third examples, further rules apply, the result of which is the deletion of the tense suffixes. These rules attach the other complementizers if the subcategorization features on the main verb have indicated that these further rules are to apply. Every verb that is preceded by a subject or followed by an object that is a sentence must obligatorily undergo complementizer-placement. The fact that *say* undergoes this rule need not be separately listed among its rule features; but the fact that *instruct* obligatorily takes *for-to* must be listed among them. This interpretation of complementation makes the claim that there are two possible ways to produce an ungrammatical structure if the phrase structure has generated N S. One is for complementizer-placement not to apply at all. In this case, of course, none of the further rules could apply. The other is for this rule to apply, but for one or more later complementation rules not to apply in an environment in which their application is obligatory; or, alternatively, for these other rules to apply in an environment where they are inapplicable. But, in fact, when we look at actual possibilities for exceptions to these rules in language, the first case is inconceivable. We can account for this case if we use this interpretation of complementizer-placement in conjunction with the concept of rule government developed by Lakoff (1965).

It is an accepted fact about language that there are exceptions to certain syntactic rules in every language. For example, in English passivization applies to most verbs, but not to a few, which are therefore considered exceptional. These verbs do not form a natural class on the basis of meaning or any other criterion; thus we find the following:

(22a)   John owns three dogs.

(22b)   John has three dogs.

(22c)   Three dogs are owned by John.

(22d)   *Three dogs are had by John.

On the other hand, a rule such as the one that changes that-finite complementizer to *for-to* applies only to certain meaning-classes of verbs:
verbs of wishing, verbs of ordering, but not verbs of communicating.
But exceptions may occur within these classes: a verb of ordering might,
for example, take *that*-non-finite or a verb of communicating *for-to*.
Rules such as passivization and complementizer-change are governed:
they depend on the presence of a specific verb in the deep structure in
order to apply. But it is possible that some verbs are marked to indicate
that, although they are contained in structures that meet the structural
description of the rule in question, this rule does not apply if they are
present.

For other rules, however, there are no exceptions possible. Such a rule
is reflexivization. This rule does not refer to any particular verb or class
of verbs, and it is inconceivable that it should fail to apply to a structure
meeting its structural description because the verb in the tree was
marked as not undergoing reflexivization. This is an example of an
ungoverned rule.

As was stated earlier, complementizer-change is governed, but
complementizer-placement is ungoverned. Complementizer-placement
applies whenever its SD is met, that is, when the structure N S is present
in the tree. No exception to this rule is possible. Hence, the theoretical
chance for three possible types of violations is never possible in fact.
But each part of the complementizer-changing rule (to be discussed later
in this section) is marked as applying only to certain classes of verbs,
according to meaning. For certain classes, the application of no part of
this rule is normal: such verbs will regularly occur with *that*-finite complementizers. For others, one or another of the four parts of the
complementizer-changing rule applies regularly. Sometimes one part of
the rule applies optionally. For example, verbs expressing communication of information normally take *that*-finite complementizers in
English. This category includes, for example, *say, tell, mention, suggest,
declare*, and many others.

(23a)   I said that John left the house.

(23b)   I mentioned that John left the house.

(23c)   I declared that John left the house.

For this class, then, there is a redundancy rule in the lexicon specifying
that if the verb in question is unmarked, it will not undergo any of the
complementizer-changing rules. Thus we have the following:

(24a)   *I said John's leaving.

(24b)   *I said for John to leave.

(24c)   *I said that John leave.

(24d)   *I said how John left.

The effect of this redundancy rule is to say that, if any of these verbs can undergo any of the complementizer-changing rules, the verb is marked for that rule. (On the contrary, for verbs of ordering, for example, where *for-to* is regular, a verb of this class undergoing *for-to* complementizer change is unmarked.) Now, although the preceding examples with *say* were ungrammatical, the following is grammatical:

(25)   I mentioned John's leaving the house.

Mention, then, can occur with the possessive-*ing* complementizer. Since it is one of these verbs of communicating, it must be marked for application of the possessive-*ing* complementizer-change. The verbs *say* and *mention* are represented in the lexicon, with respect to the complement rules, as follows:

(26)   *Say*   *Mention*
         $V_{communication}$ $V_{communication}$

         u *for-to*   u *for-to*

         u poss-*ing*   m poss-*ing*

         u *that*-C   u *that*-C

         u *how*-finite   u *how*-finite

In this way, the two concepts of rule government and markedness, used in conjunction, can explain how it is that we find some exceptions to some of our rules, and yet not all the exceptions theoretically possible, and how it is that some rules never have exceptions at all.

If no complementizer-changing rules apply, the final form of the sentence contains *that* plus a finite verb. But frequently one or another of the complementizer-changing rules is applied, to produce sentences like the following:

(27a)   I like it *for* Mary *to* beat the Marquis with that dish towel.

(27b)   I want you *to* tell him what I think of you.

(27c)   I expect *for* it *to* rain any second.

(27d)   I can't countenance John'*s* leav*ing* home every day.

(27e)   Selma doesn't like them do*ing* that.

(27f)   I insisted *that* he lea*ve* that raven alone.

(27g)   This college requires it of every classicist *that* he pas*s* an oral examination in Old High Umbrian before his second semester of study.

These are examples of the chief additional complementizers found in English.[7] In the sentences (27a)–(27e) the complementizer-changing rule has altered both *that* which preceded the S and the finite verb of that S. In (27a)–(27c) *for* has replaced *that, to* has been inserted before the verb, and the verb is no longer finite: it has no tense or person marker on it. In (27b) *for* is not present. The deletion of *for* occurs by a rule to be discussed later. In (27d)–(27e) a possessive ending (*'s*) has replaced *that*, and the ending *-ing* has been added to the verb, which is also no longer finite. In the last two cases *that* remains unchanged; but the verb is no longer finite, and person and tense no longer appear in the surface structure. (We know they must be present in the deep structure; thus, we know that a verb in the past tense underlies *leave* in (27f) and that its subject is third person singular, and therefore it would normally end in *-s*.)

The first rule we are discussing, complementizer-placement, operates obligatorily in these environments.

Rule (1) Complementizer-Placement

$$X_1 - it - \# - S - \# - X_2 \rightarrow 1 - 2 - \emptyset - that + 4 - \emptyset - 6$$
$$1 \quad 2 \quad 3 \quad 4 \quad 5 \quad 6$$

It is at present an open question as to how *that* is adjoined to S. There are two possibilities that are equally likely. Perhaps *that* is adjoined by a convention suggested by Chomsky (in the spring of 1966), the effect of which is that a new node is created above the S node by the adjunction, which is also labeled S. In this interpretation, the surface structure of *I said that he was here* is as shown in diagram (28).

Alternatively, *that* may be adjoined below S, rather than above it, to become a sister of NP and VP of the lower sentence. If this is the case, the resulting surface structure of the sentence just given is represented by diagram (29).

At present, there are no arguments supporting either of these possibilities over the other. Rule (1) removed the sentence boundaries present in the deep structure around the lower sentence. If a sentence appears in the surface structure with the boundaries still present, it is automatically ungrammatical. Hence, this rule must have applied. At this point

(28)

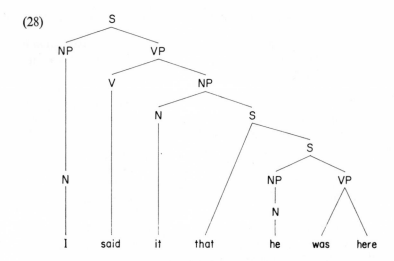

in the derivation we have structures like those of the sentences of (21). If the verb of the higher sentence is marked as having to undergo any of the complementizer-changing rules, one of these then applies.

(29)

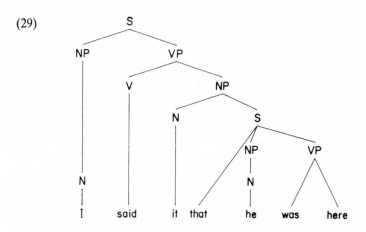

Rule (2) Complementizer-Change

(a) *for-to*
$$X_1 - that - NP - VP - X_2 \rightarrow 1 - \emptyset - for + 3 - to + 4 - 5$$
$$1 \quad\ \ 2 \quad\ \ 3 \quad\ \ 4 \quad\ \ 5$$

This rule erases *that*, and it adjoins *for* to the noun phrase and *to* to the verb phrase of the lower sentence. The choice of adjunction type for Rule (1) does not affect this rule or the subsequent complementizer-changing rules, because these complementizers are adjoined differently in any case. Diagram (30) is the structure of the sentence *I like it for*

(30)

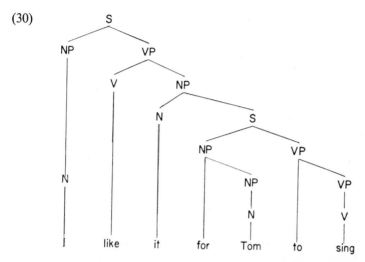

Tom to sing after (2a) has applied. *For Tom* is an NP, and *for* is part of NP. This accords with the fact that in many languages the complementizer corresponding to *for* appears as a case attached to all nouns that are part of this NP. Likewise, *to* is part of the VP, and appears in many languages as an infinitive ending that is morphologically part of the verb.

Rule (2) Complementizer-Change

(b) possessive-*ing*

$$X_1 - that - NP - VP - X_2 \rightarrow 1 - \emptyset - poss. + 3 - ing + 4 - 5$$
$$1 \quad 2 \quad 3 \quad 4 \quad 5$$

Later rules attach poss. after NP, as '*s*, and attach *ing* to the right of the verb. Otherwise, the surface structure of a sentence to which Rule (2b) has applied is identical to (30). In both these complementizers, as was mentioned before, the verb is non-finite: it has no tense or person-number endings. The difference between *to* and *-ing* in this connection is merely that *-ing* undergoes an additional rule in English attaching it morphologically to the stem of the non-finite verb, while *to* remains independent. This distinction is paralleled in the first part of the complementizers: *for* in English remains an independent word, while possessive eventually becomes a morphological and inseparable suffix of the noun. In other languages complementizers which appear to correspond morphologically to both *to* and *-ing* are added to the stem and are inseparable.[8]

We can deal with the third of the frequently found complementizers in a similar fashion. In this case, *that* is not changed, and however we have adjoined it in the first place, *that* remains adjoined that way. There is no word parallel to *to* or *-ing*: nothing with phonological shape is added to the verb phrase. But Rule (2c), like (2a) and (2b), removes all tense and person-number markings from the verb; it also makes the verb non-finite. To express our intuition that there is a relationship between what happens as a result of Rule (2c) and what happens as a result of Rule (2a) or (2b), we can treat the non-finiteness of the ending as due to the action of an abstract complementizer represented as C. This C is exactly parallel to *to* and *-ing* in that, by whatever process (cf. note 8), it removes finite endings from the verb; it differs from them in that this complementizer leaves no phonological trace in the superficial form of the verb. Thus, it is an abstract complementizer where the others are concrete. Rule (2c), then, is as follows:

Rule (2) Complementizer-Change

(c) *that*-non-finite

$$X_1 - that - NP - VP - X_2 \rightarrow 1 - 2 - 3 - C + 4 - 5$$
$$ 1 \quad\;\; 2 \quad\;\; 3 \quad\; 4 \quad\;\; 5$$

The intermediate tree for the sentence *I demand that he leave* is seen in (31). The remaining parts of the complementizer-changing rule change

(31)

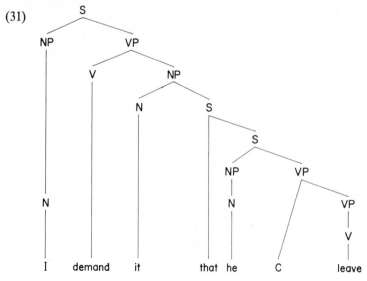

that to any of various other particles: *if, when, how,* etc. The verb remains finite. The final complementizer-changing rule will operate for all of these infrequent types.

Rule (2) Complementizer-Change

(d) *how*
if-finite
when

.
.
.

$$X_1 - that - S - X_2 \rightarrow 1 - how - 3 - 4$$
$$1 \quad 2 \quad 3 \quad 4$$

.
.
.

where *how,* etc., are adjoined to S in the same way that *that* is. The tree resulting from the operation of Rule (2d) is identical to (28), except that *that* is replaced by one of these particles. We have discussed in this section the various complementizing morphemes that are found in English. There are four major ones: *that*-finite, *for-to,* poss-*ing* and *that*-non-finite. Which of these will be found with a given embedded sentence depends on the subcategorization features in the complex symbol of the main verb of the sentence. These features indicate which of the two rules relating to complementizers may apply to a sentence in subject or object position with respect to this verb. After complementizer-placement has applied, obligatorily, and complementizer-changing rules, if any are applicable, have applied, the resulting structure is still not the superficial form of a sentence. Other rules, optionally or obligatorily, apply to these complement-containing sentences. The bulk of this chapter will be devoted to an examination of the rules that apply to complements.

2.5 Equi-NP-Deletion

This rule, equi(valent)-noun-phrase-deletion, applies to structures produced by the operation of the Rule (1) and Rule (2a) or (2b). Its operation produces contrasts like the following:

(32a)   Mary hates for John to send her aspidistras.

(32b)   Mary hates to send John aspidistras.

In (32a), the subject of the embedded sentence, *John*, is present in the surface structure. But in (32b) there is no subject of *send* present. But we know that its subject is *Mary*. Traditional grammar deals with such cases by saying that in sentences like (32b), the subject of *send* is "understood." In our terms, this means that the subject of (32b) is present in the deep structure but deleted by transformational rule and not present in the surface structure. There is syntactic evidence as well that *Mary* is present at some point in the structure of (32b). This proof is clearer in languages that make distinctions of gender. Thus, in Latin the following sentence is grammatical:

(33a)   Iulia mavult esse pulchra. 'Julia prefers to be beautiful.'

But the following is not:

(33b)   *Iulia mavult esse pulcher.

In the latter sentence, the adjective is masculine in gender, while *Iulia* is, of course, feminine. The noun *Iulia* must have been present in the lower sentence of (33a) at some point in the derivation so that the agreement rules could operate.

There is also evidence in English, in sentences like the following:

(34a)   Mary likes it for John to talk to himself.

(34b)   *Mary likes it for John to talk to herself.

(34c)   Mary likes to talk to herself.

(34d)   *Mary likes to talk to himself.

The rule deleting the subject of the embedded sentence, equi-NP-deletion, operates, as its name implies, only in case the subject of the lower sentence is identical to that of the higher sentence, so that the former, when deleted, can be supplied. This rule is stated as follows:

Rule (3) Equi-NP-Deletion

$$X_1 - NP_1 - X_2 - \left. \begin{matrix} for \\ poss \end{matrix} \right\} - NP_2 - X_3 \rightarrow 1 - 2 - 3 - 4 - \emptyset - 6$$
$$\quad 1 \quad\quad 2 \quad\quad 3 \quad\quad 4 \quad\quad\quad 5 \quad\quad 6$$

This rule operates only in case Rule (2a) or (2b) has already applied. As an example of how this rule operates, let us take the sentence *I like to eat kittens*. The deep structure of this sentence is represented by the tree in diagram (35). Rule (1) operates on this tree, and then Rule (2a), to give the intermediate structure shown in diagram (36).

(35)

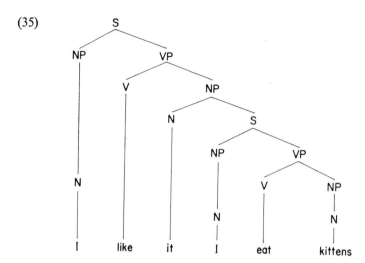

(36)   I like it for me to eat kittens.

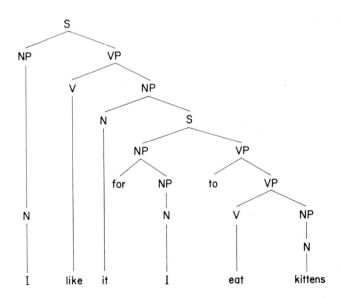

Equi-NP-deletion can apply here, since the subjects of the two sentences are identical. This leaves the tree shown in diagram (37). Later rules will convert (37) to the superficial form *I like to eat kittens.*

(37)   I like it for to eat kittens.

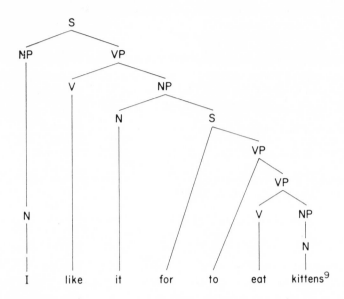

2.6 *It*-Substitution

The next rule we shall discuss is *it*-substitution (or *it*-replacement). This rule accounts for the existence of sentences like the following, where, although the subject of the lower S is present, the complementizer *for* or poss is not present in the surface structure.

(38a)   Mary likes herself to be considerate.

(38b)   Mary likes Fred to be considerate.

(38c)   John was right to go.

(38d)   John seems to be the mad strangler.

(38e)   Mary believes Fred to have shot Al Capone.

(38f)   Mary believes herself to have invented the mini-skirt.

These sentences contrast with others like (39a), in which Rule (3) has applied, as well as others like (39b), in which the complementizer may still be present.

(39a)   Mary likes to go.

(39b)   Mary likes (it) for Fred to go.

In the latter case, *it* may still be present in the surface structure, but when the complementizer is not present, it may not.

(39c)   *Mary likes it Fred to go.

The sentences of (38) contrast as well with sentences in which *it* must be present and in which the subject noun in the lower sentence is still preceded by a complementizer. The meanings of the following sentences are the same as those of (38c) and (38d), respectively:

(40a)   It was right for John to go.

(40b)   It seems that John is the mad strangler.

Notice, too, that in (38a) and (38f) *herself* is a reflexive, while the following sentences are not grammatical:

(41a)   *Mary likes for herself to be considerate.

(41b)   *Mary believes that herself invented the mini-skirt.

The nonoccurrence of the sentences of (41) can be explained by the fact that reflexivization never occurs across sentence boundaries, with certain well-defined exceptions (Ross, 1967) which do not include cases like the preceding. In (41), the *Mary* of the lower sentence is not in the same simple S as is the *Mary* of the higher sentence. Hence, *herself* is impossible here; we find only *she*. (In the second example of (41), equi-NP-deletion must always apply.) These facts suggest that, in fact, in (38) the subjects of the lower sentences are no longer dominated by the lower S. They must now be in the same simple S as the subject of the higher sentence. When we discuss *for*-deletion later, we shall show that the absence of *for* in these sentences is additional evidence that these nouns are no longer in their original position as subject noun phrases of the lower sentence.

The subject NP of the lower sentence is substituted for *it* of *its* by the *it*-substitution rule. *Its* can be either the subject or direct object of the sentence. This substituted NP becomes syntactically independent of the sentence to which it belonged in the deep structure, and it behaves as if it were the subject or direct object of the higher verb, rather than the subject of the lower verb. For this reason, sentences like (41c) are ungrammatical; *it* is replaced by NP as a result of the operation of this rule, and the NP of the lower sentence always is preceded by a complementizer unless this rule has been applied.

The rule that produces sentences like those of (38) appears at the end of this paragraph. It is unique among the rules given here in that the proper statement of it demands a double structural description. The structure that is to undergo the rule is broken up by this rule in two different ways. The rule first looks to see if the left-hand side of the SD is applicable to the sentence, and then it checks the right-hand side. Three elementary operations are involved in this rule; in performing the first two, substitution and deletion, the rule uses the left-hand side of the structural description; for the third operation, adjunction, it uses the right-hand side. This double structural description could be avoided if there were two separate *it*-substitution rules, one for subjects and one for objects; but to do this would be to miss a generalization, that *it*-substitution is the same process whether applied to subject complements or to object complements.

Rule (4) *It*-Substitution

$$X_1 - it - \left.{\begin{array}{c}for\\poss\end{array}}\right\} - NP - VP - X_2; \; NP - VP$$

$$1_I \quad 2_I \quad 3_I \quad\quad 4_I \quad 5_I \quad 6_I \quad 1_{II} \quad 2_{II}$$

where $2 - 3 - 4 - 5$ is an NP
$\quad\quad\quad 3 - 4 - 5 \quad$ is an S
$\quad\quad\quad 4 - 5 \quad\quad$ is an S

substitute 4_I for 2_I
delete 4_I
adjoin $3_I - 4_I - 5_I$ to 2_{II}
delete $3_I - 4_I - 5_I$

There is another reason why we want the subject of the lower sentence to be the direct object of the verb, in an object complement, after the application of Rule (4). This argument involves the rule for passivization, which will be discussed later.

The result of the passivization transformation is to exchange the subject of a sentence with its direct object. This means that, if passivization has taken place, the whole NP of the subject is exchanged with the whole NP of the direct object. In English, when complement-containing sentences are passivized, in the majority of object complements two forms of passivization are possible. The following sentences are, in order, the active sentence and the two possible corresponding passives:

(42a)   Mary said that John was a fool.

(42b)   It was said by Mary that John was a fool.

(42c)   John was said to be a fool by Mary.

Sentence (42b) is traditionally called the impersonal passive, (42c) the personal passive. In (42b) the direct object noun phrase of the sentence is *It that John was a fool*: that is, the whole NP dominating *it* and the embedded sentence. (A later rule moves *that John was a fool* after the verb.) In (42c) *John* is the noun that has been exchanged with the subject, and it is the superficial subject of this sentence. This means that, when the passivization transformation applies, *John* must be in direct object position, as a NP independent of the sentence of which it was the subject in the deep structure. *It*-substitution has applied to it. Notice, besides, that

(42d)   *Mary said John to be a fool

is ungrammatical in English, although *Mary believes John to be a fool* is acceptable for some speakers at least, and *John is said to be a fool* is completely grammatical. These facts tell us certain things about the interrelationship of complementizer-change and *it*-substitution.

According to the structural description of *it*-substitution in Rule (4), this rule can apply only if Rule (2a) or (2b) has previously applied. Moreover, for most verbs to which one of these rules has applied, it must apply. (*Like* and *expect* are, for some speakers, among the few exceptions.) For a verb like *believe*, application of Rule (2a) is optional. If it has applied, Rule (4) is obligatory; if not, it cannot apply. Hence, in the active, there is a choice of *I believed that John was rich* and *I believed John to be rich*. We can draw tree diagrams (43a) and (43b) for these sentences after the application of Rule (4) to the second.

(43a)   I believed that John was rich.

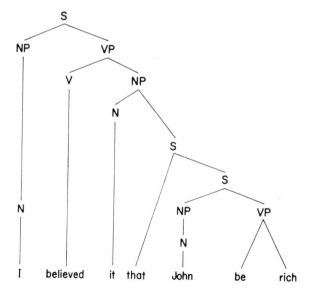

(43b)   I believed John to be rich.

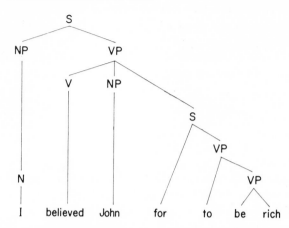

But with a verb like *say* the situation becomes rather more complicated. If passivization is not to apply, none of the complementizer-changing rules may apply. If, however, the deep structure is such that passivization must apply, then Rule (2a) may optionally apply. If it applies, then *it*-substitution must apply. Hence we must know whether passivization must apply or not, before we know whether, in a given instance, a verb like *say* can undergo Rule (4).

It-substitution and Rule (3), equi-NP-deletion, are mutually exclusive. If one has applied, the other cannot; the application of Rule (3) removed the noun phrase that is required to meet the SD of Rule (4). But both Rule (3) and Rule (4) require that either Rule (2a) or Rule (2b) has applied. For most verbs equi-NP-deletion is obligatory. An example is *demand*: if the subjects are identical, Rule (2a) must apply, and so must Rule (3):

(44a)   I demand to go.

(44b)   *I demand that I go.

(44c)   *I demand for me to go.

(44d)   *I demand myself to go.

In such a verb, Rule (4) can never apply. Hence (44d) is ungrammatical. In other verbs, although the structural description is met, Rule (3) cannot apply. In this case, Rule (4) must apply, for example,

(45a)   *I said to have gone.

(45b)   *I believed to have gone.

(45c)   *I believed for me to have gone.

There is a third class of cases, for which Rule (3) is optional if the structural description is met. Examples are *wish* and *like*.

(46a) I wish to go.

(46b) I wish myself to go.

(46c) *I wish for me to go.

(46d) I like to go.

(46e) I like myself to go.

(46f) *I like for me to go.

For *like* and *wish* either equi-NP-deletion or *it*-substitution must apply if subjects are identical. Hence (46c) and (46f) are ungrammatical. But if the subjects are not identical, then of course equi-NP-deletion cannot apply. In this case *it*-substitution is also optional.

(46g) I wish for John to go.

(46h) I wish John to go.

(46i) I like (it) for John to go.

(46j) I like John to go.

There is a further argument for the existence of Rule (4), which makes the subject NP of the lower sentence a constituent independent of the embedded S. The argument involves the rule of verb-gapping. This rule deletes the main verb in the right-hand member of two conjoined sentences, under identity with the verb in the left-hand sentence. But if in the superficial structure of the right-hand sentence there are three constituents, verb-gapping cannot take place. For example, (47a) can be reduced to (47b).

(47a) I saw John and Bill saw Harry.

(47b) I saw John and Bill, Harry.

But (47c) cannot be reduced to (47d).

(47c) I gave John a nickel and Bill gave Harry a dime.

(47d) *I gave John a nickel and Bill, Harry a dime.

This is because (47c) has a three-way split in the derived constituent structure of the right-hand side. For the same reason, the first of these sentences is grammatical, but the second is not:

(48a) I believe that John is rich, and Bill that Arthur is poor.

(48b) *I believe John to be rich, and Bill, Harry to be poor.

Evidence like this indicates that there is a rule that has operated to produce *Bill believes Arthur to be poor* the effect of which is to bring *Arthur* out of its embedded sentence and make it an independent constituent, making a structure such as *Bill believes Arthur to be poor* unable to undergo verb-gapping. *It*-substitution, as it is characterized in Rule (4), performs this function.

2.7 Flip

Although Rule (5), flip, cannot be stated formally, it accounts for variations like the following:

(49a)   John's shooting of Mary surprised me.

(49b)   It amused me to hear Harry tell those jokes wrong.

(49c)   It always infuriates me to have to call him up at 1 A.M.

These verbs also occur in a different construction, which resembles the passive:

(50a)   I was surprised at John's shooting Mary.

(50b)   I was amused to hear Harry tell those jokes wrong.

(50c)   I am always infuriated to have him call up at 1 A.M.

These are not true passives, however. In the first place, true passives usually occur with the preposition *by*. These occur with *at*, sometimes *of*, *with*, or *in*.

(51a)   I was surprised *at* John.

(51b)   I am ashamed *of* Harry's actions.

(51c)   Mabel was infuriated *with* Alphonse.

(51d)   We are all interested *in* his amatory proclivities.

Moreover, the following sentences are grammatical, but they do not have the same meaning as they would if the preposition were *at, with,* etc.

(52a)   I was surprised by John.

(52b)   I was amused by the Girl Scouts.

Sentences like (51) cannot occur with certain adverbs of time or place, while those like (52) can.

(53a)   *I was surprised at John every day at 5 o'clock.

(53b)   I was surprised by John every day at 5 o'clock.

The active form of such sentences is also found:

(53c)   John surprised me every day at 5 o'clock.

Sentence (53c) corresponds in meaning to (53b), not (53a), which is ungrammatical. These facts suggest that only the sentences with *by* are the true passives of such verbs. Additionally, sentences with *by* can be intensified only by the use of *very much*. Sentences with *at, with,* etc., can be intensified by *very* alone.

(53d)   I was very surprised at John.

(53e)   I was very much surprised by John.

(53f)   *I was very surprised by John.

This is related to the fact that we do not find *very* used alone as an intensifier of verbs, nor *very much* as an intensifier of adjectives.

(53g)   *I very like John.

(53h)   *His face was very much red.

Notice that the sentences with *at, with,* etc., can occur only if the subject is animate. The quasi-active form of these can occur only if the direct object is animate.

(54a)   I was surprised at his fear of Tabasco sauce.

(54b)   His fear of Tabasco sauce surprised me.

(54c)   *His fear of Tabasco sauce was surprised at me.

(54d)   *I surprised his fear of Tabasco sauce.

Although it appears that the direct objects of the forms with *at,* and the subjects of the corresponding "actives," may be concrete nouns, this is, in fact, not true. In a sentence like *I am surprised at you, you* actually means something like *what you did* or *the way you are* and is abstract, an embedded sentence. In this respect, too, such sentences are different from those with *by,* where the object of the preposition *by* is the noun itself. Also, passives cannot occur if the subject and object in the deep structure are identical, as in the following:

(55a)   *I was washed by myself.

(55b)   *I was surprised by myself.

But the following can occur:

(55c)   I was surprised at myself.

Alongside of the types that occur with *at*, etc., we find the following:

(56a)   It is surprising to me that John gave up his earldom.

(56b)   That Hector put up with that treatment is astounding to me.

But we do not find this:

(56c)   *John is surprising to me.

In the last case the noun itself, rather than the noun as a reduced form, is the subject of the sentence. The existence of sentences like (56a) and (56b) among this category leads us to include other similar types as related phenomena. For example, we have these:

(57a)   It seems to me that John is a fool.

(57b)   It appears to me that Harry was lying.

We also have forms that have undergone *it*-substitution:

(58a)   John seems to me to be a fool.

(58b)   Harry appeared to me to be lying.

Sentence (49a), *John's shooting Mary surprised me*, and all the sentences of this type are related to sentences of the type of (50a), *I was surprised at John's shooting Mary,* by the flip transformation. The underlying structure for both these sentences is

(59)   I surprise at it   S
                        ⎯⎯⎯⎯⎯⎯⎯⎯
                        John shoot Mary

This structure also underlies nominalizations, in which the deep structure subject of these sentences appears as the subjective genitive of the nominalized verb. The objective genitive is not found.

(60a)   My surprise at John's shooting Mary.

(60b)   *John's shooting Mary's surprise of me.

This is additional evidence that the animate noun is, in fact, the deep-structure subject in both (49a) and (50a). The exact form of the flip transformation is unclear, but we know what it operates on and what it produces. Flip operates on the deep structure given earlier to produce (49a), if the verb *surprise* chosen is non-stative; or, if it is the stative *surprise* (marked [+ adjective]), then the transformation produces

John's shooting Mary was surprising to me. That is, if the verb is adjectival (or one of a few exceptional verbs not adjectival, such as *seem*), flip inserts *to* before the deep-structure subject, before putting it in direct object position. If the verb is adjectival, the participial ending and the verb *to be* are added. Otherwise, the forms remain the same. Then subject and direct object are interchanged. The preposition *at* or *with* is deleted before the new direct object. If flip does not operate on a verb like *surprise*, then (50a) is the result. In this case, another rule inserts the past participle ending *-ed* and the verb *to be,* but this rule is not the same as the rule for passivization, for the reasons given earlier. For a few verbs, of which *seem* is one, flip must operate. For a sentence like (58a), we assume the following deep structure:

(61)   I seem it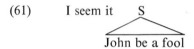

Seem may optionally undergo *for-to* complementizer-change. Its subsequent behavior relative to flip and other transformational rules is dictated by whether it has undergone *for-to* complementizer change or whether it appears with a *that*-finite complementizer. First, let us take the case in which it has undergone *for-to* placement. In this case, *it*-substitution obligatorily applies. This gives us the intermediate structure shown in diagram (62). Now flip operates on this, exchanging the

(62)   I seem John for to be a fool.

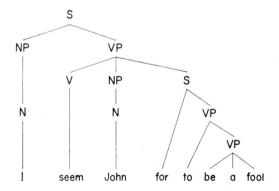

direct object, *John* and *I*. At the same time, *to* is inserted before the new object, *me*. This gives us the final form, *John seems to me to be a fool.*

If, on the other hand, *that*-finite is the complementizer, *it*-substitution of course cannot apply. Flip now exchanges the direct object, in this

case *it S*, and the subject *I*. This yields the structure shown in diagram
(63). After this, a later rule, extraposition (discussed in Section 2.9)

(63)

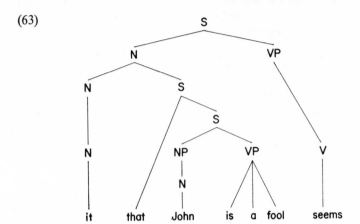

applies. This rule takes the lower S and removes it from the NP that
dominates it, and adjoins it under the higher S, as a sister constituent
of NP and VP. The derived structure *It seems that John is a fool* is,
then, as given in diagram (64). *Seem,* like a number of other verbs of

(64)

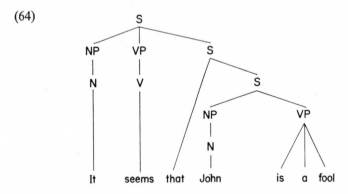

mental state, undergoes a rule called *not*-transportation. (See Klima,
1965.) This rule will be discussed in the fourth chapter, but its relevance
here is that the rule must be constrained so as to apply only to a small
class of object complements.

(65a)   I think John isn't here.

(65b)   I don't think John is here.

Notice that it applies to *seem*.

(65c)   It seems to me that John isn't here.

(65d)   It doesn't seem to me that John is here.

If we do not assume the existence of flip, *seem* is a verb with a subject complement and is the only such case (besides *appear*, another flip verb) to which *not*-transportation applies. To consider these as subject complements, the form of the *not*-transportation rule would have to be greatly complicated and perhaps would become impossible to express. Hence, the fact that *seem* and *appear* undergo *not*-transportation suggests that they are underlying object-complement verbs: *I seem it S*, rather than *it S seems to me*. This is further evidence for flip.

2.8 Passivization

That active sentences and passive sentences are somehow related is well known. What is less well known is precisely what the relationship between them is. The passivization transformation, Rule (6) of the complement-related rules we are discussing, is one of the most mysterious rules of the transformational component. We know, to be sure, that it exists; we know approximately what it does to the deep structures on which it operates and what superficial structures it produces. But we do not know, and can barely begin to guess, the actual form of this rule and the kind of deep structures on which it operates.

The earliest attempts to formalize the passive transformation are invalidated because they are plainly *ad hoc* and because they produce the wrong constituent structure. This is true of the formulations by Chomsky (1957), (1965a), and Rosenbaum (1967). A recent suggestion by Postal (oral communication), discussed at length by Lakoff and Ross (in preparation), is that passivization occurs in a sentence if in the deep structure it is embedded in another sentence containing the verb *to be*. Thus, a sentence such as *The ball was seen by the boy* would be derived from an underlying structure of approximately the following form:

(66)   It   S   is

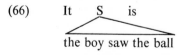

the boy saw the ball

The passive transformation, operating on this structure, first exchanges the subject of the lower sentence and its direct object. Then it attaches the participial ending *-ed* to the main verb of the lower sentence,

perhaps by a special complementizer-placement rule, in which -*ed*
functions like -*ing*, and the first part of the complementizer (like poss,
for example) never appears because *it*-substitution obligatorily applies.
Postal further hypothesizes that *by* is present in the deep structure of all
sentences preceding their subjects, as a nominative case marker. (That
is, according to this analysis, *John hit the ball* is really present in the
deep structure as *By John hit the ball*.) It is not, of course, present before
objects. It is usually deleted, but not if passivization occurs or in nominalizations: *The assassination of Kennedy by Oswald*, from *By Oswald
assassinated Kennedy*. The derived structure is *The ball be+past
see+en by the boy*. Morphological rules operate on this to yield the
correct surface structure.

This treatment accounts for a number of facts in English and other
languages. It accounts for the presence of *be*, the presence of *by*, and
the nominative of the superficial subject. It does not account for the
existence of a relationship between passive and reflexive in many
languages or the relationship between passives and impersonal constructions.

It was further noted by Postal that sentences like the following are
ungrammatical in English, as are their translations into any language:

(67a)   *The girl was shot by herself.

(67b)   *John and Mary were washed by themselves.

These nonsentences show that passivization and reflexivization are
mutually exclusive. An explanation for this is suggested by Lakoff
and Ross (in preparation) and originally proposed by Postal. They
suggest that there is a constraint on coreferential noun phrases—noun
phrases that refer to the same thing—in all languages, precluding the
existence of transformational rules that move one coreferential NP over
another.

2.9 Extraposition

If *it*-substitution has not applied to a sentence, *it* will still be present
immediately preceding the complementizer. In some of these cases the
resultant structure is not permissible as a sentence of English. Either
of two later rules must apply in such cases. One of these rules is extraposition. This rule moves an embedded sentence away from *it*, to the
right of the main sentence. It operates on structures like the following:

(68a)   It that John shot Bill is unlikely.

(68b)   It that John was here yesterday was believed by Alexander.

(68c)   I liked it that he sent those orchids very much.

Extraposition operates on structures like these as follows:

Rule (7) Extraposition

$$X_1 - it - S - X_2 \rightarrow 1 - 2 - 4 - 3$$
$$ 1 2 3 4$$

This rule can apply to the output of Rule (6), passivization, as (68b) illustrates. It would not apply to the corresponding active *Alexander believed it that John was here yesterday*, because X_2 cannot be null. But it can apply to object complements in case there is an adverb to the right of the embedded sentence, as in (68c). The application of extraposition to (68c) produces the following sentence:

(69)   I liked it very much that he sent those orchids.

Extraposition is normally optional, but in the case of a few verbs it is obligatory.[10]

2.10 *It*-Deletion

In English, *it* is never found immediately preceding the complementizer *that* in subject complements. By subject complements we mean here not only deep-structure subject complements but also derived subject complements, such as passives and flips. For object complements after most verbs *it* must be deleted, but there are exceptions. Thus the following sentences do not occur:

(70a)   *It that John is the mad strangler is possible.

(70b)   *It that John is the mad strangler is believed by Harry.

(70c)   *It that John is the mad strangler seems to be true.

(70d)   *I said it that John is the mad strangler.

(70e)   *I want it for John to confess that he is the mad strangler.

The following, however, are found:

(71a)   I doubt it that Harry is the mad strangler.

(71b)   I like it that Harry is the mad strangler.

Rule (8) *It*-Deletion

$$X_1 - it - S - X_2 \rightarrow 1 - \emptyset - 3 - 4 \text{ if } 2 - 3 \text{ is an NP}$$
$$1 \quad 2 \quad 3 \quad 4$$

This rule must be ordered after passivization and flip in order for the rule to operate obligatorily on sentences that have undergone either of these rules.

(71c)   *It that Harry is the mad strangler is doubted by everyone.

If extraposition, which is optional, has not applied, then *it*-deletion must operate on all but the exceptional verbs.

2.11 Preposition-Deletion

There are a few other rules that must operate to produce grammatical sentences. Compare the following sentences:

(72a)   We all are aware of it that it was necessary for Stanley to eat the cheese.

(72b)   We all are aware that it was necessary for Stanley to eat the cheese.

(72c)   We all are aware of the necessity for Stanley's eating the cheese.

(72d)   *We all are aware of that it was necessary for Stanley to eat the cheese.

(72e)   *We all are aware the necessity for Stanley's eating the cheese.

Also compare the following:

(73a)   John and Frodo planned on doing it.

(73b)   John and Frodo planned to do it.

(73c)   John and Frodo planned that Alice should do it.

In these sentences the verb may or may not be followed by a preposition. We shall have more to say in Section 2.14 about how the preposition comes to be in that position; but the problem now is whether we are to assume that the preposition is inserted in case it is followed immediately by a noun phrase, or whether it is deleted if it is not. We shall give reasons later for believing that, in fact, the preposition is always present but is deleted if it is followed immediately by S. (This will be true also for sentences like (73b), which at this stage in the derivation is actually *John and Frodo planned on for to do it*, with *for to do it* being dominated by S.) This rule, preposition-deletion, is the ninth in our list of rules, and its form is as follows:

Rule (9) Preposition-Deletion

$$X_1 - \text{prep.} - S - X_2 \rightarrow 1 - \emptyset - 3 - 4$$
$$1 \quad\quad 2 \quad\quad 3 \quad\, 4$$

It-deletion must apply before this rule, or else sentences like (72b), (72c), and (72d) would not undergo this rule, as *it* is not dominated by S, but by NP.

2.12 *That*-Deletion

There are found in English alternations of the following type:

(74a)   I said that Mary had stolen the peanut butter.

(74b)   I said Mary had stolen the peanut butter.

(74c)   It's likely that Sidney was just putting you on again.

(74d)   It's likely Sidney was just putting you on again.

But we do not find sentences like the following:

(75a)   *I like it John left.

(75b)   *Everyone agreed on it John was the father of the kittens.

In order for *that* to be deleted, it must be immediately preceded by a verb.

Rule (10) *That*-Deletion

$$X_1 - V - \textit{that} - S - X_2 \rightarrow 1 - 2 - \emptyset - 4 - 5$$
$$1 \quad 2 \quad 3 \quad\quad 4 \quad 5$$

For a number of verbs this rule cannot operate even though the structural description is met, for example:

(76a)   *It happened John left.

(76b)   *It is unlikely John is here.

Such verbs will have to be specially marked in the lexicon as not undergoing this rule. Otherwise, the rule is optional.

2.13 *For*-Deletion

At this stage of the derivation of a sentence there are still ungrammatical structures, such as these:

(77a)   *I want for to go.

(77b)   *I want Harry for to go.

For must be present at the time of application of Rule (9), and therefore the rule deleting *for* is ordered after Rule (9).[11] This rule will also operate on sentences that have undergone Rule (2b), possessive -*ing* complementizer-change, and either Rule (3) or Rule (4), such as the following:

(78a)   *I don't like 's doing that.

(78b)   *I don't like John 's doing that.

It will yield, respectively, *I want to go, I want Harry to go, I don't like doing that, I don't like John doing that.*

Rule (11) $\left. \begin{array}{c} For \\ Poss \end{array} \right\}$-Deletion

$$X_1 - \left. \begin{array}{c} for \\ poss \end{array} \right\} - VP - X_2 \rightarrow 1 - \emptyset - 3 - 4$$
$$ 1 \quad\quad 2 \quad 3 \quad\quad 4$$

Since this rule deletes *for* and poss. only before VP, it does not apply. This is additional motivation for *it*-substitution. Except for some superficially obvious cases, we have not discussed here the reasons why the rules are ordered as they are. For discussion of this point see Lakoff and Ross (forthcoming) and Ross (1967). Tree diagrams (79a)–(79n) illustrate the derivation of sentences according to the preceding rules.

(79a)   I want to do that.

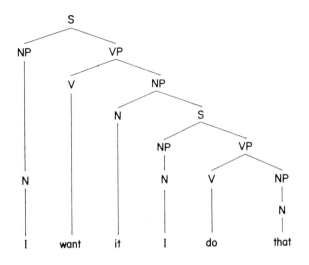

(79b)   Rule (1)

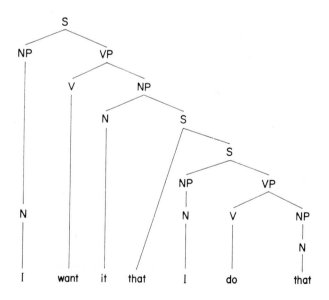

(79c)   Rule (2a)

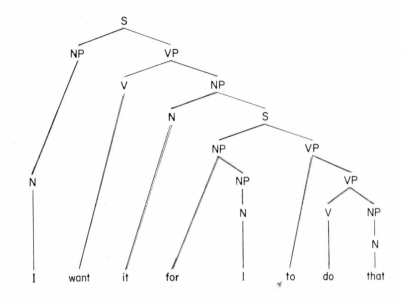

(79d)   Rule (3)

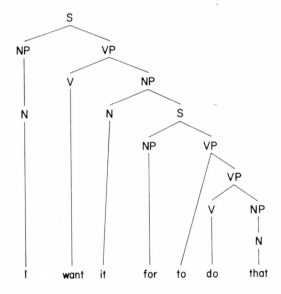

Rules (4) through (7) are not applicable.

(79e)   Rule (8)

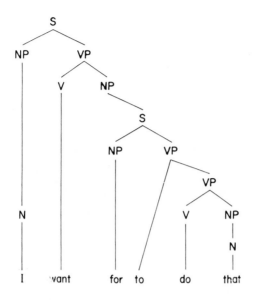

Rules (9) through (10) are not applicable.

(79f)   Rule (11)

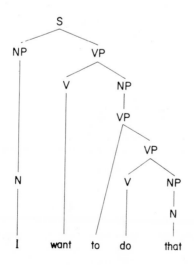

(79g)   It is likely that he is the mad strangler.

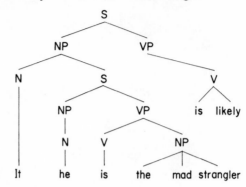

(79h)   Rule (1)

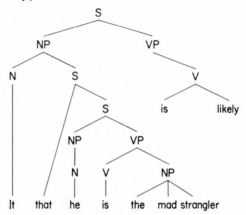

Rules (2) through (6) are not applicable.

(79i)   Rule (7)

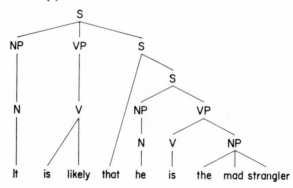

Rules (8) through (11) are not applicable.

(79j)   He is likely to do that.

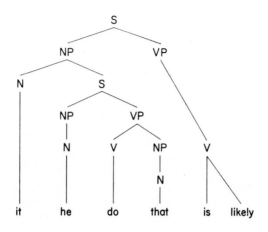

(79k)   Rule (1)

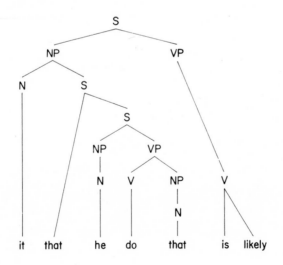

(79l)   Rule (2a)

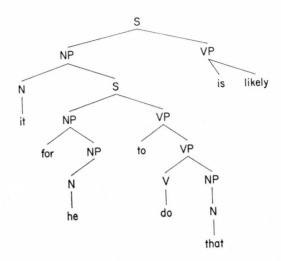

Rule (3) is not applicable.

(79m)   Rule (4)

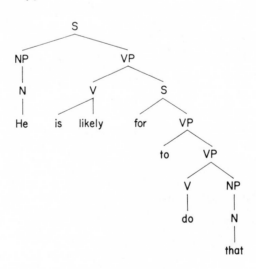

Rules (5) through (10) are not applicable.

(79n)   Rule (11)

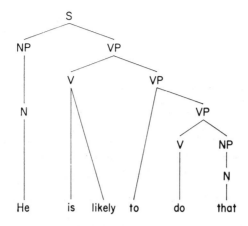

2.14 Other Complement Types

It is evident that there are a number of cases of complementation in English which the preceding rules and deep structures do not satisfactorily explain. Among them are sentences like the following:

(80a)   John was persuaded by me to do that.

(80b)   The soldiers were ordered by the general to retreat.

(80c)   Hedda was dared by Louella to write that.

We do not find the following:

(81a)   *It was persuaded by me that John do that.

(81b)   *It was ordered by the general that the soldiers retreat.

(81c)   *It was dared by Louella that Hedda write that.

Compare, as a contrast, the behavior of a verb like *expect*.

(82a)   I expected John to do that.

(82b)   John was expected by me to do that.

(82c)   It was expected by me that John would do that.

This fact by itself is not sufficient to necessitate a revision of the categories of complements. If this were the only difficulty, we could easily mark all such verbs in the lexicon as having to undergo *it*-substitution mandatorily. Another curious fact about all these verbs is that the subject of the higher verb cannot be identical to the subject of the lower verb.

(83a)   *I persuaded myself to do that.

(83b)   *The general ordered himself to retreat.[12]

(83c)   *Louella dared herself to write that.

There is, moreover, one more strong argument that such verbs are of a different class than the others discussed before. The indication that this is true is contained in the following sentences:

(84a)   I persuaded John to be examined by the doctor.

(84b)   I persuaded the doctor to examine John.

Sentence (84a) can be true without (84b) being true; that is, these two sentences must have different deep structures. Compare the following:

(85a)   I expected John to be examined by the doctor.

(85b)   I expected the doctor to examine John.

In these two sentences, neither can be true if the other is false. The sentences *may* then have identical deep structures. Rosenbaum set up the following trees representing the deep structures of (84a) and (84b), respectively. (Details are omitted for the sake of simplicity.) The sentences of (85) have identical deep structures except that (85a) must undergo passivization.

(86a)

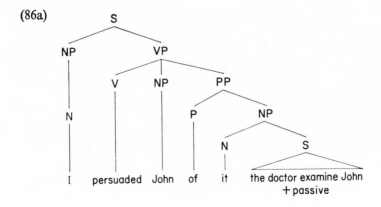

(86b)

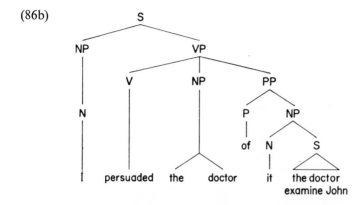

Some of these verbs can be explained by the assumption that there is more structure in them than appears superficially. Because of this structure these verbs can be accounted for without placing a new rule, VP → V VP PP, in the base component. For example, it has been suggested by Lakoff (1965) that *persuade* is actually composed of a causative verb and a lower verb. According to this interpretation, a sentence such as *I persuaded John to go* has the deep structure shown in (87).

(87)

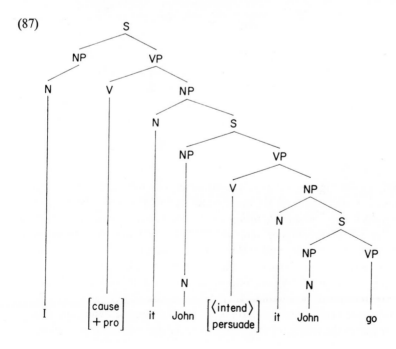

Here *persuade* is actually the result of the combination of a causative abstract verb[13] and a verb with the features (syntactic and semantic) of *intend* and the phonology of *persuade*. Thus, for *intend* and for any verb with the syntactic features of *intend*, there is a constraint that the subject of *intend* and the subject of the lower verb be identical, so that **I intended for John to go* and **I persuaded John for Bill to go* are both ungrammatical. *For-to* complementation applies to the lowest and next-higher sentences, *John go* and *John intends it S*. Equi-NP-deletion obligatorily applies after this, yielding the intermediate structure (after *it*-deletion and pruning rules) shown in (88). *It*-substitution can now

(88)

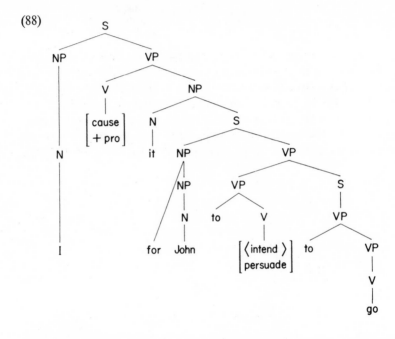

apply in the higher sentence, substituting *John* for *it*, the object of the causative abstract verb. By the second part of this rule, the VP of the original lower sentence *John intended to go* is extraposed and attached to the VP of the higher sentence. *For*-deletion and various pruning rules take place here, and the resultant structure is illustrated in diagram (89). To this structure the plugging-in rule applies. We shall discuss this rule briefly here and both give the rule itself and discuss it at greater length in Chapter 4. Its effect in the present derivation is to remove the verb from the verb phrase of the lower sentence and attach it, or rather the matrix of features syntactic, semantic, and phonological

(89)

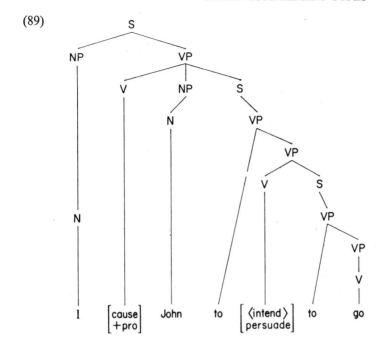

that composes it, under the causative pro-verb. A rule is needed here
to delete the complementizer *to* that was originally in front of < intend >. The VP node dominating *to* and <intend> is therefore
pruned. The derived structure now is shown in diagram (90). This is
the superficial structure of this sentence. A similar derivation can be

(90)

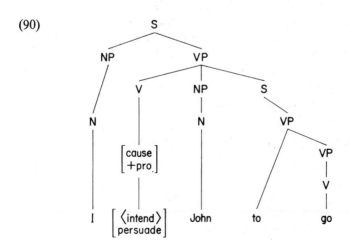

performed, but will not be here, for *I persuaded John that Fred was wrong*. The deep structure of this sentence is given in (91). In this meaning, there is no constraint of identity between the subject of

(91)

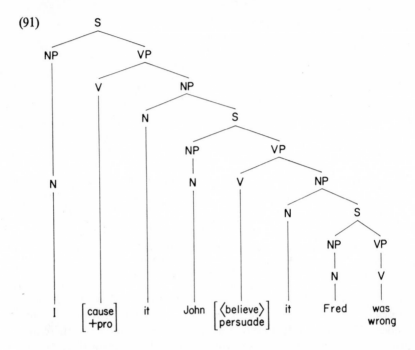

< believe > and of the lowest sentence, and there is a *that*-finite complementizer. *Persuade* in this case has the syntactic properties of *believe*. In this way the difference between the two uses of *persuade* can be accounted for formally. But all verbs of this type, unfortunately, cannot be handled as easily as *persuade*, and some problems remain for *persuade* as well.[14] They may contain causatives, but even if we could make that claim definitely (and there is no proof of this), we have no idea what the underlying verbs are.

2.15 Rosenbaum's Oblique and Verb Phrase Complements

Rosenbaum had, in all, seven classes of complement types. The first of these was the intransitive verb-phrase complement. This category included such verbs as *endeavor, tend, begin, manage*. In all of these, the subject of the higher verb had to be identical to the subject of the lower verb, and equi-NP-deletion was obligatory.

(92a)   *John endeavored for Bill to rob the bank.

(92b)   *John began for Bill to rob the bank.

Sentences containing these verbs do not undergo passivization:

(93a)   *To rob the bank was endeavored by Bill.

(93b)   *To rob the bank was begun by Bill.

Most cannot occur with *it* as a direct object, unlike the other types of complements we have been discussing:

(94a)   *John endeavored it.

(94b)   *John tended it.

(But (94c), *John began it*, is grammatical.) They do not occur in pseudo-cleft sentences.[15] Hence, as Rosenbaum hypothesized, there was no NP dominating the embedded S in complements of these verbs. For *John endeavored to rob the bank*, Rosenbaum set up the deep structure illustrated in diagram (95).

(95)

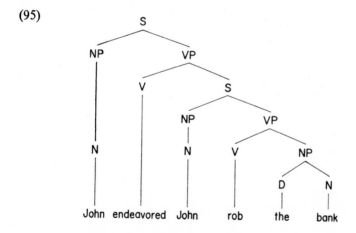

A second type, closely related to this, was the transitive verb-phrase complement. This category included verbs like *order, defy, dare* (transitive). The personal passive may occur with these:

(96a)   John was dared to rob the bank by Harry.

(96b)   The soldiers were ordered to shoot.

But the impersonal passive does not occur.

(97a)   *It was dared John to rob the bank.

(97b)   *It was ordered for the soldiers to shoot.

In these the NP direct object of the main verb was identical to the subject NP of the lower verb. Again, *it* is not found as a direct object, nor are pseudo-cleft sentences grammatical. Rosenbaum assigned to *John dared Bill to go* the deep structure shown in diagram (98). His third

(98)

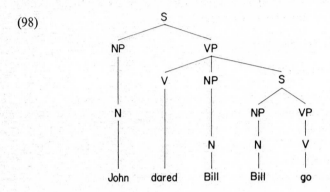

class was related to the first two. This was his oblique verb-phrase complement. These were like the transitive verb phrase complement except that the object noun phrase was the object of a preposition. A verb taking this type of complement is *prevailed upon* in the sentence *I prevailed upon Harry to surrender*, as illustrated in (99).

(99)

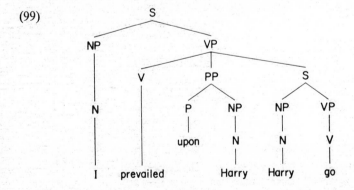

The remaining four classes of complements, according to Rosenbaum, all contain S dominated by NP. The first of these is the object complement. This comprises the largest class of cases. In structure it is just like the complements we have been assuming. Thus, *I doubt that he will shoot Alice* has the deep structure shown in diagram (100).

(100)

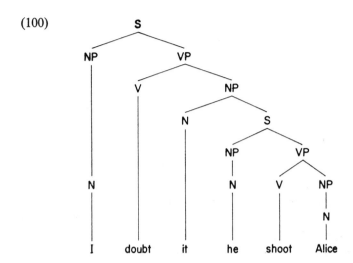

The next class is Rosenbaum's transitive oblique NP complements. *Persuade* is an example of this category. These could not undergo impersonal passivization: **It was persuaded John to go.* The direct object of *persuade* was an animate noun phrase, and the complement was contained in a prepositional phrase following this NP. In Section 2.14 Rosenbaum's proposed deep structure for a verb of this class is given.

Another class is that of intransitive oblique NP complements. This class is similar to the simple object complements except that the direct object NP is preceded by a preposition. *Decide on, conceive of,* and *agree to* are examples of this class. Rosenbaum assigned this deep structure to *We decided on it that Harry was wrong.* This is shown in diagram (101).

Rosenbaum's final class was that of subject NP complements. His treatment of these was like the one already given.

It has been shown by Lakoff (1965) that most of these divisions that were proposed by Rosenbaum were unnecessary and complicated the deep structure unduly. Instead of a complicated base component, Lakoff would have only two, or perhaps three, complement types and a slightly more complicated transformational component and lexicon. He accomplished the removal of four of the complement types needed by Rosenbaum by making use of the concept of rule government and the exception mechanism he set up. Since both of these are needed

(101)

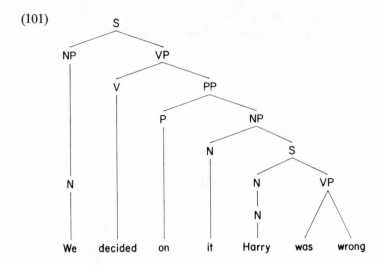

independently of the complement system, he was not complicating the grammar by these changes. Moreover, there is evidence, also presented by Lakoff, that Rosenbaum's division of complements was not only unnecessary but, in a number of instances at least, incorrect.

To return to the first category, the intransitive verb-phrase complements, this can be shown to be a superfluous category. They are few in number, although they are the simplest type of complement structurally and might therefore be assumed to be at least as common as the others. Of the ten or twelve verbs in this class, some have synonyms that are put by Rosenbaum into the NP-complement category because they can take *it* as direct objects or can passivize:

(102a)   *I endeavored it.

(102b)   I tried it.

(102c)   I attempted it.

Since this is true, and since it would be odd if very close synonyms had strikingly different deep structures, it is better to assume that both *endeavor* and *try* are NP object complements and that *endeavor* is marked in the lexicon as having to meet the structural description of *it*-deletion. This means that it must be followed by *it S*. Hence, *I endeavored it* (or *the murder, the robbery*) is ungrammatical, because there is no S following the noun. There will also be a redundancy rule stating that every verb that must meet the structural description of *it*-deletion must undergo equi-NP-deletion. It is also true that any sentence to which *for to* complementizer-change and equi-NP-deletion have applied cannot be passivized, so that the lack of a passive is thus taken care of automatically by the same redundancy rule that prevents the derivation of **To go was hoped by John* from *John hoped to go.*

A few of the verbs in this class can be dispensed with for still other reasons. *Begin, tend, stop,* and others can be shown to be, for independent reasons, underlying subject complements. *John began to see the light* is really derived from tree diagram (103). The second class of

(103)

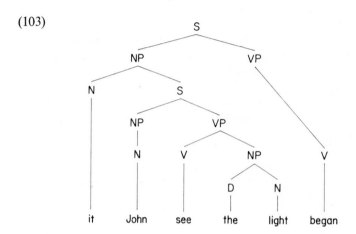

verbs can be handled partly by assuming that they, too, must meet the structural description of *it*-deletion. This puts them in the same class as *persuade.* They will be handled when they can be by the same arguments by which *persuade* was handled: some appear to be causatives, although their structure is uncertain. The next class, the oblique verb-phrase complements, are, by the same arguments, brought into the same class as the intransitive oblique NP complements like *decide on.* All will be handled in the same way.

Preposition-deletion has been discussed in Section 2.11. Rosenbaum set up a special class of complements comprising this type of structure. But it has been pointed out by Postal (lecture in class, summer 1964) that this is unnecessary and that a significant simplification of the grammar could be achieved if the category were eliminated. The argument is summarized here.

Postal argued that the preposition was not an independent unit and that the node "prepositional phrase" did not exist. Instead, every verb is entered in the lexicon with a notation indicating that it is followed by a preposition. For regular verbs this preposition is *of.* For other classes of verbs it is one of several other prepositions. So *decide* has *on*, *hope* has *for*, and so forth. This preposition is usually deleted by a transformational rule except under certain conditions. It is never deleted if the verb is nominalized:

(104a)   My hope for peace

(104b)   Our decision on the plan

(104c)   Our choice of the book

In other environments, such as the one specified in the preposition-deletion rule, all prepositions are deleted. In still other environments some remain, and some are deleted. It is this apparent irregularity that led Rosenbaum to postulate a separate class for these verbs in which the prepositions were not deleted. An example of such an environment is before *it*. In this environment *of* is deleted, but the other prepositions remain.

(105a)   They decided on it.

(105b)   We hoped for it.

(105c)   We chose it.

For a few verbs *of* is not deleted.

(106)   I can't conceive of it.

A verb like *conceive* must be marked in the lexicon as not undergoing *of*-deletion. In this way, both the intransitive oblique NP complement and the oblique VP complement are shown to be cases of ordinary object complementation. Therefore, we are left with three classes: object complements, subject complements, and transitive oblique complements like *persuade* and *defy*. Some, perhaps eventually all, of these can be shown to be related to ordinary object complements plus causatives.

In this chapter we have discussed the analyses of complement constructions in English as proposed by Rosenbaum, Lakoff, and Ross. In the next chapter we shall consider the complement constructions found in Latin to see whether they resemble those we have examined here and how much of the deep structure and transformational component that relates to complementation in English can be justified for Latin.[16]

Notes

1. It has been proposed (Lakoff, 1965) that adverbial clauses arise through complementation. This is true in the case of adverbs of time, place, manner, etc. In these cases, what is, in the superficial structure, the main clause is in the deep structure a sentence embedded in the adverbial element. For example, the sentence

   I shot John in the yard

   is derived from the deep structure

   It   S   was in the yard

   I shot John.

   There is some evidence for this analysis, both within English and in exotic languages. In various African, Asian, and Indian languages, it appears that the only way to say, for example, *I shot John in the yard* is to say something equivalent to *My shooting John was located in the yard.* The effect of this analysis, coupled with various reductions of other complex sentence types, is to reduce deep-structure simple sentences to subject–verb–direct object and to say that no sentence contains anything but these three elements in the deep structure. There is, of course, no limit on the potential number of embeddings tolerated per deep-structure complex sentence. Thus Ross (in the fall of 1966), for example, produced evidence that there are at least eight sentences underlying the surface sentence *Floyd broke the glass.*

2. It can easily be shown that the rules $S \rightarrow NP\ VP$, $VP \rightarrow V\ NP$ and $NP \rightarrow N\ (S)$, which generate complement structures, are recursive. We find sentences like the following:

   It was amusing for the Marquis to ask the girl to say that it was obvious that she was enjoying herself.

   The rules just given have been used four times to produce these sentences.

3. It is important to distinguish, in this discussion, between language-specific morphological features and probably universal syntactic features. It is a well-known fact, for example, that in Algonquian the words for "strawberry" and "elbow" have an ending that marks them as animate nouns, while the words for "raspberry" and "knee" are marked as inanimate. But this is merely morphological; we should consider a semantic distinction on this basis very strange indeed, and it probably does not exist anywhere. One of the ways of distinguishing semantic animacy and inanimacy is whether the noun can occur as the direct object of *grow* or *be alive*. If in Algonquian it were impossible to say "The raspberry is alive," but one could say, "The strawberry is alive," then the semantic features would, in fact, be different. But this seems most unlikely.

4. For example, there follow a list of English verbs taking object complements, with their Latin counterparts also taking object complements and a list of English verbs taking subject complements, with their Latin counterparts. No cases are known where a verb taking in the deep structure a subject complement in English corresponds to a Latin verb taking a deep-structure object complement, and vice versa.

Object-Complement Verbs

English	Latin
say	dico
think	puto
know	scio
hear	audio
order	impero
believe	credo
hope	spero
persuade	persuadeo
try[a]	conor[a]
decide	constituo
see	video
dare[a]	audeo[a]

All these verbs are object complements; proof of this is that all can undergo either personal or impersonal passivization or both, in both Latin and English. (Exceptions to this rule are marked [a]; the reason why they are exceptional will be discussed later. Since subject complements are intransitive, they cannot be passivized.)

Subject-Complement Verbs

English	Latin
be likely	veri simile est
be possible	fieri potest
happen	accidit
befall	contingit
follow	sequitur
be clear	liquet
be agreed	constat
be evident	manifestum esse

All these verbs are considered "impersonal": that is, their subject is the neuter pronoun *id*, with which they agree (for example, manifest*um*). Of course, none can be passivized. They are all third person, again in agreement with *id*, while object complements may be in any person.

5. Sentences such as the following may appear to be counterexamples to this statement:

I believe John.

But further examination will show that these are not true counterexamples. They are derived, by a process that is not clear at present, from sentences of the form *I believe what John said*. Thus, the following sentence is acceptable where the occurrence of *him* is made possible by the earlier occurrence of a verb of saying:

John said that the sky is falling down, and if you don't believe *him*, go read the *Times*.

Compare:

* John thinks the moon is made of Kraft Pasteurized Process Cheese, and if you don't believe him, try some yourself.

(To be more accurate, rather than *say* here we should postulate a verb of communication. Thus, *report, write, inform*, and a number of others can all occur in the second of the three sentences given earlier.) These examples show that, in fact, our claim is essentially correct: *believe* can take as an object only an abstract noun phrase. Other apparent counterexamples of this sort are undoubtedly to be handled in the same way.

6. An additional rather complex argument for this treatment of complementizer-placement was noted by Lakoff (oral communication). It is based on his concept of markedness. This concerns the possible number of violations of the complementizer rules. If *that*-insertion were, as suggested by Rosenbaum, parallel to *for-to* placement and the other later rules, then there would be more possibilities for an ungrammatical structure than are actually ever found in any known language or that are conceivable. If, for example, *that*-finite placement and *for-to* placement were parallel, a given sentence with the deep structure

could violate the rules in any of three ways: marked as having to undergo *for-to* and being unable to undergo *that*-finite, it might: (1) not undergo *for-to* and not undergo *that*-finite; (2) undergo both *for-to* and *that*-finite; (3) undergo *that*-finite and not *for-to*. The fourth remaining logical possibility, undergoing *for-to* and not *that*-finite, produces in Rosenbaum's system the grammatical sequence *I want to go*, after the operation of later rules. But the first two possibilities listed are inconceivable. Rosenbaum's theory of complementizer-placement gives no grounds on which to reject (1) and (2). But if we consider *that*-finite placement an ungoverned rule to which no exceptions are possible, then (1) would be automatically ruled out. Of course, (2) is what happens in our system, but one process after the other rather than simultaneously. *For-to* cannot apply unless *that*-finite has applied. If (3) happens, because of the stipulation in the verb's complex symbol that *for-to* must be applied, the resultant string is ungrammatical. In our system, the fourth possibility is, as was said, impossible.

7. These are not the only complementizers found in English. Other rarer ones are found with a few verbs.

    1. I hated it *when* Harry came in at five A.M. on Wednesday.
    2. Did you like it *how* Elizabeth Taylor socked him vigorously in the movie?
    3. Clarissa always liked it *if* they sent her flowers.
    4. I couldn't stand it *where* she got lost in her own bathroom in the Bloomington Hilton.

    Notice that in sentences in which *where*, *when*, and *how* are really used as adverbs of place, time, and manner, they cannot co-occur with prepositional phrases of place, time, or manner, respectively, as they do here, indicating that here they are being used as complementizers, rather than as adverbs.

    5. *I know when Harry came in at five A.M. on Wednesday.
    6. *I wonder how she socks him vigorously in the movie.
    7. *I asked where she got lost in the bathroom in the Bloomington Hilton.

8. This description of the operation of Rules (2a) and (2b) bypasses a problem that is, at present, interesting but unresolvable. In the deep structure, verbs are generated with tense specified, probably as a feature of the verb:

$$\text{go} \atop [+ \text{present}]$$

Person-number agreement is, of course, not indicated in the base but is rather added later by agreement rules, according to the subject NP. The complementizers *for-to* and possessive-*ing* share the property that, when they are chosen, the embedded verb loses all these distinctions, becoming *non-finite*, as was noted in the text. Non-finiteness, then, is introduced by the complementizer chosen, and we ought probably to understand our *for-to* and poss-*ing* representations as abbreviations for fuller expressions: *for-to* + non-finite, and possessive-*ing* + non-finite.

It is not clear just how these complementizers impose non-finiteness on the verb. In the case of tense, we can imagine a rule that deletes the tense feature in the environment of the non-finite marker, except that there is no other example of a syntactic rule that deletes features (as opposed to segments). If the agreement rules precede complementizer-placement and complement-change, then a similar solution could be envisioned for person-number. But again, in this case too, it is not clear how the rule could be written to recognize the features in question as the ones to be removed, while leaving other features present, such as, in Latin, conjugation-class ending and aspect if this is a feature. Another possibility is to add [+ non-finite] as a feature to the verb's complex symbol as part of the complementizer-changing rule and leave the other features there to be realized later in the grammar as segments. The segments, then, could be deleted later in the presence of the feature [+ non-finite]. Infinitive and participial endings could then be added. The trouble with this possibility is its awkwardness: additional rules are required, where intuition suggests that there is only one actual process. At present, however, we can neither suggest a better solution nor choose between these two rather unsatisfactory proposals.

9. The node NP of the subject of the lower sentence, in the deep structure *I* of *I eat kittens*, has been deleted in accordance with Ross's tree-pruning convention (Ross, 1967). An NP node that, because of deletions performed on it, no longer branches is deleted.

10. For example, it applies obligatorily to the following intermediate structures (in the writer's dialect):

    1. It that John shot Harry happened.
    2. It that John is the head of the CIA is likely.

It is optional in sentences like the following:

    1. It that John was here yesterday is inconceivable.
    2. It that Harry dropped the H-bomb on Memorial Hall is curious.

If the sentence is one where the operation of extraposition is optional, and it does not apply, then Rule (8), *it*-deletion, must apply. If extraposition has applied, then (8) cannot apply, of course.

11. *For* must still be present when preposition-deletion, Rule (9), applies because of tree-pruning conventions. If *for* had been deleted before the operation of Rule (9), the NP dominating it would also have had to be deleted. Then the S dominating both this NP and the VP of the lower sentence would automatically be pruned. Rule (9) requires the presence of S to the right of the preposition to be deleted.

12. It is frequently argued that one rather often finds sentences in which this restriction is ignored: *I persuaded myself to go to the police, I ordered myself to march straight up to President Johnson and tell him what I thought of his Vietnam policy,*

I dared myself to walk alone across the Boston Common at midnight. But in such cases, the effect is usually humorous or semihumorous: the speaker sees himself as split into two people, one of whom is exhorting the other to do something. There is a sort of inner dialogue here with one speaker playing two parts. This may or may not be different from the construction found in, for example, *I wanted myself to go, I believed myself to be a fool*; in the latter two examples, the distinction seems less clear, if it exists at all.

13. A great deal more will be said in later chapters about forms such as those marked + Pro in diagrams (87), (88), (89), (90), and (91). These abstract verbs, or pro-forms, are thought of as representations of verbs with the general meaning and sometimes the syntactic properties of a whole class of verbs: they contain all the semantic features this class of verbs shares in common but no special ones of their own. They have no phonological features and are deleted by various transformational rules late in the syntactic component of the grammar.

14. Unfortunately, this tentative analysis is not completely devoid of problems. For example, if *persuade* in one meaning and *believe* are to share deep-structure similarities and some syntactic similarities, why is *I don't believe it of him* grammatical, but not **I couldn't persuade Mary of it of him?*

15. The term "pseudo-cleft sentence" has been used recently principally by Rosenbaum, Lakoff (1965), and Ross (1967). It describes sentences like the following:

1. What I did was go to the movies.
2. What she is now is happy.
3. What I know is that virtue will triumph.
4. What I planned was to invite them all to the party.

But we do not find the following:

5. *What I endeavored was to go.
6. *What I dared was to shoot Bill.

Ross derives these sentences from, for example, for (1), *The thing I did was to go to the movies.* Previous analyses derived *What* from *It that.* Ross discusses these analyses in full in the work cited and gives reasons for preferring his.

16. The analysis of complements presented in this chapter, and underlying the assumptions of the following chapters, should not be considered as a complete description of the phenomena of complementation. At the present time, unfortunately, enough is known to convince workers in this field that an analysis such as the one given here is, in many respects, not thorough or deep enough to account for many significant facts; but, on the other hand, very little is known or even hypothesized about what a more complete theory of complementation would contain. Therefore this analysis is presented with the hope that it will be taken with a grain of salt; as it stands, it is probably not really wrong—it does not directly contradict any data—but rather is not wholly correct, in that it is essentially an intermediate level of analysis, somewhere between the deeper analysis that would be necessary for a complete solution, and a wholly superficial solution. A truly correct solution should echo some of our intuitions about the nature of the complement system.

For example, it has been pointed out by Kiparsky (oral communication) that, in many cases, the choice of complementizer is not optional but is rather governed by semantic factors. As an example, in the sentence *I like it that John swims fast*, the complementizer *that* appears to carry with it the implication that the act has been performed at some time by the subject of the embedded sentence. But in *I like people to swim fast*, *to* carries no such implication. Hence, in a contrary-to-fact sentence, *for-to* is a possible complementizer with *like*, but *that* is not:

I would like it for John to swim fast, but he refuses to try.
*I would like it that John swims fast, but he refuses to try.

But this distinction is not carried through everywhere: there are instances of *for-to* being used to express the idea that an action was performed, as well as cases where *that*-finite does not necessarily indicate that the action in the embedded sentence took place.

All reasonable men believe John to be a fool.
I would say that John is trustworthy, but he isn't.

Therefore, although there is clearly some relationship between the complementizer chosen and the semantics of the sentence (a relationship that our treatment cannot take account of, except in its use of redundancy rules applying to semantic classes), not enough is known about the facts at present for us to be able to make use of this information. Therefore, it seems wiser not to incorporate these undoubtedly correct, but still poorly understood, intuitions into our treatment at present. It is probable that, as we become better able to deal with the relationship between syntax, semantics, and morphology, we shall be able to extend this sort of treatment by taking intuitions such as Kiparsky's into account. One does not exclude the other.

3. Complementation in Latin

In the preceding chapter we presented an analysis of complement constructions in English and some of the evidence motivating that analysis. Although some of the evidence was based on very subtle grammatical judgments of native speakers of English, much of it did not require a native speaker's intuition but could have been found by even a non-native speaker with a good command of the language. In this chapter we shall examine the Latin complement system. Since there are no native speakers of Latin, we cannot hope to find evidence equivalent to what we can find in English, even though such evidence may sometimes be required to decide between two competing grammatical analyses. However, we know enough about Latin to enable us to outline the principal facts concerning complementation in that language. As we shall see, the evidence that is available for Latin leads us to believe that the rules of complement formation in that language are essentially the same as those in English.

A conclusion such as this would be startling to the traditional grammarian accustomed to thinking of the grammar of Latin as very different from that of English. The reason Latin syntax has appeared so different from that of English is that it has always been approached in the wrong way. Philologists attempt to work on syntactic problems as if they were outgrowths of the morphology of a language. Syntax itself usually consists, for them, of little more than word order and the placement of enclitics. We have little to say on these topics. But what we are dealing with here under the name of syntax is the same topic that is dealt with by many philologists under various morphologically based subheads: "The Prolative Infinitive," "The Infinitive of Indirect Discourse," "The Subjunctive of Command," "The Potential Subjunctive," and so forth. The result of dividing the subject of complementation into a large number of unrelated morphological facts is that the relationships among, for example, subjunctives and infinitives have never been fully explored as they should have been. The real relationship between the infinitive and the finite verb is not a subject for study to classical philologists. Then when they approach Vulgar Latin and see the infinitive of indirect discourse change to *quod* plus a finite verb, they cannot account for the change satisfactorily, since accusative-infinitive and *quod*-finite are unrelated morphologically. Within classical Latin they are unable to find any relationship between the accusative-infinitive of *volo me esse consulem* and the nominative-infinitive of *volo esse consul*. They resort to calling the second a borrowing, which does not tell us how it is related to the first. Similarly, they are unable to find a relationship between either of these sentences and their English counterparts.

Our belief is that these facts are not to be relegated to the morphology, to be dealt with as separate parts of the language. We feel that the subject of syntax is the way sentences are formed in a language. The nature of the subjunctive and its relationship to the indicative and to the infinitive are not questions of morphological endings but of the function of the word containing these endings in the sentence containing that word. A sentence cannot be segmented into discrete, independent elements.

In the previous chapter we discussed a number of related sentence types in English. To state the relationships among these types, we had to set up certain deep structures and certain transformational rules. In this chapter, we shall show that a great many of the relationships between sentences that we found in English also hold in Latin. Using similar arguments, we shall demonstrate that essentially the same deep structures and transformational rules as we found in the case of English complement constructions also occur in Latin.

It appears to be the case, in complement constructions, that the deep structures that had to be set up for English are identical to those we must set up for Latin. One could argue similarly that the deep structures underlying relative clauses and coordinate sentences in the two languages are also identical. If it is the case, as many people now believe, that complementation, relativization, and conjunction are the only means of recursion in a language and that other ways of producing complex sentences from simple ones—the addition of adverbial clauses, for example—are merely types of complementation, then it would appear that English and Latin share the same phrase structure rules defining deep structure.[1]

3.1 Latin and English

That the same recursive properties that exist in English are found in Latin—including, of course, complementation—can be clearly seen from such sentences as the following:

(1a)   Volo Marcum ire. 'I want Marcus to go.'

(1b)   Volo ire. 'I want to go.'

(1c)   Dico me esse consulem. 'I say that I am consul.'

(1d)   Marco impero ut eat. 'I order Marcus to go.'

(1e)   Accidit ut Marcus iret. 'It happened that Marcus went.'

Sentences like these operate under the same constraints as do sentences containing complements in English. The verb of the main sentence, again, must be one that can take abstract objects or subjects. Hence, just as sentences like those of (5) in Chapter 2 are ungrammatical, sentences like the following are not possible in Latin:

(2a)   *Edi Marcum venire. 'I ate that Marcus was coming.'

(2b)   *Caeruleum est ut Marcus eat. 'It is blue that Marcus is going.'

Therefore, it is evident that for a sentence like (1a) we can set up a deep structure similar to that which we would set up for its English translation. This is shown in diagram (3). That *Marcum* is, in the deep

(3)

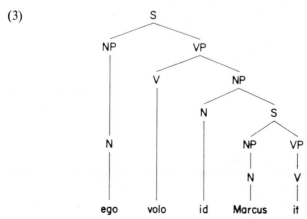

structure, the subject of *ire* and that *ire* represents a finite verb with third person endings is indicated by the fact that (1a) alternates with another sentence type in Latin:

(4)   Volo ut Marcus eat. 'I want Marcus to go.'

In this sentence, *Marcus* remains the superficial subject of the lower sentence. The verb retains its finite endings. Hence, from a sentence such as (4) we can tell that it is correct to set up *Marcus it* as a single constituent, S, dominated by NP (that it is one is not evident from *Volo Marcum ire*). On the other hand, *eat* in (4) is a subjunctive, which is not the basic form of the verb. (The basic mood of a verb is, of course, the indicative.)

3.2 Complementizer-Placement

Since the indicative has always been assumed to be the basic form of the verb, if we are looking for a complementizer that is comparable to *that*-finite in English, which we gave reasons for considering as basic, we shall try to find one in which the indicative endings are present. This is true in the following sentences, of which (5b) is Vulgar Latin:

(5a)   Accidit quod Marcus Publium vidit. 'It happened that Marcus saw Publius.'

(5b)   Dico quod Marcus bonus est. 'I say that Marcus is good.'

This complementizer, *quod*-finite, is found in classical Latin only in subject complements, and even there not as frequently as other complementizers.[2] The fact that it is relatively uncommon is, however, no reason why it should not be considered basic. The complementizer-changing rules simply operate obligatorily in more classes of verbs in Latin than in English. (In Vulgar Latin, however, for many of these classes of verbs these rules become optional or nonapplicable.) Our arguments for having a basic complementizer added by a complementizer-placement rule, and then changed where necessary by later complementizer-changing rules, are just as valid in Latin as in English. It can be shown that in Latin as well as in English only two types of violations, rather than the three logically possible if *quod*-finite were on an equal footing with the others, are ever found (cf. Chapter 2, note 6). For these reasons, we assume that the first of our rules in Latin is essentially identical to that of English, except that *quod* appears instead of *that*. It is stated as follows:

Rule (1) Complementizer-Placement

$$X_1 - it - S - X_2 \rightarrow 1 - 2 - quod + 3 - 4$$
$$1 \quad 2 \quad 3 \quad 4$$

Just as in English, this complementizer is adjoined to S. This rule yields structures comparable to the sentences (21) of Chapter 2.

(6a)   Volo quod Marcus it.[3]

(6b)   Volo quod ego eo.

(6c)   Dico quod ego sum consul.

(6d)   Accidit quod Marcus it.

3.3 Complementizer-Change

Except for (6d), and (6c) in Vulgar Latin, these sentences are not grammatical as they stand. Hence, we hypothesize rules that change *quod*-finite to the other complementizers found in Latin. The question is whether these rules are like Rule (1), essentially identical in form in Latin and English, or whether the shape of these rules is quite different in Latin from that of English.

One of the complementizer-changing rules converts a deep-structure nominative subject to an accusative and adds to the verb an infinitive ending. This complementizer has been identified with *for-to* of English, and, indeed, there are considerable similarities. Cases in Latin are analogous in many ways to prepositions in English: the English rule adjoined a preposition to NP, creating a new NP node above the old one. It thus expresses the intuition that, if *John* in *I expect for John to go* is an NP in the deep structure, *for John* is an NP in the derived structure. Likewise in Latin, if *Marcus* in *Volo Marcum ire* is an NP, so is *Marcum* in the derived structure. Hence, the adjunction of accusative to NP is similar to that of *for-to* NP in English. The question is whether the treatment of the two is identical: *for* is a segment, an independent word. But accusative is just an ending on a noun and is probably to be thought of as a feature added to that noun's stem.[4] In that case, the adjunction would not create a new NP node, as there would be no branching of accusative-*Marcus* as there is of *for John*. In the deep structure, the proper noun *Marcus* has a number of features in its complex symbol: [+ concrete], [+ human], [+ singular], [+ masculine], and perhaps others. The new case feature is added transformationally at the bottom of these. Hence, in this interpretation, after accusative-infinitive placement, the NP would look like diagram (7). If, by later

(7)

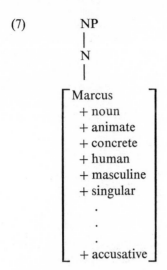

transformations, the case marking of this noun is changed, the rule changing the case will erase [+ accusative] and substitute the new case marking.

In the verb phrase, the treatment of infinitive in Latin seems very much like the treatment of *to* in English. In Latin, the rule attaches the infinitive ending *-se* to a non-finite form of the verb. The only difference between Latin and English here is that in English, *to* remains a morphologically independent word, while in Latin *-se* is adjoined to the verb, like *-ing* in English. It is adjoined to the right of the verb stem, also like *-ing*. We shall handle *-se* placement as we handled *-ing* placement in English: we shall introduce *-se* just as we introduced *to*, but a later rule will move *-se* to the right of the verb stem and attach *-se* to it. It carries with it a non-finite marker: all tense and person-number endings are deleted when this is adjoined to a verb. This is true in English too (cf. Chapter 2, note 8). The only distinction that can be made in the infinitive is one of aspect. Hence, although the verb embedded in *want*, or *volo*, must be future, this future tense is deleted in *Volo Marcum ire* and *I want John to go*. (Infinitive may be a feature of the verb, as accusative is a feature of the noun; or it may be a segment added to the right of the verb stem. There is not enough evidence at present to enable us to make a non–*ad hoc* decision.) The rule for accusative-infinitive complementizer-change is as follows:

Rule (2a) Accusative-Infinitive Complementizer-Change

$$X_1 - quod - \text{NP} - \text{VP} - X_2 \rightarrow 1 - \emptyset - 3 - \text{C} + 4 - 5$$
$$[+ \text{acc.}]$$

1   2   3   4   5

(C = -*se* + non-finite)

The operation of this rule on the derived structure produced by the operation of complementizer-placement on the deep structure of diagram (3) gives the structure illustrated in (8).

(8)

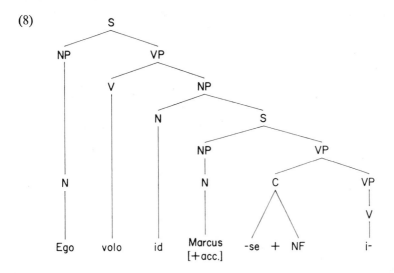

There is no complementizer in Latin comparable to poss-*ing*. There is, however, in Latin one that is not really analogous to anything in English. This is found in sentences like the following:

(9a)   Volo ut Marcus eat. 'I want Marcus to go.'

(9b)   Accidit ut Marcus iret. 'It happened that Marcus went.'

(9c)   Marco imperavi ut iret. 'I ordered Marcus to go.'

(9d)   Rogavi ut abiret. 'I asked that he leave.'

The introductory word of this complementizer is *ut*. The verb has a special suffix, the subjunctive, and also person-number tense distinctions. This third kind of complementizer can be called *ut*-subjunctive.

This complementizer is frequently found with verbs that correspond to English verbs occurring with *that*-non-finite. But *ut* is not equivalent in meaning to *that*: its meaning, when not used as a complementizer, is "how." Subjunctives are finite: they express tense distinctions (at least present-past, as there is no future subjunctive) and person-number distinctions. Perhaps subjunctive is to be considered comparable to *should* or *would* in English (as in "I wish he *would* go "); if so, then *that ... should* is another complementizer in English. But it is most reasonable at this time to assume that *ut*-subjunctive is not parallel to anything in English, just as possessive-*ing* appears not to be parallel to anything in Latin. *Ut* is adjoined to S replacing *quod*; probably, subjunctive is added as a feature of the verb, as accusative was added as a feature of the noun. Under this assumption, the rule that changes *quod*-finite to *ut*-subjunctive is written as follows:

Rule (2b) *Ut*-Subjunctive Complementizer-Change

$$X_1 - quod - \text{NP} - \text{VP} - X_2 \rightarrow 1 - ut - 3 - \text{subj} + 4 - 5$$
$$1 \quad 2 \qquad 3 \qquad 4 \qquad 5$$

The tree representing the derived structure at this stage in the derivation of *Volo ut Marcus eat* is as given in (10).

(10)

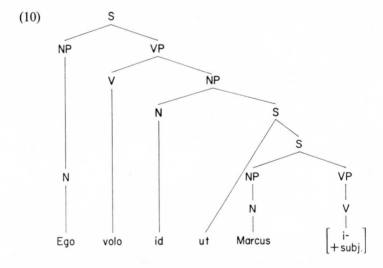

The complementizer-placement and complementizer-changing rules in Latin, then, are similar to those in English. But the domain of the various rules is different in the two languages: for example, verbs of saying (when not passivized) in English may not undergo any of the complementizer-changing rules, but in classical Latin, all such verbs (*dico, aio, nego,* etc.) must undergo Rule (2a), accusative-infinitive complementizer-change. It is this difference as to which parts of Rule (2) may apply to a given meaning-class that makes this part of the syntax of Latin so different in superficial appearance from its English counterpart. But the only real difference is that in Latin Rules (2a) and (2b) apply far more frequently and obligatorily than the corresponding complementizer-changing rules apply in English. In English *that*-finite is found frequently in the surface structure. In Latin it is found only with certain subject complements. This discrepancy is not brought about by the existence of different complementizer-changing rules in the two languages but rather by a difference in the lexical redundancy rules that state which complementizer-changing rules must apply to verbs of a general meaning-class. The redundancy-rule mechanism, dependent on the concept of markedness and rule government, was discussed briefly in the preceding chapter (see Section 2.4). It can be shown that the changes in complementizer-placement and complementizer-change rules that occur between classical and Vulgar Latin, and between the latter and Romance, are not to be interpreted as resulting from changes in the transformational component: they are not, that is, the result of any change in the form of Rule (1), or any part of Rule (2). These changes are to be interpreted as brought about by changes in the redundancy rules. This is in general true of all the governed rules that have been studied. In the sixth chapter evidence will be presented to support this claim with respect to changes from Latin to Spanish, for many of the rules discussed in the second chapter. For the present, we should like to discuss how the concept of redundancy rules is applied to the complementizer system of Latin and how this can be used to explain the changes found in one meaning class in Vulgar Latin. We do not attempt to give a reason for this change, as we cannot give reasons why any change took place; moreover, frequent attempts by philologists to give reasons are to be discounted. We merely show that there is a way to handle certain kinds of syntactic changes within transformational theory.

For verbs of saying, in classical Latin, the redundancy rule states that Rule (2a), complementizer-changing, must apply if the verb is regular. Anything else is exceptional. When *dico* is listed in the lexicon, its grammatical properties are listed in terms of markedness: *dico* is marked for a rule if the redundancy rule governing its meaning-class dictates that verbs of this class do not undergo the rule, and this verb does, or if the redundancy rule dictates that verbs of this class must undergo the rule, and *dico* does not. Otherwise it is unmarked. The markings, of course, apply only to governed rules. Hence, no verb is marked for Rule (1). But any verb which takes an abstract subject or object must be marked as undergoing or not undergoing Rule (2). Verbs of saying, in classical Latin, may only occur with accusative-infinitive: for this class, then, undergoing Rule (2a) is unmarked. The redundancy rule, stated informally, expresses this fact:

Redundancy Rule A

For verbs of saying: If a verb is unmarked for (2a), it obligatorily undergoes (2a): if marked for (2a), the verb does not undergo it.

The verb *dico* is entered into the lexicon of a typical speaker of classical Latin as follows:

u Rule (2a)
u Rule (2b)

This notation indicates that *dico* behaves perfectly regularly for its class. All we need to know to use this verb correctly is the redundancy rule and the fact that *dico* is unmarked. There are no examples in Latin of any verb of this class which is irregular. In the hypothetical case that one existed, it would still necessarily undergo Rule (1). It would be marked for Rule (2a) and would therefore not undergo it. If it were unmarked for Rule (2b), it would not undergo (2b) either; it would undergo only (1). But if it were doubly marked, for (2b) as well as (2a), it would take *ut*-subjunctive. (We are speaking here of verbs of communicating, with *dico* in the meaning of *say that*, rather than *say to*.) It may seem that something of this sort is happening in Vulgar Latin, as for example, in the *Satyricon* of Petronius. The speakers of the dialect represented in the *Cena Trimalchionis* can apparently use all verbs of this class either as they are used in classical Latin, with accusative-infinitive, or with *quod*-finite. But this change is not to be interpreted as a change in the lexical properties of each of the individual verbs of this class. That is, we are not claiming that for Trimalchio, *dico* was listed as m Rule (2a). This would be the correct interpretation if *dico* alone behaved in this way. But it appears that the whole class of verbs of saying and thinking could occur with both the complementizers mentioned. This suggests that it is the redundancy rule that has changed, and that both the complementizer-changing rule and the lexical entries for these verbs remain just as they were in classical Latin. For Trimalchio and his guests, Redundancy Rule A is replaced by Redundancy Rule B.

Redundancy Rule B (Vulgar Latin)

For verbs of saying: If a verb is unmarked for Rule (2a), the verb optionally undergoes the rule. If a verb is unmarked for Rule (2b), it may not undergo the rule.

There are, as for classical Latin, no verbs of this class attested which are marked for either of these rules. The further changes that occur in verbs of this class in Romance will be discussed in the sixth chapter.

So far, we have been discussing the behavior of meaning-classes of verbs in which all the verbs in a class behaved in the same way with respect to a rule. But this is not the only situation that is possible. In Latin, as in English, there are verbs that are themselves irregular with respect to the rules we have been discussing: although most verbs of a given meaning-class occur with one complementizer, these irregular verbs will always, or usually, occur with another. This situation is found in Latin with verbs of ordering. For most of these verbs, Rule (2a) may not apply, and Rule (2b) must. Thus the following sentences are grammatical:

(11a)   Marco imperavi ut veniret. 'I ordered Marcus to come.'

(11b)   Marco mandavi ut veniret. 'I ordered Marcus to come.'

But for most speakers of classical Latin, the following were not:

(11c)   *Imperavi Marcum venire.

(11d)   *Mandavi Marcum venire.

On the other hand, the verb *iubeo*, also with the meaning *order*, works in the opposite way:

(12a)   *Marco iussi ut veniret.

(12b)   Iussi Marcum venire. 'I ordered Marcus to come.'

For verbs of ordering, the redundancy rule follows:

Redundancy Rule C

For verbs of ordering: If such a verb is unmarked for Rule (2a), it does not undergo it; if it is marked for (2a), it must undergo it. If it is unmarked for (2b), it must undergo it; if marked for Rule (2b), it cannot undergo it.

Impero, then, is entered in the lexicon as follows:

> *Impero* (verb of ordering)
> u Rule (2a)
> u Rule (2b)

It is thus completely regular. *Iubeo*, on the other hand, is entered in the following way:

> *Iubeo* (verb of ordering)
> m Rule (2a)

It is unnecessary to mark this verb for Rule (2b): it must obligatorily undergo (2a) and therefore cannot undergo (2b). In this way, we can state what we know about these verbs: that *impero, mando,* etc., are regular, and *iubeo* is irregular, with respect to the application of complementizer-change.[5] A third possibility, not found, is that a verb of this class might be marked for both Rules (2a) and (2b): that is, it might undergo neither and thus take *quod*-finite.

We have shown that complementizer-placement and complementizer-change, the first two rules for complementation, as they are found in Latin, operate on deep structures like those of English and produce derived structures very much like those of English though not identical to them. Not surprisingly, the rules themselves are very similar in the two languages. Infinitives and subjunctives are shown to be merely ways of subordinating one sentence to another and are mutually exclusive: a subjunctive infinitive, though theoretically possible on morphological grounds, is never found. Now we shall examine the structures produced by the operation of the first two rules, to see whether any of our further rules must necessarily operate on them.

3.4 Equi-NP-Deletion

Consider the following sentences:

(13a)   Volo Iuliam esse bonam.

(13b)   Volo esse bonus.

(13c)   Volo me esse bonum.

(13d)   *Volo esse bonum.

Just as we know that the embedded sentence of (13a) has a subject, *Iulia*, we know that the embedded sentence of (13b) has one as well. We also know that the subject of (13b) is masculine, as opposed to that of (13a), which is feminine. The same is true for (13c), but there the subject is present. The meaning of (13b) is identical to that of (13c). Therefore, it is evident that the deleted subject of (13b) must be the same as the subject present in (13c): *ego*. It is deleted by the same rule as is found in English, equi-NP-deletion. The statement of Rule 3 is approximately the same. But the segment numbered 4 (for) in the rule given in Chapter 2 is not present here. Instead, the whole NP is erased —including, of course, the [+ accusative] feature. If the NP is deleted, then there is no [+ accusative] left with which to perform agreement across copula, and *bonus* remains in the nominative. Agreement across copula, then, is ordered after equi-NP-deletion. If, on the other hand, this rule does not operate (it is optional for verbs of wishing), then agreement across copula is obligatory: *Volo me esse consul* is ungrammatical.

Sentence (13d) is generally considered ungrammatical. There are one or two instances of it in later writers such as Pliny. The fact that for Pliny (13d) was grammatical may indicate that he could optionally change the order of his rules so that agreement across copula applied before this rule but after complementizer-change.

In English there is no class of verbs that must undergo *for-to* complementizer-change, giving them the correct structural description for undergoing equi-NP-deletion but must not undergo it. In classical Latin there is such a class of verbs: verbs of saying and thinking.

(14a)   Dico me esse consulem.

(14b)   *Dico esse consul.

A redundancy rule for verbs of this class must indicate that they cannot undergo equi-NP-deletion, even though they meet the structural description. Verbs like *be able*, *try*, and the like are the only ones in Latin which obligatorily undergo this rule. Hence, the domain of the rule in English is considerably wider than it is in Latin. But it must apply sometimes in Latin in order to produce sentences like (13b).

3.5 *It-Substitution*

In English it was possible to tell whether Rule (4), *it*-substitution, had applied in object complements by seeing whether the complementizer *for* (or poss.) was still present in the surface structure as it would be only if equi-NP-deletion had not taken place. If the complementizer were still present, then *it*-substitution could not have applied. In Latin there is no such simple test. We have shown that the complementizing morpheme in Latin which corresponds to *for* is simply the case-marking accusative. But if *it*-substitution applied and the subject of the lower sentence became the direct object of the verb of the higher sentence, it would appear as an accusative in the surface structure too. Hence, a sentence like (15a) tells us nothing about whether this rule has applied, although its counterparts (15b) and (15c), respectively, are sentences to which *it*-substitution has and has not applied.

(15a)   Exspecto Marcum venturum esse. 'I expect Marcus to come.'

(15b)   I expect John to come.

(15c)   I expect for John to come.

Therefore, it appears that the only place in which unambiguous evidence as to whether this rule applies is to be found is in subject complements. If *it*-substitution has applied to them, the subject of the lower sentence will in the surface structure be in the nominative case; otherwise, it will be accusative, the case representing the complementizing morpheme. We can test this in three cases of subject complementation: one case is that of personal passives, in which the subject of the lower sentence must undergo *it*-substitution at some point in order for it alone to be in direct object position in the higher sentence and thus to be able to be exchanged for the subject of the higher sentence and finally substituted again for the subject *it* of the passive (according to Postal's formulation, discussed in Section 2.8). A sentence like *Marcus dicitur esse consul*, 'Marcus is said to be consul,' indicates that *it*-substitution must be a rule of Latin. For example, consider the following sentences, in which the personal passive is found. This is more frequent in Latin than the impersonal passive with verbs of saying and thinking.

(16a)   Qui unus omnium iustissimus fuisse traditur. (Cic. Sest. 67, 141) 'Who alone is said to have been the most just of all.'

(16b)   Themistocles suasisse existimatur Atheniensibus ut . . . (Quint. 9, 2, 92) 'Themistocles is thought to have persuaded the Athenians that . . .'

(16c)   Illi socius esse diceris. (Pl. Rud. 1, 2, 72). 'You are said to be an ally of his.'

But with verbs of this class the impersonal passive too is found, indicating that for some speakers of classical Latin, at least, *it*-substitution was optional for these verbs.

(17a)   Galbam, Africanum, Laelium doctos esse traditum est. (Cic. Tusc. 1, 3, 5) 'It has been related that Galba, Africanus and Laelius were learned men.'

(17b)   Huic [insulae] milia DCCC in longitudinem esse existimatur. (Caes. B. G. 5, 13) 'It is thought that this island is 800 miles in length [lit., 'that there are 800 miles to this island . . .'].'

(17c)   Dicitur eo tempore matrem Pausaniae vixisse. (Nepos, Pausanias, 5, 3) 'It is said that the mother of Pausanias was alive at this time.'

A second environment where *it*-substitution is evident is that of certain verbs that undergo flip, thus putting the deep-structure object in superficial subject position. These cases are like passives in that they can be either personal or impersonal. If they are personal, that indicates that *it*-substitution has applied. We shall present later in the chapter evidence that flip is necessary in Latin; here we shall assume that it can take place and produces structures like the following when *it*-substitution applies:

(18a)   Ut beate vixisse videar, quia . . . (Cic. Lael. 4, 15) 'That I may seem to have lived happily, because . . .'

(18b)   Ut exstinctae potius amicitiae quam oppressae esse videantur. (Cic. Lael. 21, 28) 'That friendships may seem quenched rather than stamped out.'

Just as in English, the impersonal form was also possible, though less common:

(19)   Non mihi videtur, ad beate vivendum satis posse virtutem. (Cic. Tusc. 5, 5, 12) 'It doesn't seem to me that virtue can be sufficient for living happily.'

There are thus some cases at least of *it*-substitution in Latin. In English this rule also applies to some deep-structure subject complements: *John is right to go; Sally is likely to be rich.* In Latin, however, the rule does not operate in this environment.

(20a)   Aequum est Marcum ire. 'It is right for Marcus to go.'

(20b)   Veri simile est Iuliam divitem esse. 'It is likely that Julia is rich.'

We do not find sentences like the following:

(21a)   *Marcus aequus est ire.

(21b)   *Iulia veri similis est dives esse.

In Section 2.14 we discussed verbs like *begin, end, tend*. These ostensibly object complements were dealt with by Lakoff as subject complements to which *it*-substitution had to apply. There are a number of strong reasons for dealing with these verbs this way. In Latin their behavior is the same as it is in English, and we should undoubtedly treat them like subject complements there too. In the surface structure they look just like their English counterparts.

(22a)   Marcus incipit currere. 'Marcus begins to run.'

(22b)   Marcus desinit flere. 'Marcus stops crying.'

If these are treated like their English counterparts, they are the only examples in Latin of subject complements which undergo *it*-substitution. Therefore, it seems that the rule must be constrained, in subject complements in Latin, so that it applies only if it is obligatory. Verbs such as *be right* and *be likely* in English undergo *it*-substitution optionally. Their Latin counterparts cannot undergo it at all. But deep-structure object complements that are superficial subjects optionally undergo this rule, and perhaps object complements in general do, though there seems to be no possibility of telling whether they do or not. If we assume that *it*-substitution operates both on deep-structure objects (such as *seem*) and deep-structure subjects (such as *begin*), then the statement of this rule in Latin must be like that for English, with a double structural description. The constituent-structure argument we gave in Chapter 2, using verb-gapping to show that if *it*-substitution had applied to object complements, there must be a third constituent, cannot be used with certainty in Latin since only a native speaker can pass judgment on subtle distinctions like this and be certain of being correct. But it is not out of the question that the following sentence, parallel to the ones given in the second chapter, is grammatical:

(23)   Marcus credit Publium esse divitem et Quintus, Gaium esse pauperem. 'Marcus believes Publius to be rich, and Quintus, Gaius to be poor.'

If this is true and such sentences are grammatical to the native speaker of Latin, *it*-substitution has not applied here. But it is not safe to draw any conclusions from the impressions of non-native speakers where these impressions cannot be validated by data.[6]

3.6 Flip

There is motivation for Rule (5), flip, within Latin in sentence pairs like the following:

(24a)   Animo autem virtute praedito . . . non admodum delectari. (Cic. Lael. 14) 'Not to be delighted overmuch with a spirit full of virtue.'

(24b)   Quam delectabat eum defectiones solis et lunae multo ante nobis praedicere. (Cic. De Sen. 14) 'How it would delight him to predict, long before us, solar and lunar eclipses.'

The second of these sentences has undergone flip; the first is the underlying form. Just as in English, the agentive found is not *ab*, 'by,' but rather the ablative alone, 'with.' This fact indicates that, in Latin as in English, we are not dealing with true passives. *Delectare* is one of the few verbs in Latin to which flip applies optionally. (In English, as was pointed out in the second chapter, all verbs of this class optionally undergo this rule.) Some verbs of this class (roughly, mental state) must undergo flip in Latin, and others are always found in their underlying form. Examples of the latter are verbs like *laetor*, 'be glad,' *miror*, 'be surprised.' These act like flips, rather than like passives or deponents: they are not deponent, because they are apparently passive in meaning. But they are not true passives, because they occur with the ablative alone, rather than the agentive.

(25a)   Laetor eo, Marcum venisse. 'I rejoice at this, that Marcus has come.'

(25b)   Miror eo, Marcum talem rem facere potuisse. 'I'm surprised at this, that Marcus could have done such a thing.'

Other verbs must undergo the rule. In this category are the so-called impersonal verbs. These verbs are all third person neuter, in agreement with *id*, 'it,' found in English in sentences to which flip has applied. These are found in sentences like the following:

(26a)   Iuvat Marcum Iuliam videre. 'It is pleasing for Marcus to see Julia.'

(26b)   Placet senatui hoc facere. 'It is the pleasure of the senate to do this.'

(26c)   Me pudet Marco hoc dicere. 'I am ashamed [lit., 'it shames me'] to tell this to Marcus.'

(26d)   Decet me hunc vestem gerere. 'It suits me to wear this clothing.'

(26e)   Licet vos esse beatos. 'It is permitted for you to be happy.'

(26f)   Oportet me Marcum videre. 'I ought [lit., 'it obliges me'] to see Marcus.'

In some verbs of this class we find rarely the passive used in an active sense, corresponding to the underlying form of the flip verb.

(27)   Miseremini sociorum. (Cic. Verr. 2, 1, 28) 'Take pity on your allies.'

(The more usual form is *Misereat vos sociorum*.) We also find passive perfects like *pertaesum est*, 'it wearied,' *pigitum est*, 'it disgusted,' *licitum est*, 'it was permitted,' for *pertaesit, piguit, licuit*. Passive forms such as this are difficult to explain in a verb with active endings elsewhere. In general, in Vulgar Latin and Romance deponent verbs lost their passive endings and became conjugated as actives (so, for example, *sequor*, 'follow,' becomes in Spanish *seguir*), rather than the other way around. Only with these flips do we find deponent endings substituted for active in part of the conjugation. (Of the few semideponents that exist outside this group, some are perhaps flip verbs with active endings in the imperfective system, and passive endings in the perfective. Thus we have *gaudeo, gavisus sum*, 'rejoice.') In Vulgar Latin, too, we find a number of cases in which these impersonal verbs have passive endings but with the same meaning as they would have without them. If we assume that flip operates in Latin as it does in English, then we can assume that these passive endings are added if flip does not apply. But perhaps this distinction breaks down in Vulgar Latin, to give forms like *pudeatur*, 'it should shame,' in Petronius (47, 4) and *paenitemini: credite evangelio*, 'repent: believe the Gospel' (*Biblia Vulgatae Editionis Evangelium Marci* 1, 15).

The flip rule that was described for English in Section 2.7 operates similarly in Latin. It attaches passive endings just as the English equivalent attached *be + ed*. It also exchanges subject and object. The rule in English attached *-ing* to the verb if it was adjectival. But in Latin there is no equivalent of this ending (perhaps related to the lack of possessive-*ing* complementizer), and therefore this part of the rule does not operate. We do find something that corresponds to the *to*-insertion rule in English:

(28a)   Mihi videtur Marcus esse stultus. 'Marcus seems to me to be a fool.'

(28b)   Feli licet regem spectare. 'A cat may look at a king.'
(Lit., 'it is permitted to a cat to look at a king.')

The *to*-insertion rule applies to some verbs of this class, as in English, but not to all. For some (such as *licet*) it is optional. For others, like *placet, videtur*, it is obligatory.

In the second chapter it was mentioned that *not*-transportation had to precede flip in order to prevent a difficulty in constraining the former rule. This appears to be true in Latin as well. Sentences such as (28) are evidence of this.

We have included *licet*, 'it is permitted,' and *oportet*, 'it is an obligation, one ought,' among the verbs that obligatorily undergo flip, and their meaning seems to allow this treatment, as these verbs, like the others, are verbs of mental state, or perception. There are various syntactic and semantic indications that these verbs should be considered as obligatory flip verbs. In the case of *licet*, we find the following four sentences:

(29a)   Licet me ire. 'It is allowed for me to go.'

(29b)   Licet mihi ire. 'It is allowed to me to go.'

(29c)   Licet eam. 'It is allowed for me to go.'

(29d)   Licet mihi eam. 'It is allowed to me to go.'

All of these are more freely translated into English as ' I may (am permitted to) go away.' But while (29a) and (29c) are synonymous as are (29b) and (29d), all four are not precisely identical in meaning. Sentences (29a) and (29c) may also have an additional dative, as follows:

(29e)   Licet matri me ire. 'It is permitted to my mother for me to go.'

In a sentence of this type, it is understood that the mother requested that her child be allowed to go. In the other two sentences, the meaning is 'It is permitted to me for me to go away.' This suggests that there is, in (29a) and (29c), a dative agreeing with the subject of the lower sentence and deleted under identity with it. The subject of the lower sentence appears as *me* of the *for-to* complement of (29a), and *ego*, later deleted of (29e), *licet (ego) eam*. There is probably a dative present in the deep structures of (29a) and (29c). This is the " unspecified person " or "someone" usually deleted both in Latin and in English, as in the English sentence "It is easy to please John," from "It is easy (for some unspecified person) to please John." The sentences here are derived from something like *licet (alicui) me ire, licet (alicui) eam*.

'It is permitted to (some unspecified person) for me to go.' Thus, we derive all cases of *licet* from an underlying **liceor*, 'I am allowed': sentences (29a) and (29c) have the following deep structure:

(30a)   [Aliquis] licetur id   S
                                ／\
                              ego eo

Sentences (29b) and (29d) share the following deep structure:

(30b)   Ego liceor id   S
                         ／\
                       ego eo

The difference between the members of each pair is that a different part of the complement-changing rule has applied in each case. We also find:

(31a)   Licet ire. 'One may go, it is permitted (to people) to go.'

This is derived from

(31b)   [Aliquis] licetur id   S
                                ／\
                           [Aliquis] it

The presence of the dative with *licet* is a strong indication that this verb has undergone flip. But in the case of *oportet*, there is no such evidence, as it occurs either with a subjunctive alone or with accusative-infinitive. The second is much commoner. The accusative must be the subject of the lower sentence, rather than the flip of the subject of the higher sentence, or we should expect to find sometimes **Me oportet eam*, which appears to be ungrammatical. If *oportet* is to be dealt with as a flip (we shall give reasons later for considering it so), then there must be a special rule that it undergoes to delete the subject of the higher sentence. This is perhaps not so unlikely, as it seems always to have to be identical to the subject of the lower sentence, with a deep structure perhaps of the following form, yielding *oportet me ire,* or *oportet eam*:

(32)   I oblige it   S
                      ／\
                     I go

The most obvious way to look at *oportet*, of course, is to assume that it takes a subject complement. If the arguments to be presented in the fifth chapter are valid, they give reasons why this solution is unsatisfactory; but those arguments cannot be used as evidence. There is another fact as well: *ut*-deletion is mandatory with *oportet* and very frequent with *licet*. It occurs in no subject complements, and it may occur in most classes of object complements, although these are exceptions. If *oportet* is to be considered a subject complement verb, we must complicate our redundancy rules so that *ut*-deletion (discussed in Section 3.11) will apply to *oportet*.

Another argument is semantic in nature. It is conceivable, of course, that a verb that takes a subject complement may have a very near synonym that occurs with an object complement. But there appear to be no cases of this, and it would seem to contradict the claim that deep structures are closely related to semantics. But *oportet* has a synonym that clearly takes an object complement. It is possible to consider *oportet* a flip and therefore a verb that takes an underlying object complement, identical in deep structure to its synonym but merely undergoing an additional transformation. It is much more likely, if we judge from analogous cases, that this is true, than that *oportet* requires a subject complement and its synonym an object complement. The synonym, *debeo*, 'ought to, should,' has in Latin, as its translation has in English, the constraint that the subjects of the higher and lower sentences must be identical, just as *oportet* has. Verbs of this type are traditionally considered auxiliaries, but arguments have been made (see Lakoff and Ross, forthcoming) that auxiliaries are not a special type of verb, but take complements just as other verbs do. Postal and Lakoff–Ross first present arguments that the nontense auxiliaries, such as *can* and *should*, work this way. According to their analysis, the deep structure of *I can see John* is

(33a)   I can it   S
I see John

The subject of the lower sentence obligatorily undergoes equi-NP-deletion. This analysis also works for *possum* in Latin and for *ought* and *should* in English, *debeo* and *oportet* in Latin.

(33b)   I ought it   S
I go

With *debeo*, the flip rule does not apply. With *oportet*, the deep structure is similar to that of *debeo*:

(34a)   Ego oporteor id   S
ego eo

Complementizer-placement applies, and then either accusative-infinitive or *ut*-subjunctive complementizer-change (for *debeo* and *possum*, only accusative-infinitive is possible). Equi-NP-deletion does not apply. Flip applies, yielding one or the other of the following:

(34b)   Id me ire oportet me.

(34c)   Id ut ego eam oportet me.

Me is then deleted by the special rule we mentioned before. *Ut* is deleted obligatorily with this verb (cf. Section 3.11). This will produce the correct surface structures.

3.7 Passivization

Rule (6), passivization, clearly operates in Latin, since sentences in Latin can be passivized just as those in English can. We discussed Postal's formulation of passivization in Section 2.8. Passivization in Latin works to some extent like that of English, but in other ways it is mysterious—just as a great deal of what happens in the passivization transformation in English is mysterious. We cannot tell at present whether the differences between the Latin and the English passive really reflect differences in the passivization rule itself, or whether they are brought about by later differences in morphological rules, while the syntactic passivization rules in the two languages are identical or nearly so. In any case, both produce sentences in which the subject and object are exchanged. Therefore, *it*-substitution is involved in passivization in both languages, accounting for the nominative ending on what is in the deep structure the direct object of the lower sentence. There is, incidentally, a rather interesting fact about Latin which perhaps lends strength to Postal's suggestion that passivization is the result of *it*-substitution in a subject complement. This application of *it*-substitution can take place only if subject and direct object in the lower sentence have previously changed their positions. It is apparently true in Latin that if the object of the verb is not in the accusative case (and thus, probably, not a deep-structure direct object), personal passivization cannot take place. The *it* of the higher sentence remains, and the object of the verb of the lower sentence remains in its original case, the dative.[7] For example:

(35a)   Marcus matri paret. 'Marcus obeys (is obedient to) his mother.'

(35b)   Matri paretur a Marco. 'His mother is obeyed by Marcus.'

(35c)   *Mater paretur a Marco.

(35d)   Matri a Marco paritum est. 'His mother was obeyed by Marcus.'

Compare the contrasting situation with a normal verb.

(36a)   Marcus videt matrem. 'Marcus sees his mother.'

(36b)   Mater videtur a Marco. 'His mother is seen by Marcus.'

In both English and Latin an agentive preposition is added to the subject noun of the lower sentence by this rule. In Latin, this is *ab* + ablative. The chief difference between the Latin passive and its English counterpart lies in the difference found in the imperfective system in Latin. In the perfective, passivization in Latin looks very much like that of English. A participial ending *-to-* is added to the verb stem and the verb *to be* (*esse*) is inserted. In the imperfective system, however, endings are added in Latin that have no counterparts in English. These are reflexes of Indo-European middle endings. Occasionally the middle was used where English uses a direct reflexive, but more frequently it was used where English merely has an anaphoric pronoun. "He scratched his head" would be translated into Greek and Sanskrit with the verb in the middle voice. In Latin these endings have become pure passives. In Spanish, however, the passive is expressed again by forms that look very much like reflexives, alternating with forms that are equivalent to *to be* + participle. The relationship between passive and reflexive is not expressed in Postal's formulation of passivization: it appears that some relationship exists, but it is not clear what that is.[8] Finally, it should be noted that, just as (37a) in English is ungrammatical, (37b) in Latin undoubtedly is, for the reason explained in the second chapter, that coreferential NP's cannot be exchanged.

(37a)   *John was washed by himself.

(37b)   *Marcus lautus est a se.

3.8 Extraposition

Since Latin is a language containing a late rule that freely (within certain limits that have not been fully studied) scrambles the order of words, we cannot tell whether Rule (7), extraposition, applies.[9] In English, a sentence like *It happened that Bill kissed Santa Claus* can be produced only if extraposition operates, separating *it* from *that* . . . *Claus*. In Latin, we have completely analogous sentences like this one:

(38)   Illud etiam restiterat, ut te in ius educerent. (Cic. Quinct. 33)
'That too remained—that they should drag you into court.'

The rule that deletes unemphatic subject pronouns in Latin usually deletes the *id* of the subject complement. But *illud* here is emphatic. This looks precisely like a case of extraposition, but the word-scrambling rule could also account for it. Therefore, if we postulated an extraposition rule for Latin, we should, considering the evidence available to us at present, merely be adding an unnecessary rule. The additional evidence required involves judgments about constituent structure which only a native speaker is qualified to make. Hence, the chances that we shall be able to verify the existence of an extraposition rule in Latin are dim. It should be noted, however, that this rule is known to operate in all the Romance languages. This is circumstantial evidence that it probably existed in Latin as well, but we cannot make that a definite claim.

3.9 *It*-Deletion

The next rule discussed in the second chapter is *it*-deletion, Rule (8). In English one of its functions is to remove the *it* of the subject complement when extraposition has not taken place, producing sentences like *That John shot Felicia is evident*. In Latin there is no need for a rule to do this; there is a rule that deletes all unemphatic subject pronouns, provided the main verb of the predicate is finite. (This proviso excludes the deletion of *me* in *dico me venire*, where *me*, if *it*-substitution has not applied, is the subject of *venire*, a non-finite verb; and in so-called independent subject infinitives, *Ego negare factum* . . . 'I keep denying that it was done.') In object complements, either *it*-deletion or *it*-substitution applies obligatorily. But we have no evidence as to how to interpret the fact that we probably do not find sentences such as

(39)   *Id scio Marcum venire, 'I know it that Marcus is coming.'

However, in Vulgar Latin, where *quod*-finite can be used with object complements, we find sentences like the following:

(40)   Id scio, quod Marcus venit.

It-substitution cannot apply in this environment, and the existence of (40) but not (39) may therefore be interpreted as indirect evidence for *it*-substitution taking place in object complements like (39). But we can make no claim on this basis for an *it*-deletion rule in classical Latin. We do, however, find sentences like the following:

(41a)   Laetor eo. 'I rejoice at it.'

(41b)   Eo laetor, Marcum venire. 'I rejoice at this, that Marcus is coming.'

(41c)   Laetor Marcum venire. 'I rejoice that Marcus is coming.'

Sentence (41c) has undergone *it*-deletion, optional for *laetor*, as it is optional for *like* in English. Its effect with *laetor* is to remove the pronoun *id*. But it is impossible to tell whether the rule is to be stated for Latin just as it is stated for English, since it is not certain where it applies and where it does not.

3.10 Preposition-Deletion

A preposition-deletion rule, like Rule (9) in English, is needed to take care of the preposition remaining in sentences like the following, after *it*-deletion has applied:

(42)   *Laetor de Marcum venire. 'I rejoice about that Marcus is coming.'

This rule is apparently just like its English counterpart.

3.11 *Ut*-Deletion

In Latin, *quod*, the equivalent of *that*, appears never to be deleted, although it appears too rarely in the classical language for us to make certain judgments.

(43)   *Accidit Marcus venit. 'It happened Marcus came,' from Accidit quod Marcus venit.

There is a Latin counterpart of the English Rule (10), *that*-deletion. There must be a rule to delete *ut*, but only under certain special circumstances, with only a few verbs. With some verbs it is very frequent, perhaps usual.

(44a)   Volo ames. (Cic. Att. 2, 10) 'I wish you to love.'

(44b)   Queramur licet. (Cic. in Caec. 41) 'We are allowed to complain.'

(44c)   Me ipsum ames oportet, non mea. (Cic. Fin. 2, 26) 'You ought to love me myself, not my possessions.'

With other verbs, it is found, but less frequently.

(45a)   Orant ignoscamus peccatum suum. (Pl., Am., 1, 1, 101) 'They
         beg that we forgive their wrongdoing.'

(45b)   Rogat finem faciat. (Caes. B. G., 1, 20) 'He asks that he
         make an end.'

(45c)   Qui postularent, eos qui sibi Galliaeque bellum intulissent,
         sibi dederent. (Caes. B. G., 4, 16, 3) 'Who demanded that
         those who had made war against them and against Gaul
         surrender to them.'

But with other verbs of the same class as some of those just given, this
rule cannot operate. For example, *postulo* and *rogo* are verbs of asking
or requesting. But other verbs of similar meaning—*peto, posco, flagito*—
cannot undergo *ut*-deletion. The rule is therefore governed. It applies
only to object complements, apparently.

(46a)   *Accidit Marcus veniret. 'It happened Marcus came.'

(46b)   *Est Marcus consul sit. 'It's so Marcus is consul.'

The rule can be stated just as it was (in Section 2.12) for English. But
a redundancy rule will state that it applies only to deep-structure
object complements. Notice that if we do not impose this constraint,
every subject-complement verb will have to be marked as not undergoing the rule, a considerable complication of the grammar. Notice
also that if *licet* and *oportet* are not treated as flips, then they are the
only verbs taking subject complements that undergo this rule; moreover, *oportet*, when it takes the subjunctive, undergoes it obligatorily.
But if they are regarded as flips, then they take deep-structure object
complements, and there is no problem, as far as this rule is concerned.

3.12 *For*-Poss Deletion

The part of Rule (11) that applies to possessive is inapplicable in
Latin since there is no possessive-*ing* complementizer. Since case
markings are removed when the noun phrases to which they are attached
are deleted, the accusative marker that is the equivalent of *for* will be
deleted by equi-NP-deletion. Therefore, there appears to be no need
for this rule in Latin.

3.13 Conclusions

We have discussed the motivations for assuming the existence in Latin of the rules needed for English complements. Most were needed, a few were not or were uncertain. But it should be made clear that the arguments that are used for determining the form and ordering of English rules are, in general, not available to the Latinist. In fact, a great many of the best arguments for ordering and form of rules in English are at present in doubt, as a result of the recent discovery (see note 6) that there may be no syntactic cycle. While the cycle seemed a certainty, the rules given in this chapter and the preceding could be ordered as they have been here. But if there is no cycle, then many of the arguments for ordering change and, with them, many of the crucial arguments dictating the actual form of the rules themselves are questionable. Even with the cycle, a number of the rules of English given in the last chapter could not be correctly formalized at present. *Ad hoc* formulations could be given for a number of these, as has been done in some studies of the syntax of English and other languages. It seems better, however, to state that certain things are not known when they are not known, rather than to set down an obviously incorrect attempt at rules about which we do not know very much. Then, if so little is known about English, which has been studied by many native speakers for many years in a transformational framework, it is foolish to expect rules and derivations in a treatment of Latin, especially as the form of many English rules was arrived at through inspection of sentences and non-sentences on which only the native speaker is able to pass judgment.

In this chapter we have not shown that the rules for complementation in Latin *must* be the same as those for English. However, many of them, and all of the more important ones, *can* be the same, and there is no reason to assume that they are very different. We have shown that essentially the same evidence that supports the analysis of English complement rules appears in Latin. From the same evidence, there is no reason to draw different conclusions. Whatever the precise formulation of English complement rules eventually turns out to be, the present evidence strongly indicates that the corresponding Latin rules will be much the same. This in itself is a rather surprising claim, if we consider the traditional view of the relationship between the syntax of Latin and that of English. We have presented evidence that the same rules may apply to deep structures in Latin as apply to those in English. Indirectly, we have presented evidence that the deep structures of Latin complements are similar and possibly identical to those of English. Otherwise, the same rules could not apply to both. With the evidence that we do have from Latin, we can make the claim that the Latin and English complement rules may be the same. We do not have enough Latin evidence to show that they *must* be the same.

The traditional grammarian believes implicitly that there is a great difference between the syntax of Latin and that of English. Asked the reasons for his belief, he cites sentences like those we have been discussing: he might, for example, mention the accusative-infinitive with verbs of saying where in English we have *that*-finite or the difference in formation of the passive in Latin and in English. We have shown that, although the corresponding constructions may be different, the transformational rules that produce them are not. The first difference we have shown to be the result of a difference in redundancy rules, rather than a difference in the syntactic component of the two languages. The second is a fact about the morphological components of the language, and not about syntax. In fact, there is no indication for any of the rules of English complementation that it must not apply in Latin. In a few cases, the evidence available to us does not conclusively demonstrate that a given rule must apply. It seems evident that in transformational terms, the syntactic components of Latin and English are very closely related. This is not what has been traditionally believed.

Notes

1. It may seem that there is an obvious counterexample to the claim that the deep structures of Latin and English are identical. This is the well-known difference between the languages in regard to word order. That is, in English the basic word order, seldom changed, is subject-verb-object (SVO). In Latin the word order is much freer, but the most frequent order, at least in the best prose, seems to be subject-object-verb (SOV). If these surface structure facts reflected a fact about the deep structure, then the deep structures of the two languages would differ markedly. In English there would be a phrase structure rule VP→V NP. In Latin the corresponding rule would be VP→NP V. Within the synchronic grammar of Latin itself, there is apparently no way to decide whether, in fact, the basic word order is SOV or SVO. If syntax operated under a simplicity criterion similar to that used in phonology, then we might be tempted to pick the order SOV, on the grounds that this was closer to the surface structure and hence required fewer rules. There appears, however, to be no reason for supposing there is any simplicity metric for syntax.

   If we look at the Romance languages, the curious fact emerges that in each of these languages the basic order is evidently SVO. In general, it seems a sensible theory to follow that if all the Romance languages share a given trait, that trait must have been present in Latin. Certainly, in Vulgar Latin, as in the *Cena Trimalchionis*, for example, sentences seem to be largely SVO. But throughout the history of Latin, Vulgar Latin was spoken alongside of classical Latin, and a reasonably literate Roman could understand and use either interchangeably. But it is absurd to think that one speaker could have in his grammar two different deep structures. This fact suggests that we should question whether SOV is, in fact, the word order basic to Latin, as has so often been claimed.

Aside from this, there is evidence from outside Latin that SVO is the basic word order in Latin. Greenberg, in his *Universals of Language*, presents some interesting and relevant statistics. In a survey of a great variety of the world's languages, he found that in every case where the basic order of the sentence was SOV, certain other facts tended to be true—among them, that postpositions were found instead of prepositions; relative clauses normally preceded the main clause; conjunctions followed, rather than preceded, the conjoined sentence. None of these is true for Latin as it is true, for example, for Japanese. It appears to be the case (cf. Ross, 1967) that in such languages, most phrase structure rules and a number of transformational rules as well are mirror images of the rules in SVO languages. This is not so for Latin, and if we were to persist in considering its basic order SOV, we should be faced with a single exception among all the languages of the world. Moreover, Greenberg also states that SOV languages cannot permute the order of objects and verbs. Hence, in an SOV language, alternative orders like SVO and SOV are not found. But in Latin, as is well known, every permutation of these three constituents is found. In SVO languages, according to Greenberg, permutation is often permissible. Thus, on the basis of universal facts so far as they are known, there is evidence that either the basic word order of Latin is SVO or Latin is an exception to a number of rules that are true for a very wide range of languages.

2. An apparent counterexample to the claim that *quod* occurs only with subject complements lies in the existence of sentences like the ones following, in which, in the surface structure, *quod*-indicative seemingly occurs followed by a complement that is the direct object of the main verb.

    1. Praetereo quod eam sibi domum sedemque delegit. (Cic. Clu. 188) 'I pass over the fact that she chose that house and home for herself.'
    2. Mitto quod possessa per vim. (Cic. Flacc. 79) 'I disregard the fact that they were seized by force.'

In none of the sentences of this type, however, does *quod*-indicative function as the complementizer governed by the main verb. Whenever it occurs in object complements, the sentence is *explicitly* factive. (The difference between an explicit factive, in which the words "the fact" appear in English, and a *presupposed* factive, in which the factivity of the sentence is assumed—as, for example, in the complements of verbs such as *regret, be self-evident,* and *confess* —is discussed by P. and C. Kiparsky in their paper "Fact," to appear in Bierwisch and Heidolph (eds.), *Recent Advances in Linguistics*, Mouton.) The difference between these Latin sentences and their English translations in this regard is simply that English expresses the word "fact" overtly in the surface structure, while in Latin it is the complementizer of the word meaning "fact"— deleted transformationally—which appears. Since this word "fact" is a nominalization of a verb "it is a fact" which takes subject complements, it is not surprising that its complementizer should appear as *quod*-indicative. Abstract structures of this type will be discussed and justified in Chapter 6. The point is that the appearance of *quod*-indicative as the complementizer of a sentence superficially the object of a main verb, in examples like the ones given before, does not contradict the claim made here.

3. The lower verb is represented here as *it*, present tense of *ire*. In reality, the verb

is *ibit*, future, in the deep structure. Verbs of wanting cannot co-occur with present tense verbs in their embeddings. (Note, however, that verbs of wishing may: *I wish I were king this very minute!* but not **I want to be king this very minute.*) This is also true of verbs of ordering and asking. There is a rule both in Latin and in English that deletes the future tense (probably a real verb dominating *ire* in the deep structure and dominated by the verb of the main sentence, here *volo*) after verbs of these classes. So the future is both required as the deep-structure tense of the lower verb (except in verbs of wishing, where past tenses are also possible) and is obligatorily deleted after them.

4. The assumption here is that no noun enters the deep structure marked with a case. By various syntactic rules cases are added to the complex symbol. If a noun already is marked for a case and a further rule applies to it attaching another case, the first case marking is automatically deleted when the second is added.

5. For some speakers of Latin, *iubeo* can occasionally take *ut*-subjunctive. For these speakers (assuming, as is undoubtedly the case, that *iubeo* accusative-infinitive was more frequent in their speech) the rule features governing *for-to* and *ut*-subjunctive were listed not as marked (as they would be if *for-to* were not possible at all for these people) but as optional. Thus we find a number of cases like the following:

   1. Iubet sententiam ut dicat. (Pl. Am. 1, 1, 50) 'He orders that he give his opinion.'
   2. . . . iubere ut haec quoque referret . . . (Cic. Verr. 2, 4, 12) 'They ordered that he bring back these things too.'
   3. Iussitque ut quae venissent naves Euboeam peterent. (Livy 32, 16) 'And he ordered that the ships that had come head for Euboea.'

6. A great deal of the justification for the formulation of *it*-substitution and the two rules that follow, flip and passivization, depends on the existence of a syntactic cycle. The nature of the cycle that had been assumed cannot be discussed at length here; see Lakoff and Ross (in preparation) for thorough discussion both of the cycle itself and the question of its existence. Lately it has been discovered that if the cycle is eliminated, various otherwise insoluble problems of syntax are solved; and at present the assumption that there is no cycle complicates only one rule (pronominalization). Hence, it is thought at this writing that there may well be no cycle. If this is indeed true, any arguments for ordering are called into question, along with arguments for the form of passivization and flip. For this and other reasons it seems wisest not to give the form of any rules unless there are strong reasons to assume that the form given was, in fact, likely to be correct. We know in general what each rule is supposed to do—what deep structures it must operate on, approximately, and what surface structures must be produced—and we know for English, at least, what constituent structure is to be assigned by these rules, at least partially. But this is not enough to enable us to write these rules correctly at present, so they are not being written at all but merely described.

7. There is another case where the dative appears with a passive form. This is the passive periphrastic, used to express need or duty, composed of the future passive participle and the verb *to be*. The person whose duty it is is in the dative. For example:

   1. Mihi eundum est ad urbem. 'I must (should, need to) go to the city.' (Lit., 'It is to be gone to the city to me.')

2. Liber legendus erat tibi heri. 'You had to read the book yesterday.' (Lit., 'The book was to be read to you yesterday.')

The dative is also sometimes found with the perfect participle:

3. Mihi deliberatum et constitutum est. (Cic. Leg. Agr. 1, 25) 'It has been deliberated and resolved by me.'

The presence of the dative in these cases is undoubtedly related to the presence of the dative with the passive of intransitive verbs. But since these constructions themselves are not understood at all, and since the passive itself is still so mysterious, it is not clear what this relationship is.

8. For example, compare passives used as reflexives with reflexive forms in Romance: *ferro accingor,* 'I gird myself [lit., 'I am girt'] with a sword'; Spanish *Me pongo la ropa,* 'I put on the clothing.' (Lit., 'put on myself'.) Also, the passive can be used in an impersonal sense, like 'people, one' in English or *on* in French: *ventum est in silvas,* 'People went into the woods.' Cf. the reflexive in Spanish, also used in this way: *Se habla español aquí,* 'Spanish is spoken (people speak Spanish) here.'

9. For discussion of possible constraints on scrambling rules, and their form, see Ross (1967).

4. Negation in Complements

4.1 Indefinites and Negation

In both English and Latin, negative sentences, when combined with others, undergo special rules. These rules are of interest in themselves, but, more than that, their reflexes occur where they are crucial in the interpretation of certain phenomena.

In both languages there is a special set of indefinite words that are found only in interrogative, conditional, or comparative sentences, and after negatives both in simple sentences and in complex sentences. We shall discuss the relationship between the appearance of the indefinites in simple and in complex sentences later. As examples, we find sentences like the following in English:

(1a)   I didn't see *any*body.

(1b)   He doesn't like *any* guava jelly *ever*.

(1c)   Does *any*body *ever* see Harry *any* more?

(1d)   I didn't see John, nor in fact did I see *any*one.

But we do not find

(2a)   *Anybody didn't see me.

(2b)   *John ever doesn't eat lamb chops.

104

In Latin, too, we find this class of words used in the same environments.

(3a)   Neque praeter te in Alide *ullus* servus istoc nomine est. (Pl. Capt. 3, 4, 58) 'Nor is there in Alis any slave besides you of that name.'

(3b)   Est ergo *ulla* res tanti, aut commodum *ullum* tam expetendum, ut viri boni nomen amittas? (Cic. Off. 3, 20, 82) 'Is, then, any matter of such importance, or any advantage so desirable, that you would lose your reputation as a good man?'

(3c)   . . . quod nemo *umquam* homo antehac vidit. (Plaut. Am. 2, 1, 16) 'What no man ever saw before.'

(3d)   Ps. Eho an *umquam* tu huius nupsisti patri? Ba. Di melius faciant (Pl. Ps. 1, 3, 95) 'Ps. Say, did you ever marry this man's father? Ba. God forbid!'

We also find these types of indefinites in complex sentences, in English:

(4a)   He is smarter than *anyone* ever.

(4b)   If *anyone* leaves this room, he will be shot.

(4c)   I don't want to do *anything*.

(4d)   I never said I saw *anything*.

(4e)   I never said I wanted to do *anything*.

(4f)   No one is so stupid as to lend John *any* money.

And in Latin we find these:

(5a)   Plus amat quam te *umquam* amavit. (Pl. Ep. 1, 1, 63) 'He's more in love than he ever was with you.'

(5b)   Hunc si *ullus* deus amaret . . . (Plaut. Bacch. 4, 7, 20) 'If any god loved him . . .'

(5c)   Neminem quidem adeo infatuari potuit ut ei nummum *ullum* crederet. (Cic. Flac. 20, 47) 'He couldn't make such a fool of anyone that he would lend him any money.'

(5d)   Negat se more et exemplo populi Romani posse iter *ulli* per provinciam dare. (Caes. B. G. 1, 8) 'He says that, by the custom and precedent of the Roman people, he cannot grant anyone passage through the province.' (Lit., 'he denies . . . that he can.')

Besides these, we find sentences in English like

(6a)   I saw no one (nothing).

(6b)   Nobody said anything.

And in Latin we find

(7a)   Nullum mittitur telum. (Caes. B. C. ii, 13) 'No weapon is thrown.'

(7b)   Milites mittunt nulla tela. 'The soldiers throw no weapons.'

(7c)   Marcus agit nihil. 'Marcus is doing nothing.'

(7d)   Nemo videt ullam puellam. 'No one sees any girl.'

(7e)   Miles numquam misit telum. 'The soldier never threw a weapon.'

Both in Latin and in English these *no*-words seem to be related to the *any* (*ullus*)-words. They are all indefinite pronouns, adjectives, or adverbs. The *any*-words occur only after negatives, interrogatives, comparatives, and conditionals, where the *no*-words never occur. Therefore, one would assume that the *no*-words are related to the *any*-words. This relationship has been discussed by Klima (1964) for English. Interestingly, the examples given previously show that the distribution and use of *ullus*-words and their corresponding negatives in Latin are virtually identical to that of English. In both languages, where the environment mentioned before is not present, indefinites may also be found, but of a different class.

(8a)   *Some*one saw him yesterday.

(8b)   I like *some* kinds of guava jelly, sometimes.

(8c)   *Some*body isn't telling the truth.

Similarly, we find

(9a)   *Aliquem* vidi heri. 'I saw someone yesterday.'

(9b)   *Quisquam* non loquitur vere. 'Somebody isn't telling the truth.'

(9c)   Hoc faciet *aliquando*. 'He'll do it sometimes.'

Returning to the phenomena illustrated in sentences (1) through (7), we find that in both Latin and English there is only one negative (or none) per sentence in the surface structure. This may be in initial position, to the left of other indefinites, or attached to an indefinite. In all cases, for an *any-* or *ullus*-word to appear, the negative must appear to the left of it.

4.2 Negation in Vulgar Latin and Romance

The principle of one negative per sentence appears not to apply to Vulgar Latin or Romance (nor, for that matter, to a number of other Indo-European languages, among them Greek and Russian, and to colloquial English). In these languages several negatives can be found within one simple sentence in the surface structure as follows:

(10a)   Neminem nihil boni facere oportet. (Petr. 42, 7) 'No one ought to do any good.' (Lit., 'no good.')

(10b)   Iura te non nociturum . . . nemini. (Plaut. Mil. 1411) 'Swear that you will not hurt . . . anybody [lit., 'nobody'].'

In Vulgar Latin the appearance of two or more negatives was apparently optional; compare this with (10b) other Plautine sentences, such as (3c). For Plautus, presumably, both these sentences could have been expressed otherwise, sentence (3c) as

(11a)   . . . quod nemo numquam homo antehac vidit

and (10b) as

(11b)   Iura te non nociturum . . . ullum (hominem)

or as

(11c)   Iura te nociturum . . . nemini.

In classical Latin (11c) is preferred. In Romance we find double negation with the meaning of a single negative much more frequently than we do in classical Latin. In fact, though sentences like (11c) are grammatical in Spanish, though not as frequent as types like (10b), those corresponding to (11b) are not grammatical. In Spanish we find sentences like (12a) and (12b) alongside of sentences like (13a) and (13b), which are less frequent.

(12a)   No viene nadie. 'No one is coming.'

(12b)   El no hace nada nunca. 'He doesn't do anything ever [lit., 'nothing never'].'

(13a)   Nadie viene 'Nobody is coming.' (vs. 'No viene nadie').

(13b)   El hace nada. 'He's doing nothing.'

4.3 Derivation of Negatives—Deep Structures

The fact that negation in classical Latin is represented differently from negation in Spanish is not necessarily a reflection of a difference in deep structure between the two languages. In fact, it cannot be: if we assumed that in Romance each negative appearing in the surface structure represented a negative in the deep structure, then sentences like (12a) and (13a) would have different deep structures. But their meanings are the same. It is better to assume identical deep structures in all cases, with one negative per simple sentence, and have the differences be brought about by differences in the transformational component.

It had been assumed until fairly recently that negation was introduced into the phrase structure rules as part of the negated sentence itself. There would then be a possible phrase structure rule, in all languages, S → (NEG)NP VP. Under this formulation, both *Nadie viene* and *no viene nadie* would represent an underlying structure like that shown in diagram (14). Likewise, any sentence with a negative in it would have

(14)

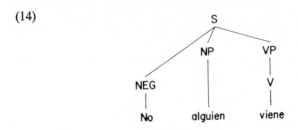

this negative at the left. So, *I am unhappy* would have the same deep structure as *I am not happy*, and the only difference between them would be that the negative undergoes an optional rule attaching it to *happy* in the first sentence and does not undergo it in the second. But sentences such as the following cast doubt on such an analysis:

(15a)   John is not happy, although the fortune teller predicted it.

(15b)   *John is unhappy, although the fortune teller predicted it.

The difference in the grammaticality of these two sentences suggests that the deep structures of the two are different, and it further suggests that *un-*, in (15b), is in the deep structure a part of the sentence *John is happy*, so that it cannot be removed from *John is happy*, in the right-hand part of the sentence.[1] Because of sentences like this, it has been proposed by

Lakoff that the deep structure of a negative sentence is actually composed of at least two sentences, the higher being something like *It S is
not so*, and the lower being the sentence or sentences negated. Under
this analysis, the sentence *John is not happy* has the deep structure
illustrated in (16). *John is unhappy*, on the other hand, contains the

(16)

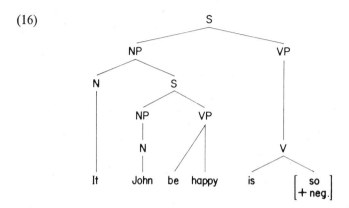

negative within the simple sentence. It is represented as a feature of
happy in diagram (17). Since [+ neg] is a feature in this sentence, it
cannot be removed by the rule that allows the negative higher sentence
to be removed to produce (15a). (See note 1.)

As diagram (16) indicates, *not so* itself is a writing of the pro-adjective
so with a negative feature. This *so*, always unstressed, and not to be
confused with the stressed *so* that appears in the surface structure in *it
is not so*, and the like, must be negated. Moreover, it is not self-
embedding, in most sentences at least; therefore we do not find **John
is not happy*, whereas we do find *John is not unhappy*. In this latter
sentence, the negative of *it is not so* does not cancel out the negative of
happy: John is not unhappy is not necessarily synonymous with *John is
happy*. These two negatives then do not equal a positive.[2]

(17)

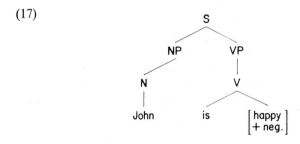

4.4 Negative-Lowering

We do not know how this higher sentence *It is not so* is transformed into *not* in the lower sentence. On the basis of the behavior of the negative in later rules, we assume that somehow the negative is taken out of its sentence and placed at the far left of the lower sentence. Other rules will place negatives from other sources in this environment too, and all these negatives will undergo later rules. If no further rules are undergone, the negative is then put before the main verb of the sentence. It should be noted that negative prefixes such as that on *happy* do not ordinarily take part in these rules.

The advantage of a formulation such as that of (14) is that it is quite simple to derive from it surface structures with negatives. On the other hand, justifying a derivation of surface structures with negatives from deep structures of the type shown in (16) is more difficult. A number of *ad hoc* suggestions can be made as to how the negative-lowering transformation is performed, but there is no reason to prefer any way over any other, with the slight evidence in any direction we have at present. Perhaps the complex of features that comprises the negated adjective is adjoined to the lower S (*John be happy*), creating a new S node above it (Chomsky-adjunction), and then deleted from the higher sentence. *It is* of the higher sentence will then be deleted in an equally *ad hoc* way. Pruning conventions will give us the approximate structure required for the operation of later rules.

Rule (1) Negative-Lowering

$$\text{It} - \text{S} - \text{is} - [^{\text{so}}_{+\text{neg.}}] \rightarrow \emptyset - 4 + 2 - \emptyset - \emptyset$$
$$\quad 1 \quad\; 2 \quad 3 \quad\; 4$$

1. Chomsky-adjoin: 4 to 2
2. Delete 4
3. Delete 1, 3

The tree diagrams (18) illustrate the steps of this derivation: The NP remaining in (18d) can probably be pruned by a rule suggested by Anderson;[3] the topmost S is pruned by the convention that whenever a node dominates itself and nothing more, it is deleted. The resultant structure is then very similar to that of (14), except that in (14) the node is daughter-adjoined below S as a sister of NP and VP, whereas in this formulation it is Chomsky-adjoined, creating a new S node.

(18a) before (1)   (18b) after (1), before (2)

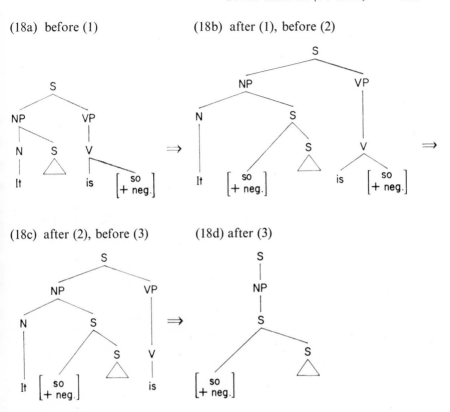

(18c) after (2), before (3)   (18d) after (3)

The negative thus lowered will participate in other rules that are to be discussed in this chapter:

Rule (2) *Some-any* change
Rule (3) Negative-attachment to *and*
Rule (4a) Negative-movement
Rule (4b) Negative-attachment
Rule (5) Negative-transportation
Rule (6) *Quin*-formation
Rule (7) *Ne*-formation
Rule (8) *Non*-placement

4.5 *Some*-Change (to *Any*)

The sentences given in Section 4.1 show that for both Latin and English there is a set of words that occur only in negative (or other specified) environments. There is also a set of words, identical in meaning to these *any*-words, which occur everywhere except in these environments. These words can be called "unstressed-*some*" words; they occur in sentences like these:

(19a)   Someone's coming up the stairs.

(19b)   Come up and see me sometime!

(19c)   He said something I didn't understand.

This unstressed *some* must be distinguished from the stressed *some*, which can occur after negations. The stressed *someone* means 'a certain person'; unstressed *someone* means 'a person, unspecified.' Unstressed-*some* words, in Latin and in English, participate in *some-any* change. In English this rule is obligatory for all such words in the presence of a negative. In Latin it appears to be optional, but it is not completely clear how the data are to be interpreted.

In Latin there are two main sets of words that correspond to *some* in English, and a number of related, rarer sets. There is also the set of *ullus* words, already listed, corresponding to *any*. The two main sets of *some*-words in Latin are the *ali*-words and the *quis*-words. *Ali*-words include: *aliquis*, 'someone'; *aliquid*, 'something'; *aliquando*, 'sometime'; *aliqui, aliquod*, 'some.' The *quis*-words are *quisquam*, 'someone'; *quicquam*, 'something.' The *ali*-words appear to correspond closely to English stressed *some*: they occur after negatives with no change in meaning. An example is found in this sentence:

(20)   Cum aliquid non habeas. (Cic. Tusc. 1, 88) 'When you do not have something.'

Here, *aliquid* refers to a specific thing. It does not mean 'When you do not have anything' (that is, when you have nothing), which would be *Cum nihil habeas*. Thus we also have the following:

(21)   Si quid in te peccavi. (Cic. Att. 3, 15, 4) 'If I have committed *some* (specifiable) wrong against you.'

(*Quid* here is the special form of *aliquid* used after a few words: *si, nisi, ne, num*.) If Cicero had written *Si ullum*..., it would have meant 'Any wrong at all.'

Quisquam, on the other hand, is similar to our unstressed *some*. The difference between its use in Latin and in English is that in Latin *quisquam* in the negative (other specified) environment optionally changed to *ullus*; in English unstressed *some* obligatorily changes to *any*. Hence, *quisquam* is translatable either as *some* or as *any*, depending on whether, in translation, it appears in *some*-environment or *any*-environment. But *ullus* is always 'any.' Hence, we find *quisquam* in sentences like the one following, where English must use an *any*-word.

(22a)   Iustitia numquam nocet *cuiquam*. (Cic. Fin. 1, 5) 'Justice never hurts anybody.'

(22b)   Si quisquam est timidus, is ego sum. (Cic. Fam. 6, 14, 1) 'If anyone is timid, I am that one.'

Ullus-words occur in identical environments, with identical meaning, as *quisquam* in (22a) and (22b). See, for example, the sentences in Section 4.1.

Rule (2), *some-any* change, operates after a number of the other rules have already operated, but before others. For example, it operates after negative-transportation but before negative-attachment. It applies optionally to *quisquam* and *quicquam* but not at all to *aliquis* and the other words in that group. The adjectives and adverbs of time and place appear not to occur at all in Latin in unstressed-*some* form. They are either stressed-*some* words (*aliqui, aliquando, alibi*, etc.) or they are *any*-words (*ullus, umquam, usquam*). Therefore, the rule need only convert *quisquam* to *ullus* and *quicquam* to *ullum*, which it does whenever there is a negative at the left of the word to be changed. It operates across sentence boundaries downward but not upward.

4.6 Negative-Attachment to *And*

Sentences like the following are not found in Latin:

(23a)   *Ullus non venit. '*Anybody didn't come.'

(23b)   *Umquam nemo venit. '*Ever nobody came.'

Sentences of the following form are found but not very frequently:

(24a)   Marcus non vidit ullum. 'Marcus didn't see anyone.'

(24b)   Marcus non vidit Publium umquam. 'Marcus didn't see Publius ever.'

(24c)   *Ullus non vidit Marcum. '*Anyone didn't see Marcus.' Sentence (24c) is completely ungrammatical. Better and more frequent than these are the following:

(25a)   Marcus vidit nullum (or neminem). 'Marcus saw no one.'

(25b)   Marcus vidit Publium numquam. 'Marcus never saw Publius.'

But sentences like these below are very frequent:

(26a)   Nec Marcus vidit ullum. 'Nor did Marcus see anyone.'

(26b)   Nec Marcus vidit Publium umquam. 'Nor did Marcus ever see Publius.'

These are, in turn, preferable to the ungrammatical:

(27a)   *Et Marcus vidit nullum.

(27b)   *Et Marcus non vidit ullum.

(27c)   *Et Marcus numquam vidit Publium.

(27d)   *Et Marcus non vidit Publium umquam.

This distribution of sentences is evidence of the operation in Latin of a rule that attaches the negative to any of several indefinite *any*-words, with various morphological changes. Besides Rule (3), negative-attachment to *any*, there is a separate rule that attaches the negative to the word for *and*, which operates first.

In the second chapter it was shown that one of the possible expansions of S was S → *and* S^n. This sort of structure can be negated in either of two ways. Either the whole structure is negated (it is not so that S and S and S), or each of the conjoined S's, or only one or several of them, can be negated separately. The second is much more common. Thus, a sentence like *John didn't see Bill, and Helen didn't look for Harriet* has the deep structure shown in (28). Sentences in English with *neither . . . nor*

(28)

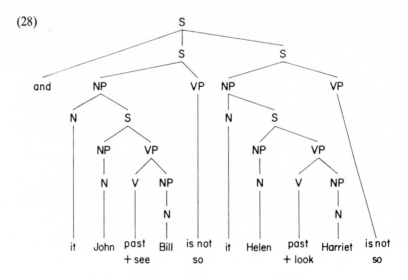

also have this structure. They do not usually come from *either ... or* in the deep structure but rather from a negation of two sentences conjoined with *and.* Thus, the sentence

(29)   Neither John nor Mary likes Harriet

has a deep structure parallel to (28). Negative-lowering takes place within both these conjoined structures, giving the derived structure, for (28), as shown in diagram (30). To this structure, as to all conjoined structures,

(30)

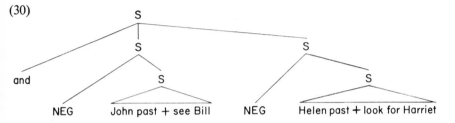

a rule applies copying *and* and adjoining it as a sister of S to the left of each conjoined S. This is illustrated in (31).

At this point in English, a rule obligatorily deletes the leftmost *and,* except in special cases where it remains and is changed to *both.* In Latin, as in many other languages, this rule does not apply. All *and*'s remain, and if *and* precedes a negative, it is combined with the negative to yield *neque* (*nec*). Otherwise, it stays as *et,* or *que.* The rule that combines *and* with the negative is obligatory, and therefore the sentences (27a)–(27d) are ungrammatical. Once the negative is combined with *and,* it ceases to take part in any of the later negative rules.

(31)

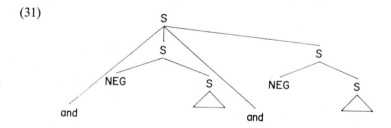

4.7 Negative-Movement and Negative-Attachment with Indefinites

The sentences of (24a) and (24b) must be related to (25a) and (25b). In these sentences, there is no conjunction. Hence, *and*-attachment, of course, does not apply. What applies instead is a sequence of two rules:

the first of them, negative-movement, moves the negative directly to the left of a word marked as [+indef.]. The second, negative-attachment, adjoins the negative to the indefinite word when the negative is immediately to the left of this word.

Rule (4a) Negative-Movement

$$\text{NEG} - X - [+\text{indef.}] - Y \rightarrow \emptyset - 2 - 1 - 3 - 4$$
$$\;\;\;\;\;1 \;\;\;\;\;\;\; 2 \;\;\;\; 3 \;\;\;\;\;\;\;\;\;\;\; 4$$

Copy 1 at immediate left of 3
Delete 1
if: *X* does not contain [+indef.]

Rule (4b) Negative-Attachment

$$X - \text{NEG} - [+\text{indef.}] - Y \rightarrow 1 - 2 + 3 - 4$$
$$1 \;\;\;\; 2 \;\;\;\;\;\;\; 3 \;\;\;\;\;\;\;\; 4$$

Adjoin 2 as a sister of 3

The latter rule operates to produce the following:

NEG + *ullus* → *nullus*

NEG + *umquam* → *numquam*

NEG + *quisquam* → *nemo*

NEG + *quicquam* → *nihil*

In classical Latin, Rule (4a) contains both an elementary operation deleting the negative at the left after it has been copied and a proviso that the rule operates only on the first indefinite word in the sentence. In Vulgar Latin and Romance, however, these conditions do not hold. The negative at the left is not erased, and thus it participates in negative-spelling, the late rule that spells the negative as *non* and moves it into position before the verb, or specifically negated word, if none of the other rules has applied. Moreover, the condition that only the leftmost of the indefinite words has the negative moved before it is not true in Vulgar Latin and Romance: every indefinite undergoes this rule. Hence, the following sentences are grammatical in Vulgar Latin:

(32a)   Nemo vidit nullam puellam numquam.

(32b)   Non vidi nullam puellam numquam.

The following are grammatical in Spanish:

(33a)   No vió nadie a ninguna muchacha nunca.

(33b)   Nadie vió a ninguna muchacha.

Therefore, it is clear that there is only a minor difference in the statement of this rule between classical and Vulgar Latin. The non-deletion of the negative and a condition on the application of Rule (4a) are what create the superficially great difference between the constructions in Latin and Romance.

Negative-movement apparently applies across sentence boundaries in a very few cases, such as with *possum*, 'be able,' and *debeo*, 'ought.'

(34a)   Neminem videre possum. 'I can see no one.'

(34b)   Nihil facere debeo. 'I should do nothing.'

Sentence (34a) is derived from a structure like

(34c)   NEG I can it S

$$I \ see \begin{bmatrix} + \ indef. \\ + \ human \end{bmatrix}$$

Both negative-movement and negative-attachment are optional in Latin. This is different from English, where negative-attachment is obligatory and negative-movement has applied. It is possible that negative-attachment was, in fact, obligatory for most speakers of Latin, since there are many fewer examples of *non* immediately preceding *ullus* than of *non . . . ullus* or *nullus*, but since there are some examples of *non* directly before *ullus*, we are forced to consider it grammatical in classical Latin and therefore to assume that negative-attachment is optional. We find in Latin sentences of the following types:

(35a)   Nullum puerum vidi.

(35b)   Non vidi ullum puerum.

(35c)   Nec ullus puer me vidit.

These are all quite common. More uncommon, but attested, are the following:

(35d)   Vidi non ullum puerum.

(35e)   Non ullus puer me vidit.[4]

All of these sentences can be derived by the use of the two optional rules and, in addition, an optional scrambling rule that may operate after them. Sentence (35a) is produced by negative-movement, negative-attachment, and then scrambling operating, the last rule moving the direct object before the verb. Sentence (35d) is the result of the operation of the negative-spelling rule alone, with none of the others being applied. Sentence (35c) is the result when neither of the two rules operates, scrambling places the subject noun phrase after the verb and the direct object before it, and the negative-spelling rule spells out the negative as *non*, without moving it before the verb (it could also have moved it, of course, producing *Me non vidit ullus puer*). Sentence (35d) comes about when negative-movement operates but negative-attachment does not. Sentence (35e) is the result of neither these rules nor scrambling operating. In this case, apparently, *Ullus puer non me vidit* is not grammatical; at least, no cases of it have been found. There may be a constraint on scrambling stating that an indefinite word cannot be moved by scrambling to a position to the left of the negative in the sentence, or perhaps a constraint of negative-moving stating that the negative cannot be moved over (to the right of) an indefinite.

We said before that if negative-movement applied, the negative was obligatorily deleted from the left in classical Latin. There are a few exceptions found, such as the one following, where the negative is moved across a sentence boundary as well:

(36)   Horam eximere nullam...non possumus. (Cic. Phil. 6, 3, 7)
         'We cannot waste a single hour.'

It is perhaps relevant that this exception occurs in the *Philippics*, where Cicero was trying to gather popular support against Antony and therefore might be using the language of the people to win them over.

4.8 Negative-Transportation

Though the preceding discussion concerns simple sentences, the facts presented show up in complements in an interesting way. Indefinites and negatives combine in various ways across sentence boundaries; the presence of negatives in higher sentences influences the form complementizers take in lower sentences (for examples, see Section 4.10). This is true both in Latin and its daughter languages, as well as in English.

In English, we find alternates like the following:

(37a)   I don't think Harry is eating anything.

(37b)   I think Harry isn't eating anything.

(37c)   I didn't say Harry was eating anything.

(37d)   I said Harry wasn't eating anything.

The meaning of the first sentence is identical to that of the second: that it is the belief of the speaker that Harry is not eating anything. Likewise, in the last sentence the speaker denies that Harry is eating anything. But in the third case he makes no claim as to whether or not Harry is eating anything. Therefore, the truth value of the first pair of sentences is identical, but not of the second pair. But in both cases, we get the change of the indefinite to an *any*-word, indicating that this rule works over sentence boundaries in at least some cases. What the difference between the two pairs indicates is that, whatever the source of (37a) and (37b) is, it is very likely the same, but that this is not the case for the other two. But it remains to be discovered which of the two, (37a) or (37b), is basic and which is derived. These examples offer some evidence:

(38a)   I didn't think Harry came until five o'clock yesterday.

(38b)   I thought Harry didn't come until five o'clock yesterday.

(38c)   I said Harry didn't come until five o'clock yesterday.

(38d)   *I didn't say Harry came until five o'clock yesterday.

(38e)   *Harry came until five o'clock yesterday.

(38f)   Harry didn't come until five o'clock yesterday.

These sentences show a number of things. First, the fact that (38a) and (38b) are both grammatical, while of the next two only the one where the negation occurs in the embedded sentence is, indicates that the structure of (38a) is actually quite different from that of (38d), which it superficially resembles. Moreover, the grammaticality of (38a) suggests that it is derived from a structure with a negated verb in the second sentence, namely (38b). Therefore, these sentences provide both a proof that (38a) and (38b) are derived from the same deep structure and transformationally related and a proof that (38a) is derived from (39b). The deep structure of both of these sentences is (much simplified) shown in diagram (39).

(39)   I thought it   S

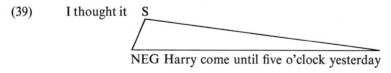

NEG Harry come until five o'clock yesterday

The rule that links sentences like (34b) to sentences like (35b), negative-transportation, operates in English as a minor rule within a small class of verbs, and not at all outside that category. (Cf. Klima, 1964.) It is minor within the class of verbs of mental activity, applying to verbs like *think, want, believe, seem,* and a few others, but not to *say, declare, imagine,* and most others. The verbs that do undergo this rule are marked for its application, while others in this class are unmarked. Verbs outside this class need not be specified either way. The choice of verbs that undergo this rule, among the members of the class, is apparently arbitrary: any of the verbs of this class might have been picked.

In Latin we find the same phenomenon restricted to the same semantic class. In the case of the English verbs these were all verbs that took *that*-finite complementizers except *want.* In Latin they are all *for-to* taking verbs. For example, *puto,* 'think,' *videor,* ' seem,' *credo,* ' believe,' and *volo,* ' want,' fall into this category. The last verb, *volo,* undergoes a special rule when negative-transportation applies to it: the negative is morphologically attached to the verb itself for most of its conjugation. Thus, *nolo,* 'I do not want,' *nolumus,* 'we do not want,' *nolunt, nolle, nolim, nolebam, nolui,* etc.; but *non vis,* 'you do not want,' *non vult,* 'he does not want.'

The rule that attaches the negative to *volo* to produce *nolo* is not the same as the rule that produces, for example, *nescio,* 'not know,' and other verbs with negative prefixes. In *nescio* the negative prefix is attached to the verb throughout its conjugation. Also, the meaning of *non scio* is different from that of *nescio* in the same way that, in English, the meaning of *not happy* differs from that of *unhappy.* A sentence of Latin can contain *non nescio,* while it cannot contain *non non scio. Nescio* is represented as inherently negative in the lexicon, whereas *nolo* is *volo* in the lexicon and becomes *nolo* by an attachment rule that is ordered after negative-transportation.

Sentences in Latin that have undergone negative-transportation resemble their English counterparts.

(40a)   Illud simul ait, se non putare illum...contempturum. (Cic. Verr. 2, 60) 'At the same time he says that he doesn't think he will despise.'

(40b)   Non mihi videtur ad beate vivendum satis posse virtutem. (Cic. Tusc. 5, 5, 12) 'It doesn't seem to me that virtue can be sufficient for living happily.'

(40c)   Nec mihi hunc errorum extorqueri volo. (Cic. Sen. 23, 85) 'Nor do I want this error to be wrung from me.'

The last example shows that negative-attachment to *and* occurs before negative-attachment to *volo*. Negative-transportation must precede both of these, of course.

In Latin, as in English, negative-transportation is optional, as the following sentence, in which it has not applied though it could, illustrates:

(41)   Me absente neminem volo intromitti. (Pl. Aul. 1, 3, 21) 'While I'm away, I want no one to be let in.'

Since negative-movement is also optional, the sentence might also have been *Me absente volo non intromitti ullum* or *Volo non ullum intromitti*. But *Volo ullum non intromitti* is probably ungrammatical (whereas, of course, *Volo Marcum non intromitti* is grammatical).

Negative-transportation can be stated as follows:

Rule (5) Negative-Transportation

$$X \,_S[\text{NP V it } [\text{NEG S}]]_{\text{NP}} \, Y$$
$$1 \quad 2 \quad 3 \; 4 \; 5 \quad 6 \quad 7$$

Chomsky-adjoin 5 to 2 through 6
Delete 5

If we have the derived structure (after negative-lowering) shown in diagram (42),

(42)   I think John isn't coming

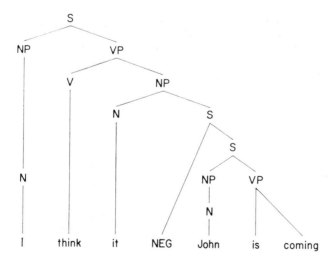

Negative-transportation converts this to the structure illustrated in (43).

(43)   I don't think John is coming.

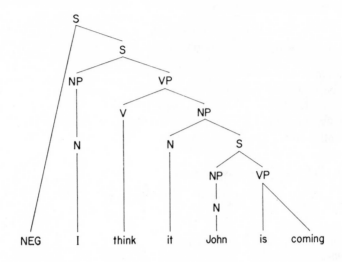

Negative transportation is an early rule in Latin, as in English. It operates before any of the rules discussed in this chapter. For many speakers of Latin, the negative could remain in the lower sentence even after it had been copied into the higher sentence if *and* was present in the higher sentence. How such a constraint as "presence of *and* in the higher sentence" is to be stated is unknown. But sentences like this one seem to suggest that it is necessary to state it somehow:

(44)   ...ut omnes intellegant, nihil me nec subterfugere voluisse reticendo, nec obscurare dicendo. (Cic. Clu. 1, 1) 'So that everyone may realize that I did not want to evade anything by being silent, nor to obscure anything by speaking.'

The derivation of this sentence is worth examining, as virtually every one of the rules discussed thus far in this chapter is involved. For (44) we set up the deep structure (omitting irrelevant structure) as in diagram (45). *And* is copied in the highest sentence, S_0, at the left of each of the lower S's (S_1 and S_2). Negative-lowering applies to the next-lowest sentences S_3 and S_4, placing the negatives to the left of S_5 and S_6, as in (46). To this structure, negative-transportation applies, but NEG is not

(45)

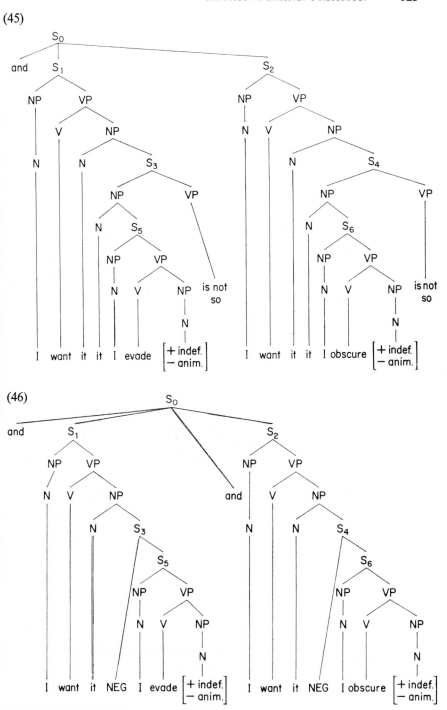

(46)

(47)

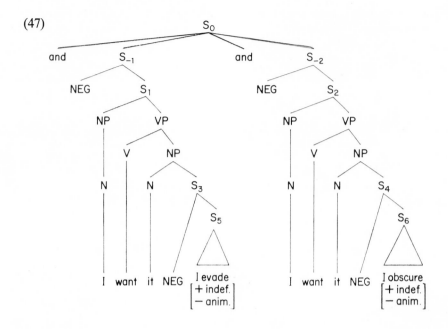

(48)

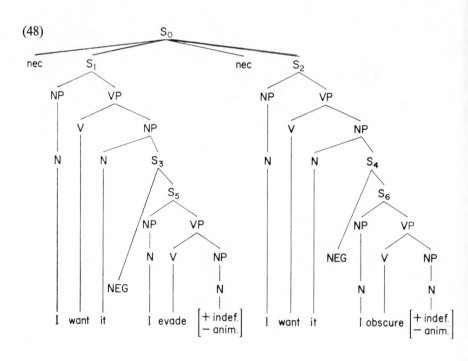

deleted from the inner sentences, as illustrated in (47). *And*-attachment now applies, as in diagram (48). After this, negative-movement applies within the lower sentences, moving NEG to a position before the indefinite inanimate noun direct objects, as in (49).

(49)

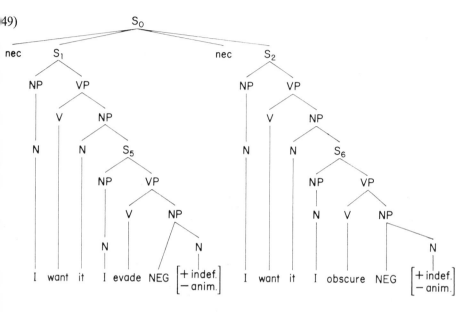

Finally, negative-attachment applies, yielding *nihil* from negative + *quicquam*. After this, scrambling rules apply, as well as verb-gapping (*volo* is deleted in the right-hand sentence, as is *nihil*). Complementizer-placement and other complementation rules apply to this structure as well, but it is not clear where they are ordered relative to these negation rules. In English negative-transportation applies almost exclusively in verbs taking *that*-finite complementizers. The exception is the verb *want*, which undergoes the rule but takes *for-to*. In Latin, where almost all verbs undergoing negative-transportation regularly take *for-to*, *volo*, 'want,' is the single exception. *Nolo*, the form of *volo*, 'wish, want,' which has undergone negative-transportation, regularly takes *for-to*, like the other verbs that undergo negative-transportation. But rarely (much more rarely than its nonnegated counterpart *volo*) it occurs with *ut*-subjunctive (*ut* is deleted, as is common with *volo*): *Nollem accidisset tempus* (Cic. Fam. 3, 10, 2) 'I wish the time had not come.'

It should also be pointed out that negative-transportation is not the only source of sentences such as the ones we have been discussing. While a sentence like

(50a)   Non putavi puerum venire, 'I didn't think the boy was coming,

can be derived from

(50b)
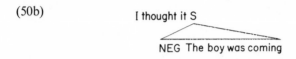

as has been discussed at length earlier, there is an alternative derivation for such sentences. Sentence (50a) may also be derived from a deep structure of the following form:

(51)
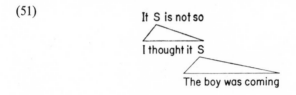

With this derivation, (50a) is not a statement of denial of belief on the part of the speaker; it merely states that the speaker thinks neither one way nor the other. But in case the verb is not a transportation verb, only the latter meaning is possible. If the verb is a transportation verb, and the higher verb is negated, negative-transportation cannot occur. Thus (52a) is grammatical, and (52b) is not.

(52a)   I didn't think John hadn't come.

(52b)   *I didn't not think John had come.

Hence, if a transportation verb is negated and the lower verb is also negated, as in (52a), the meaning of the sentence is that the speaker is neutral, not that he is denying not thinking. But it appears that there are cases in which this assertion is not strictly true: there are cases in which both the higher and the lower sentences contain negations but in which the sentence as a whole may be either the denial of a denial or a neutral statement.

(53a)   I didn't think nobody had arrived.

This sentence can either be neutral, 'It isn't so that I thought nobody had arrived,' or it can mean 'I thought somebody had arrived.' For any speaker of English for whom the second meaning is grammatical, the negative sentence *It S is not so* must be able to dominate itself, but probably only if the embedded sentence contains an indefinite, unless (52a) is also ambiguous in a similar way. The deep structure of (53) under this second interpretation, is

(53b)

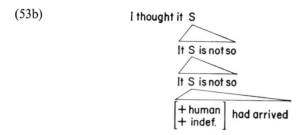

Another fact related to negative-transportation is that, if the subject of a lower sentence is an indefinite and the lower sentence in the surface structure contains no negative, the negative in the higher sentence is not ambiguous: it must be the result of negative-transportation, as in (54):

(54)   I didn't think anyone had arrived.

These facts are probably true for Latin as well, but the testimony of a native speaker is crucial.

In English, and probably in Latin as well, there are certain environments where negative-transportation cannot take place. Compare the following sentences, pointed out by Susumu Kuno:

(55a)   I couldn't keep from thinking that I hadn't succeeded.

(55b)   *I couldn't keep from not thinking I had succeeded.

This is also the case with the following:

(56a)   I prevented John from thinking that James was not a spy.

(56b)   *I prevented John from not thinking that James was a spy.

(56c)   I denied that I thought John wasn't a fink.

(56d)   *I denied that I didn't think John was a fink.

(56e)   I doubted that John thought Bill wasn't coming.

(56f)   *I doubted that John didn't think Bill was coming.

These sentences illustrate the fact that negative-transportation cannot occur if the verb dominating the transportation verb is one of a class usually called "inherently negative meaning verbs." These sentences will be dealt with in a later section, but the reason that they are "inherently negative" is that their deep structures contain a negative sentence, which is part of the meaning of the verb. Since there is already a negative sentence dominating *think* in the previous example sentences, whenever *think* is dominated by one of these inherently negative verbs, the negative of the lower sentence cannot be transported into the higher sentence. If it is, the ungrammaticality that results is the same as that of (52b), where transportation has occurred in an already negated verb.

In this section we have discussed one of the ways in which negation and complementation affect each other. Negative-transportation occurs in Latin only with a *for-to* complementizer, as a minor rule for a small class of verbs. It also must operate before any of the other negation rules discussed in this chapter have operated, both in Latin and in English. We have also pointed out some constraints on the occurrence of negative-transportation in English. It is not possible to ascertain whether they occur in Latin.

4.9 Doubly Negated Simple Sentences

Under this heading, we include sentences in Latin such as:

(57a)   Nihil non ad rationem dirigebat. (Cic. Brut. 37, 14) 'Everything steered one toward reason.' (Lit., 'nothing did not steer.')

(57b)   Nemo Arpinas non Planco studet. (Cic. Planc. 9, 22) 'Everyone in Arpinum is fond of Plancus.'

(57c)   Probi mores numquam non plurimum profuerint. (Quint. 7, 2, 33) 'Upright character is always a great advantage.'

We also include sentences in which the sentential negation occurs before the negated indefinite, with different meaning.

(58a)   Video de istis abesse non neminem. (Cic. Cat. 4, 5, 1) 'I see that some of them are absent.' (Lit., 'that not nobody of them...')

(58b)   Non nihil me consolatur, cum recordor... (Cic. Fam. 4, 14, 12) 'Something consoles me, when I recall...'

We said in Section 4.3 that usually the negative abstract form, *not so*, was not self-embedding. We found one exception to this in the last section, when there was an indefinite present in the sentence, in both Latin and English. In (57) and (58) we find another exception, also in the presence of indefinites, but confined to Latin. It will be clear that these Latin sentences cannot be literally translated into grammatical and intelligible English, because in English there is no relaxation of the constraint against self-embedding of *not so* in this environment, where there is in Latin.

For sentences like (57a) through (57c), where the indefinite is followed by *non*, we can suggest no deep structure that is correct, or even promising. It should be noted that synonymous sentences exist in Latin, for example:

(59)   Nihil est quin ad rationem dirigat.

The analysis of sentences of this sort, too, is unclear. All that we know is that the presence of *quin* indicates that there are two negatives present and one is attached to a verb of inherently negative meaning which does not appear overtly in the surface structure, since this is so in all other cases where we find *quin*. But what this structure is and whether it is the same as, or even close to, the deep structure that must be postulated for (57) we cannot even guess.

The derivation of the sentences of (58) is hardly clearer, but there appears to be one possibility. That is that a sentence such as *Non nemo venit*, 'Someone is coming,' has the deep structure shown in (60).

(60)
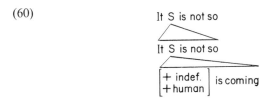

This structure could only be usable, however, if there were a syntactic cycle. Recent evidence, referred to in previous chapters, indicates that there quite possibly is not. If this is true, this formulation cannot be correct. It requires, first, that negative-lowering apply to lower the negative of the middle sentence to the left of the lowest sentence. After this, negative-movement and negative-attachment apply in the lowest sentence. Finally, negative-lowering takes place in the highest sentence, bringing the negative in it to the second, and only other remaining, sentence. There is nothing left for it to attach to, and so it becomes *non*. But this negative and the negated indefinite *nemo* as well are subject in sentences like these to a most peculiar constraint: they cannot undergo scrambling such that either would move over the other. It is impossible to imagine how scrambling could be stated to prevent this from happening. But since scrambling never changes meaning (this is the basic distinction between a "free-word-order" language and one without free word order), *non nemo,* 'someone,' can never change to *nemo non,* 'everyone,' although both *nemo* and *non* are free to scramble with the other words in the sentence so long as one does not move over the other. Because the deep structure we have proposed tentatively gives no way of explaining this fact, it is probably not correct. These sentences are not relevant to the study of complements; they are mentioned here merely to point out that they are interesting examples of apparent exceptions to the statement that two negatives do not exist within a deep-structure simple sentence and that they are undoubtedly not real exceptions, although we do not know what they are.

4.10 *Quin*

In Latin we find under highly specific circumstances a complementizer that has not been mentioned previously, *quin*-subjunctive. It is found with verbs that sometimes take *for-to* and sometimes *ut*-subjunctive, but *quin*-subjunctive is found only when the higher verb itself is negated, and this verb is one that has inherent negative meaning. In order to understand what *quin* really is and why it occurs where it does, as well as to account for the alternations between this and the other, commoner complementizers, we shall have to examine the notion of "inherently negative" meaning.

We find *quin* used after verbs meaning 'doubt' (*dubito*), 'prevent' (*prohibeo, impedio, deterreo*), 'refuse' (*recuso*), 'deny' (*nego*), 'be unaware' (*ignoro*), and in certain other, less clear cases, when the main verb is negated or questioned.

(61a)   Non dubitabat quin ei crederemus. (Cic. Att. 6, 2, 3) 'He didn't doubt that we believed him.'

(61b)   Nec quin erumperet prohiberi poterat. (Livy 26, 4, 4) 'Nor could he be prevented from breaking out.'

(61c)   Respondit se negare non posse quin rectius sit exercitum mitti. (Livy 4, 36) 'He replied that he could not deny that it was better for an army to be sent.'

(61d)   Quin loquar haec... numquam me potes deterrere. (Pl. Am. 2, 1, 10) 'You can never prevent me... from saying this.'

(61e)   Neque vero Caesarem fefellit quin initium victoriae oriretur. (Caes. B. C. 3, 94, 3) 'Nor, in fact, did it escape Caesar's notice that the start of victory was beginning.'

(61f)   Quis ignorat quin tria Graecorum genera sint? (Cic. Flacc. 64) 'Who is unaware that there are three kinds of Greeks?'

(61g)   Non recusat quin iudices. (Cic. Deiot. 43) 'He does not object to your judging.'

When the main verbs are not negated, and sometimes even when they are, we find other complementizers than *quin*. Sometimes we find *for-to*:

(62a)   ... qui Bibulum exire domo prohibuissent. (Cic. Fam. 1, 9, 7) 'Who had prevented Bibulus from leaving his house.'

(62b)   Quis ignorabat, Q. Pompeium fecisse foedus ... ? (Cic. Rep. 3, 18) 'Who was unaware that Q. Pompeius made a treaty ...?'

(62c)   Tu ne qua parentis iussa time neu praeceptis parere recusa (Verg. Aen. 2, 6, 07) 'Do not fear any of your mother's orders, nor refuse to obey her instructions.'

(62d)   Alteri negant quidquam esse bonum nisi quod honestum sit. (Cic. Fin. 2, 21, 68) 'The first group deny that anything is good except what is honorable.'

(62e)   Nefarias eius libidines commemorare pudore deterreor. (Cic. Verr. 1, 5, 14) 'I am prevented by shame from mentioning his unspeakable acts of lust.'

(62f)   Quid est igitur, quod me impediat ea quae probabilia mihi videantur sequi? (Cic. Off. 2, 2, 18) 'What is it, then, that prevents me from pursuing those actions which seem to me worthy of approval?'

(62g)   Gratos tibi esse qui de me rumores afferuntur, non dubito. (Cic. Fil. Fam. 16, 21, 2) 'I don't doubt that the rumors that are spread about me are agreeable to you.'

Besides *for-to*, we also find *ut*-subjunctive used as a complementizer after some of these verbs. But it is always negated and found as *ne*-subjunctive.

(63a)   Potuisti prohibere ne fieret. (Cic. in Caec. 33) 'You could have prevented it from happening.'

(63b)   Sententiam ne diceret recusavit. (Cic. Off. 3, 27, 100) 'He refused to give his opinion.'

(63c)   Haud ferro deterrere potes, ne ametur. (Pl. Truc. 5, 37) 'You cannot prevent her from being loved, even with a sword.'

There is still another complementizer found with these verbs, both where the main verb is negated and where it is not, *quominus*-subjunctive.

(64a)   Neque te deterreo, quominus id disputes. (Cic. Att. 11, 8) 'Nor do I prevent you from arguing about it.'

(64b)   Nec recusabo, quominus omnes mea legant. (Cic. Fin. 1, 3, 7) 'I won't object to everyone reading my works.'

(64c)   Prohibere quominus in unum coirent. (Livy 25, 35, 6) 'They prevented them from coming together.'

With *dubito*, 'doubt,' there is the additional possibility of an indirect question following the main verb.

(65a)   Dubitabam, tu has ipsas litteras essesne accepturus. (Cic. Att. 15, 9) 'I doubt if you will receive this very letter.'

(65b)   Dubitate, si potestis, a quo sit Sex. Roscius occisus. (Cic. Rosc. Am. 78) 'Have doubts, if you can, about who killed Sextus Roscius.'

(65c)   Non dubito quid sentiant. (Cic. Fam. 15, 9) 'I have no doubts about what they feel.'

It should be noted that *dubito* has two chief meanings: first, it means 'doubt,' as in all the preceding examples; second, it means 'hesitate.' In the latter meaning, it behaves rather like *recuso*, 'refuse,' and other negative-meaning verbs that imply the nonperformance of an action, except that where *recuso* takes *ne* or *quin* most frequently, *dubito* regularly takes *for-to*, rarely *quin*.

(66a)   Quid dubitas uti temporis opportunitate. (Caes. B. C. 2, 34) 'Why do you hesitate to take advantage of a favorable opportunity?'

(66b)   Nec dubitare illum appellare sapientem. (Cic. Lael. 1) 'Nor to hesitate to call him wise.'

(66c)   Dubitandum non existimavit quin proficisceretur. (Caes B. G. 2, 2) 'He did not think he should hesitate to set forth.'

The data we have set forth may be summarized as follows:

1. Negative-meaning verbs are of two types:
    a. Types like *ignoro*, in which the negative is a feature of the main verb. Thus, *ignoro* = (approximately) $[\langle \substack{scio \\ +neg.}\rangle]$.
    b. The second type, such as *impedio*, *dubito* (doubt), *recuso*, the formation of which will be discussed later.

2. For the second type, and sometimes for the first type as well, if the negative-meaning main verb itself is negated, the complementizer *quin*-subjunctive is often found.

3. For these verbs, *quin* is always optional when the verb is negated. When the verb is not negated, *quin* cannot occur. (We include questions, usually rhetorical, in speaking of negations.)

4. When *quin* does not occur, there are several possibilities:
   a. *For-to*: for all these verbs except a nonnegated *dubito*. For *dubito*, either an indirect question or *for-to* is possible. For negated *dubito*, *quin*, *for-to*, and indirect question are the only possibilities. *Quominus* and *ne* are not found with this verb at all.
   b. *Ne*: for verbs of preventing, and refusing, but not the others.
   c. *Quominus*: for verbs of preventing and refusing only.

Thus the verbs we have discussed may be tabulated:

Verb	Negated	Not Negated
deterreo, recuso, impedio, prohibeo	quin, quominus, ne, for-to	quominus, ne, for-to
dubito, 'doubt,'	quin, for-to indirect question	indir. question
dubito, 'hesitate'	quin, for-to	for-to
ignoro	quin, for-to	for-to
nego	quin, for-to	for-to

Some of these possibilities are, of course, much rarer than others. Thus, most grammars state that *dubito*, in the meaning 'doubt,' cannot be followed by *for-to*. But we find several instances of it in classical Latin, and therefore we must include it among the possible choices.

If we look at the morphological structure of *quin*, *quominus*, and *ne*, we find that all of them contain a negative element. And when the verbs *prevent*, *doubt*, *refuse* and the rest are analyzed, it becomes clear that there is a negative present somewhere in them. Also, we find sentences in English like the following:

(67a)   I prevented John from shooting anybody.

(67b)   I doubt that anyone is telling the truth.

(67c)   I refuse to answer any questions.

(67d)   I denied that anyone had told me that.

The presence of *any* indicates that there is a negative in the lower sentences of these complements, which does not appear overtly in the surface structure in English. This negative is part of the meaning of the verb. Thus, *doubt* is probably represented in the lexicon more or less as follows:

doubt
⟨think⟩ ∥ It S is not so

This notation means that *doubt* has the meaning 'think' and the constraint that when it occurs, the negative sentence *it is not so* must occur beneath it. *Prevent* and *deny* are represented in similar ways:

prevent
⟨cause⟩ ∥ it S is not so

it S happen

(That is, *prevent* means 'cause not to happen.')

deny
⟨say⟩ ∥ it S is not so

Refuse, too, will be represented with an obligatory negative in the next-lower sentence. But we do not know exactly what the structure of this verb is.

In the case of *doubt* in English, as well as *dubito* in Latin, either the deep structure given before or another is possible. The second deep structure substitutes for the negative *it S is not so* an indirect question. With this deep structure, *doubt* means 'be uncertain whether.' In this meaning we find *I doubt if, I doubt whether* in English. Note that **I don't think whether John is coming* is ungrammatical, so that it is unlikely that *I doubt whether John is coming* is derived from this source. Whenever *doubt* in English, or *dubito* in Latin, is followed by an interrogative word, we can be sure that it is this second deep structure that underlies *doubt*. In Latin, *doubt* with the meaning of 'be uncertain' is found both with the positive *dubito* and the negative *non dubito*; but *doubt* meaning 'think that ... not' is found only as *non dubito* (*quin, for-to*). Hence, we do not find *dubito* (not negated) *for-to*. We do not find *ne* and *quominus* with either *non dubito* or *dubito*; this verb may not undergo those complementizer-changing rules.

For the second meaning of *doubt*, 'be certain,' in Latin, compare (65b), where this must be the meaning, with (61a), where the first meaning is found. Note also that, in English, 'be uncertain whether' can be followed by two types of complements: either a questioning of belief

('I am uncertain whether John is coming') or hesitation about a course of action ('I am uncertain whether to tell John the news'). This latter use is very close in meaning to 'hesitate,' and hence the fact that there are two meanings of *dubito* in Latin, 'doubt' and 'hesitate,' can be explained.

To return to the negative-meaning verbs, we suggested that *quin* and *quominus*, as well as *ne*, contained in them the negatives that these verbs have as part of their meaning. That is, for the sentence *Non dubito quin Marcus veniat*, 'I don't doubt that Marcus is coming,' *quin* is both complementizer (*that*) and negative. Historically, *quin* is derived from an old instrumental of the interrogative *quis* and means 'how?' The *-n* is a reduced form of *-ne*, the negative particle that is found combined with other particles to form the negations of Latin. *Quominus* is derived from *quo*, an ablative form of the interrogative, also meaning 'how?' and *minus*, literally 'less,' but used as a negative, 'not.' *Ne* is, of course, the negated form of *ut*. The negatives *-ne*, *minus*, and that present in *ne* represent the negatives that are part of the meaning of these verbs. Thus, we can represent the deep structure of *Non dubito quin Marcus veniat* as in diagram (68). We can represent the deep structure of *Non impedio*

(68)

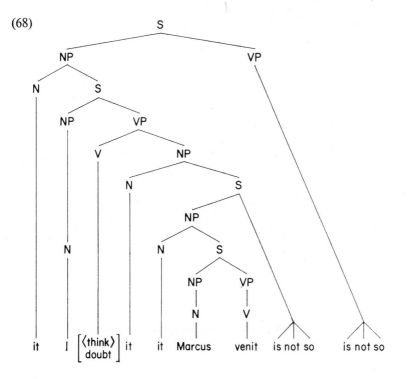

quin veniat, 'I don't prevent him from coming,' as in diagram (69).

(69)

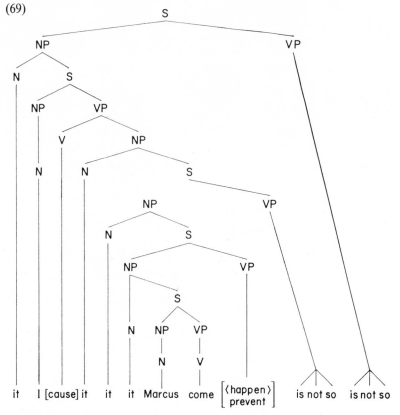

There are syntactic motivations for these deep structures, discussed in Lakoff (1965). For example, no word can be the direct object of *prevent* that cannot also be the subject of *happen* (*occur*):

(70a)   I prevented the explosion.

(70b)   The explosion happened.

(70c)   *I prevented the idea that John was king.

(70d)   *The idea that John was king happened.

Notice also that we do not find: **It hǎppened* (where *happened* has the meaning of *occurred*) that *John didn't shoot Harry*. The *happen* of *prevent* means *occur*. Thus we have the following:

(71a)   *I prevented John from not killing Harry.

(71b)   *Marcum impedivi ne Publium non necaret.

This is true even when there is an indefinite in the lowest sentence.

(72a)   *I prevented John from doing nothing.

(72b)   *I prevented no one from seeing John.

(These are at least marginal in the meaning, *I didn't prevent John from doing anything.* In this case, the indefinite is always stressed.) With *doubt*, a negative is permitted in the lower sentence only in case there is an indefinite present.

(73a)   *I doubt that John didn't go.

(73b)   I doubt that John saw nobody today.

This is also possible in Latin.

(74)   Non hercle dubito, quin tibi ingenio nemo praestiterit. (Cic. Rep. 1, 23) 'Of course I don't doubt that no one excelled you in wisdom.'

For this sentence, we must set up a structure with a self-embedded negative as shown in (75). Negative-lowering applies to the bottom

(75)

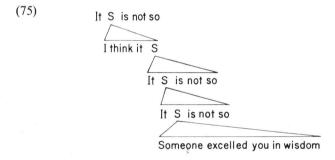

sentence. Because the verb *dubito*, when negated, undergoes *qui*-subjunctive complementation and because *qui* obligatorily undergoes a rule attaching *-ne* to it early in the rules, the negative directly below *I think it S* will never be able to undergo lowering. Of course, it never does undergo it.

Returning to our earlier classification of negative-meaning verbs, we can divide type 1(b) into action-negative-meaning verbs, such as the verbs 'prevent, refuse,' and saying and thinking negative-meaning verbs, 'deny, doubt.' We can set up redundancy rules for each class, dictating which of the possible complementizers they will take.

It should be noted that the complementizers *qui*-subjunctive and *quo*-subjunctive are of very limited occurrence, and are found only with verbs of negative meaning and in a few other, less well understood constructions.

Redundancy Rule D

For verbs of action-negative meaning (*prohibeo, impedio, deterreo, recuso*):

If negated:	u *qui*-subj. comp. change	optional *qui*-subj.
	m *qui*-subj. comp. change	*qui*-subj. not applicable
	u *quo*-subj. comp. change	optional
	m *quo*-subj. comp. change	*quo*-subj. not applicable
	u *ut*-subj. comp. change	optional
	m *ut*-subj. comp. change	*ut*-subj. not applicable
	u *for-to*	optional
	m *for-to*	*for-to* not applicable

If not negated: the same as above, except *qui*-subjunctive is not applicable. *Impedio, deterreo, prohibeo,* and *recuso* are all unmarked for all these rules.

Redundancy Rule E

For negative-meaning verbs of saying and thinking (*nego, dubito*):

If negated:	u *qui*-subj.	optional
	u *for-to*	optional
	u *quo*-subj.	not applicable
	u *ut*-subj.	not applicable

If not negated: The same, except *qui*-subjunctive is not applicable. This applies only to *nego*, as *dubito* with this meaning is found only negated. These verbs, too, are unmarked for all rules.

There are further rules dependent on which complementizer-changing rule is chosen. For example, if *quo*-subjunctive is chosen, the negative must be *minus*. If it is *qui*, *-ne* is the only possibility, and if it is *ut*, this complementizer is combined with the negative to produce *ne*. It will be evident that, if *for-to* has been chosen, there is no negative present at all. But if any of the others has been chosen, the negative must be present in the surface structure. Since the sentences are identical in meaning regardless of which complementizer has been chosen, there must be a negative in the deep structure even when the complementizer is *for-to*. It could be objected that there really is no negative present in the deep structure, at least not one that has syntactic effects, and that the *-n* of *quin* and *minus* are not syntactically relevant. One might support this claim by pointing to the English counterparts of these verbs, which give no overt indication that they contain a negation. But this is true only of modern English, at least for *doubt*. If one looks at slightly older English, the deep structure of *doubt* looks more like that which we have postulated for both Latin and English. In the writings of Jonathan Swift, one frequently comes across sentences like the following:

(76)   He doubted it would be impossible for me to swim to shore.
        (Gulliver's Travels, Part IV, Chapter X)

Such a sentence is puzzling to the modern reader. Its meaning must be, in modern English, 'He doubted that it was possible...,' but the sentence appears to say the opposite. The only possible explanation, it seems, is that there is a negative present in the deep structure of this sentence. In Swift's grammar—as in Latin grammar with *dubito*, when *quin* (or *quominus* or *ne* with other verbs) was used—the negative was not deleted after *doubt*. In modern English there is a rule that deletes this negative in all negative-meaning verbs after *some-any* change but before negative-lowering can take place. This rule operated in classical Latin only when *for-to* was the complementizer chosen, but it was obligatory if *for-to* were chosen. We can illustrate the working of this rule in a few sample derivations: In the sentence the deep structure of which appears in (68), *Non dubito quin Marcus veniat*, the first relevant rule that applies is negative-lowering, applying in both the higher and lower sentences, as shown in diagram (77). The redundancy rule for

(77)

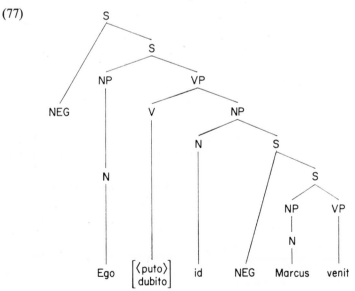

verbs of this class states that negative-deletion applies only when the verb has been taken from the lexicon with the rule feature governing *for-to* complementizer-change marked for the application of this rule. Since *doubt* here has been selected with the rule feature u *qui*-subjunctive, negative-deletion cannot take place, and negative-lowering applies. The next relevant rule is complementizer-placement and, after this, complementizer-change, which attaches *qui*-subjunctive to the embedded sentence above the negative. This is illustrated in diagram (78). After this, a special, obligatory rule converts *qui* + negative to *quin*.

(78)

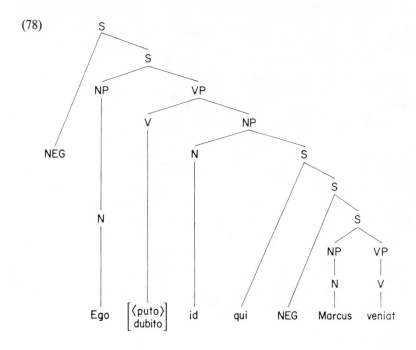

(If *dubito* were a verb that could select *quo*-subjunctive, and had done so, *quo* would be left alone, but the negative would be converted in the morphology to *minus*.)

To see how the rules operate if a *for-to* complementizer is chosen, let us take the sentence *Prohibeo Marcum exire*, 'I prevent Marcus from leaving.' This sentence has the deep structure shown in (79). The bracketing of [*cause*] indicates that this verb is an abstract verb.[6] Since this occurrence of *prohibeo* is marked as undergoing *for-to* placement, negative-lowering cannot apply. Instead, negative-deletion applies, removing the negative and leaving the structure illustrated in diagram (80).

(79)

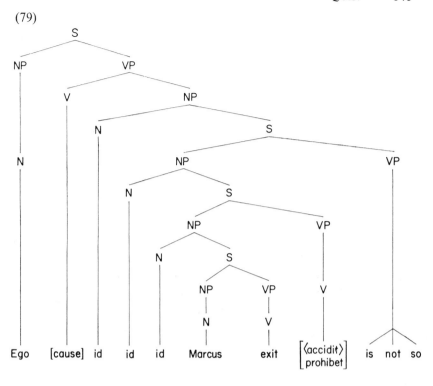

(80)

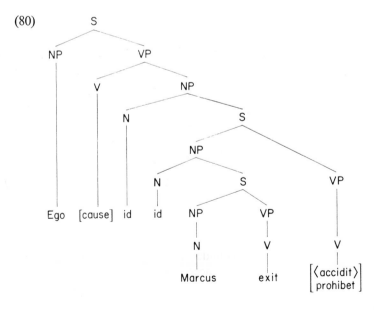

Complementizer-placement and complementizer-change now apply. In constructions of this sort we must impose a constraint on complementizer-change between the higher and the lower verb: if [*cause*] is marked as undergoing *for-to* complementizer-change, then the lower verb, with the meaning of 'happen' and the phonology of 'prevent,' must undergo the same rule. If any of the subjunctivizing complementizer-changing rules are indicated for [*cause*] (*ut*-subj., *qui*-subj.), then *happen* with the phonological matrix of *prevent* must undergo *ut*-subjunctive complementizer-change. (The real verb *accido*, 'happen,' in Latin can undergo either none of the complementizer-changing rules or *ut*-subjunctive complementizer-change. It cannot undergo *for-to*. But other verbs of its class [subject complement verbs] can take *for-to*.) In this case, *for-to* is put on both the higher and lower sentences of diagram (81).

(81)

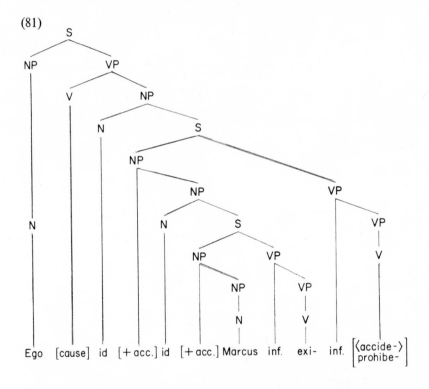

At this point in the derivation, plugging-in applies. This rule has been mentioned briefly in Section 2.14, in the discussion of verbs like *persuade*. It operates in a wide range of structures, in English and in Latin, wherever there is both a causative abstract verb (or an inchoative abstract verb) and a real verb marked as being able to undergo this rule. Examples of such verbs are

$$\begin{bmatrix} \langle \text{believe} \rangle \\ \text{persuade} \end{bmatrix} \quad \begin{bmatrix} \langle \text{intend} \rangle \\ \text{persuade} \end{bmatrix} \quad \begin{bmatrix} \langle \text{believe} \rangle \\ \text{convince} \end{bmatrix} \quad \begin{bmatrix} \langle \text{intend} \rangle \\ \text{convince} \end{bmatrix}$$

The verb now under discussion

$$\begin{bmatrix} \langle \text{happen} \rangle \\ \text{prevent} \end{bmatrix}$$

with, of course, its Latin equivalents

$$\begin{bmatrix} \langle \text{accido} \rangle \\ \text{prohibeo} \end{bmatrix} \quad \begin{bmatrix} \langle \text{accido} \rangle \\ \text{impedio} \end{bmatrix} \quad \begin{bmatrix} \langle \text{accido} \rangle \\ \text{deterreo} \end{bmatrix}$$

is of this class. A verb to be discussed later in the chapter

$$\begin{bmatrix} \langle \text{accido} \rangle \\ \text{efficio} \end{bmatrix}$$

is also one of this class, as are all verbs underlying forms with causative, or inchoative suffixed in any language. Plugging-in operates after complementizer-placement and change, taking the verb of the lower sentence, if it is marked as undergoing the rule, and putting it underneath the causative inchoative abstract verb of the higher sentence. The complementizer that remains when the verb is moved out of its sentence is deleted.

Plugging-in

$$W - [[\begin{matrix} V \\ + \text{caus} \\ + \text{pro} \end{matrix}] - X - V - Y]_{\text{NP}}]_{\text{VP}} - Z \rightarrow 1 - 2 + 4 - 3 - \emptyset - 5 - 6$$

$$1 \qquad\quad 2 \qquad\quad 3 \quad 4 \quad 5 \qquad 6$$

Plug in below 4, 2

The structure resulting from the application of plugging-in to (81) is given in diagram (82).

Now various rules operate to delete both *it*'s and one of the accusative markers. This derivation, with *for-to*, offers no clue as to which of the complementizers *for* is deleted. But in the sentence *Non prohibeo quin Marcus exeat*, 'I don't prevent Marcus from going,' the choice is clearer. We start out in this case with the same deep structure as in (79), except that the highest sentence, with [*cause*], is itself negated. Because [*cause*] is negated, it can be selected from the lexicon with the complementizer *qui*-subjunctive. *Happen*, in this case, will have the complementizer

(82)

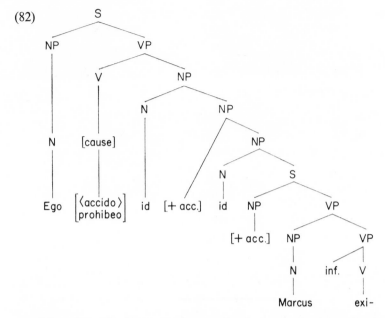

ut-subjunctive. The first rule that applies in case *qui*-subjunctive is the complementizer is negative-lowering. This is shown in (83). Next, complementizer-placement and complementizer-change apply, as in (84).

(83)

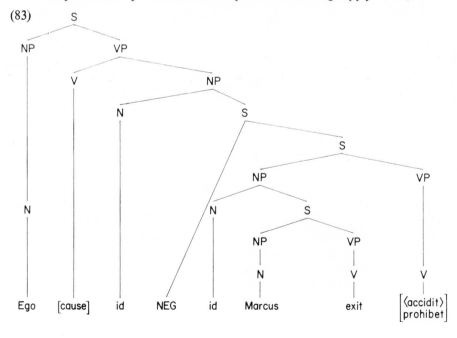

84)

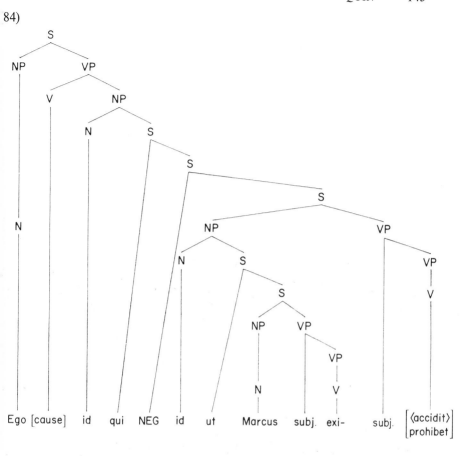

Plugging-in applies, as illustrated in (85).

The structure now has one negative and two complementizers, *qui* above the negative and *ut* below it. (If the complementizer of [*cause*] were *ut*-subjunctive, there would at this point be two *ut*'s.) The negative-attachment rule, which attaches the negative to *qui* to produce *quin*, specifies, for this and other cases, that the negative immediately follows *qui*. Moreover, the rule that will turn the negative to *ne* is also specified as applicable only when the negative is immediately preceded by *ut* and in position after the main verb of the sentence. (This will be discussed in the next section of this chapter.) For these reasons, unless we want to write a second, special *quin*-formation rule and a separate *ne*-formation rule only for verbs of preventing, it seems necessary to assume that the higher complementizer remains, and the lower is deleted. Thus, the *ut* of the lower sentence is deleted, but the subjunctive of the lower sentence remains; the *ut* of the higher sentence is kept, but the subjunctive

(85)

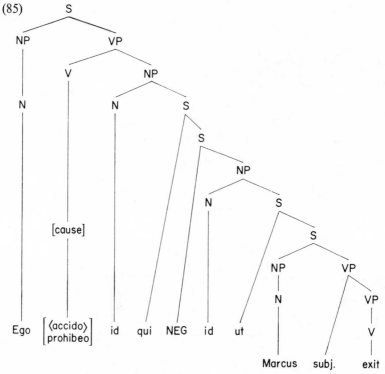

of the higher sentence, attached to *happen*, is deleted. Hence, the lower *ut* is deleted, and *id* is also deleted. Negative is attached to *qui*. The resultant surface structure is shown in (86). If *ut* had been chosen, *ne* would, of course, be the final form of the complementizer plus negative.

(86)

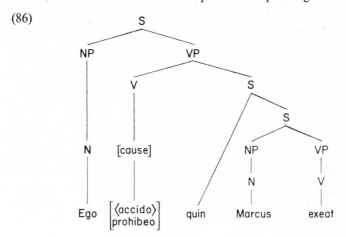

We have shown in this section how a number of different types of sentences containing *quin*-subjunctive may be derived. In these sentences *quin* is the combination of a special complementizer, *qui*, found after negated verbs of negative meaning, plus the negative implied in these verbs. There are, however, numbers of cases in which *quin* occurs which our rules do not predict. The fact that our rules cannot produce *quin* in these cases does not indicate that the rules are wrong. The fact is that we do not have any idea of what the deep structure of such sentences is, and therefore we cannot write rules relating these deep structures to surface structures. Examples of such sentences are the following:

(87a)   Nemo est tam fortis quin rei novitate perturbetur. (Caes. B. G. 6, 39) 'No one is so brave as not to be disturbed by the unexpected.'

(87b)   Nihil abest quin sim miserrimus. (Cic. Att. 11, 15, 3) 'Nothing is lacking for me to be most miserable.'

(87c)   Nego ullam picturam fuisse quin abstulerit. (Cic. Verr. 2, 4, 1) 'I claim that there was no picture he wouldn't steal.'

In these cases, either there is no overt negative-meaning verb, or if there is one, it has a structure that is not clear, as in (87b). In all three cases the main verb is negated. If this were not the case, we should find *qui non* instead of *quin* in all, as in this sentence:

(88)   Sunt qui rei novitate non perturbentur. 'There are those who are not disturbed by the unexpected.'

In two of these sentences, too, the negative found in *quin* appears in English translations in the surface structure. This indicates that there is at least some sort of difference between these and the other *quin* cases: in these, negative-deletion has applied in English. Perhaps this is because the verbs are not those with inherently negative meaning. (In (87b), however, the negative is not present in the translation: *absum* is a negative-meaning verb but of a different type from *prevent*, or *doubt*.) Further work is needed in order to answer these remaining questions.

A final problem with *quin* concerns cases where it appears and, according to our rules, definitely should not. These are cases like *quin* after *non ignoro*, of example (61f), and with *non dubito*, where *dubito* means hesitate, as in (66c). In these verbs, the deep structure we postulated did not contain a negative sentence directly below the main verb, the negative of which could be lowered and thus be in position for becoming the -*n* of *quin*. The negative meaning in these verbs is introduced as a feature on the main verb itself:

(89)   ignoro   dubito
$$\begin{bmatrix} \langle know \rangle \\ + neg. \end{bmatrix} \qquad \begin{bmatrix} \langle be\ certain \rangle \\ + neg. \end{bmatrix}$$

These verbs, then, ought not to occur followed by *quin*, but occasionally (quite rarely) they do. All that can be suggested to account for this occurrence is that, in those dialects of classical Latin in which *non ignoro quin* and *non dubito* ('hesitate') *quin* were grammatical, the negative feature on the verb might be copied at the left of the lower sentence, and *qui*-subjunctive might then become a possibility since the lower sentence was negated. This is plainly an *ad hoc* solution, but no better one suggests itself.

4.11 *Ut Ne* and *Ut Non*

We have discussed the properties of the complementizer *ut*-subjunctive in the third chapter at considerable length, but there was one very significant point about this complementizer that was not discussed. This is the fact that, when the lower sentence, with *ut*-subjunctive complementizer, has been negated, either of two negations may occur (excluding the possibility of attaching the negative to an indefinite). The negated sentence may contain *ne* (very occasionally *ut ne*), usually to the left of the rest of the embedded sentence. Or it may contain *ut*, then *non* in the position in which *non* would ordinarily appear if *ut* were not present (that is, most frequently, directly in front of the verb). The division is not arbitrary: with exceedingly rare exceptions, a verb or a construction will occur with either *ne* or *ut non* everywhere. Whether a verb takes *ne* or *ut non* can be predicted, it is generally agreed by all grammarians, from the meaning-class of that verb. Thus, for example, verbs of ordering and wishing will always take *ne*:

(90a)   Suis imperavit ne quod omnino telum reicerent. (Caes. B. G. 1, 46) 'He ordered his men not to throw back any weapons at all.'

(90b)   At ne videas velim. (Pl. Rud. 4, 4, 23) 'But I'd like you not to see.'

But impersonal verbs of various sorts take *ut non*:

(91a)   Nec fieri possit, ut non statim alienatio facta sit. (Cic. Lael. 21, 76) 'It is not possible that separation should not be made at once.'

(91b)   Quando fuit ut quod licet non liceret? (Cic. Cael. 20, 48) 'When was it the case that what is permitted was not permitted?'

(91c)   Magnificum illud etiam Romanisque hominibus gloriosum ut
          Graecis de philosophia litteris non egeant. (Cic. Div.
          2, 2, 5)
          'That magnificent idea, and a glorious one for the Roman
          people, too, that they are not lacking in Greek philosophical
          literature.'

Many grammarians have attempted to find a precise meaning difference by which verbs that take *ne* could be distinguished from those
taking *ut non*. But the diversity of the two categories prevents this.
Verbs of wishing behave in at least one respect more like verbs taking
non than like certain other verbs taking *ne*, such as verbs of ordering:
they can occur with the complement in any tense. Verbs of ordering
must take a complement referring to the future. If the distinction really
were semantic, it would be very subtle, indeed, to have caused so much
discussion and confusion among generations of philologists. But the
Romans themselves appear to have made very few, if any, mistakes
until the Vulgar Latin period. There the *ut non* type was generalized;
this is probably to be attributed, not to confusion between *ne* and *non*
(for *ut non* was never, to my knowledge, replaced by *ne*), but rather to the
fact that the rule changing *non* to *ne* first became optional, then was
lost. Since the semantic grounds for a distinction are so slim, we should
do well to look for syntactic motivation for the distinction between
ne and *non* after *ut*.

The distinction I should like to propose is relatively simple. *Ne*
occurs when *ut* introduces an object complement. *Non* occurs when *ut*
introduces a subject complement. There are a few exceptions, which
occur randomly, rarely, and not with any verbs more than with any
others. They occur almost always, in classical prose, in the environment
before indefinites where, as we have shown earlier, several other negation-
related rules are also sometimes relaxed. These cases will be discussed
later.

Since the distinction between *ne* and *non* after *ut* is syntactic, we can
give a rule that will change the negative at the far left to *ne* in the proper
environment (when its sentence is dominated by the verb phrase).
Any negative not operated on by this rule will undergo negative-
movement and negative-attachment (if there is an indefinite present) or
will change to *non* and, usually, be placed before the verb of the lower
sentence.

Rule (7) *Ne*-Formation

$$X\,[ut\ \text{neg. S}\,]_{\text{VP}}\ Y \rightarrow 1 - 2 - ne - 4 - 5$$
$$1\ \ 2\ \ \ \ \ \ \ \ 3\ \ \ \ \ 4\ \ \ \ \ \ \ 5$$

This rule will produce sentences like the following:

(92a)   Imperavi ne Marcus veniret. 'I ordered that Marcus not come.'

(92b)   Imperatum est Marco ne veniret. 'Marcus was ordered not to come.' (Lit., 'it was ordered to Marcus not to come.')

(92c)   Impero ne quis veniat. 'I order that no one come.'

(92d)   Impero ne quid Marcus faciat. 'I order that Marcus not do anything.'

This rule must operate before either negative-movement or negative-attachment, or sentences like (92c) and (92d) would not occur, and we get rather, *Impero ut nemo veniat, *Impero ut Marcus necet neminem. With verbs after which *ut non* is regular the latter two types are always found. There are exceptions which occur in so-called "independent" subjunctives. In the next chapter we shall present evidence that the occurrence of *ne* and *non* in sentences of these types, where there is no overt evidence that the embedded sentence is a subject or an object complement, is predictable in the same way as it is in nonindependent subjunctives, for the same reasons. But in independent subjunctives we sometimes find exceptions to this rule, especially where there is an indefinite in the lower sentence. Why we should expect *ne* (*ne quis*, *ne quid*, etc., which, in fact, we usually find) will be discussed in the next chapter. We list here, however, some apparent exceptions.

(93a)   A legibus non recedamus. (Cic. Clu. 155) 'Let us not depart from the laws.'

(93b)   Non te credas Davom ludere. (Tar. And., 787) 'Don't believe Davos is fooling you.'

(93c)   Et me non facias ringentem. (Petr. 75, 6) 'And don't make me grit my teeth.'

(93d)   Vos quoque non caris aures onerate lapillis ... munditiis capimur: non sint sine lege capilli. (Ov. A. A. 3, 129) 'Also, do not load down your ears with precious stones ... we are charmed by neatness: do not let your hair be in disarray.'

(93e)   Non ancilla tuum iecur ulceret ulla puerve. (Hor. Ep. 1, 18, 72) 'Do not let any slave girl or boy make your heart sick with love.'

These examples, where there is no indefinite, but there is an abstract verb that would ordinarily be followed by *ne* but where *non* occurs instead, almost exhaust the list of such forms. There are more numerous cases where negative-attachment has occurred, although *ne* formation should have operated instead:

(94a)   Nihil ignoveris... nihil gratiae concesseris... misericordia commotus ne sis... in sententia permaneto. (Cic. Mur. 65) 'Forgive nothing... make no concession to favor... do not be moved by pity... stay firm in your decision.'

(94b)   Nullam aciem, nullum proelium timueritis. (Livy 2, 12, 11) 'Fear no battle-line, fear no battle.'

(94c)   Ne transieris Hiberum... nusquam te vestigio moveris. (Livy 21, 44, 6) 'Do not cross the Ebro... do not move a step in any direction.'

(94d)   Moratus sit nemo quo minus abeant. (Livy 11, 13) 'Let no one delay them from leaving.'

Notice, too, that in (94c), although Livy permits himself to violate the rule in the second part of the sentence, where there is an indefinite, he does not permit the violation in the first part, where there is none. This suggests that the rule converting the negative to *ne* was optional, for some speakers of classical Latin at least, under several conditions: either the verb was an abstract verb, or the lower sentence contained an indefinite, or, most commonly, both. A later rule converts *ut ne* to *ne* in most cases, though there are a few instances where this rule, too, does not operate—also, interestingly, in the presence of an indefinite.

(95a)   Haec mihi nunc cura est maxima, ut ne cui meae longinquitas aetatis obstet. (Ter. Hec. 4, 2, 19) 'This is now my greatest concern, lest my old age may not interfere with anything.'

(95b)   Cura et provide ut ne quid ei desit. (Cic. Att. 11, 3, 3) 'See to it, and look out that he lack nothing.'

We know a fair amount about the ordering of *ne*-formation. We know, for example, that it must occur after complementizer-change, since *ut* must be mentioned in the rule. It must follow *nec*-formation: *Impero ne venias nec abeas*, 'I order that you not come and that you not go away,' rather than *Impero ne venias et ne abeas*. (*Neve*, sometimes found in sentences of this type instead of *nec*, is presumably formed by a variant of *nec*-formation.) Complementizer-placement is after *nec*-formation, since *ut* and *quod* will be attached to the left of the negative and above it, between the negative and *and*. This would interfere with the working of the rule as it is stated, and any other statement is more complicated. But any rule that changes the position of the deep-structure subject and predicate must go after *ne*-formation. Flip, passivization, and extraposition, if it exists in Latin, are such rules. For example, passivization must follow *ne*-formation because we find sentences like (92b) when verbs or ordering are passivized, never **Imperatum est ut non veniret*, although in the superficial structure the complement is in subject position. Flip is ordered after *ne*-formation because of sentences like this:

(96)   Senatui placuit ne Catilina loqueretur. 'It was the decision of [lit., ' was pleasing to'] the senate that Catiline not speak.'

We showed in the third chapter that verbs such as *placeo*, 'please,' were flips, as the presence of the dative indicates. The complement is an object of the verb in the deep structure and hence is negated by *ne*. In the next chapter we shall cite some evidence that flips of abstract verbs provide.

In the last section, in the discussion of *prevent*, the deep structure of this verb was set up with the negation as the direct object of *cause*. After negative-lowering, the negated sentence remained the object of the higher verb. Hence, when *ut*-subjunctive was chosen as the complementizer, *ne* was found as the negated form, never *ut non*. If it were the lowest sentence that was negated, *ut non* would have been found instead.

There is an example of such a case, in fact, This example may at first seem to be a counterexample of our claim that *ut non* results from a negation of a subject complement. We are referring to sentences like the following:

(97a)   Rerum obscuritas facit ut non intellegatur oratio. (Cic. Fin. 2, 15) 'The obscurity of the subject matter causes the speech not to be understood.'

(97b)   Demosthenes perfecit meditando ut nemo planius locutus esse putaretur. (Cic. de Or. 1, 260) 'Through practice, Demosthenes brought it about that no one was thought to have spoken more clearly.'

This construction, with a transitive verb (usually *facio* or one of its compounds) and *ut non* can be explained, however, without violating the condition we suggested before. Note that in English we find sentences like these:

(98a)   It happened that John did not catch his plane last night.

(98b)   The weather caused John not to catch his plane.

We also find sentences like the next one, in which *miss* contains in it a negative, something like 'not catch,' in this case:

(98c)   It happened that John missed his plane.

This sentence is parallel to

(98d)   The weather caused John to miss his plane.

Facts like these appear to suggest that in all these sentences the negative is not introduced in a sentence above *happen*. Otherwise, the last two sentences, where the negative must be below *happen*, would not be synonymous with the first two, where in the surface structure it is not clear where the negative is, but is rather introduced below *happen* in (98a) and (98c). This is admittedly not strong evidence at all and is put forward here only as a suggestion of how this question ought to be investigated. The solution we are about to suggest is *ad hoc*, because there is not enough syntactic evidence to support it; but it is being proposed because it, or something like it, is undoubtedly the correct solution. The deep structure shown in (99) is proposed for the sentence *Marcus effecit ut Publius non exiret*, 'Marcus brought it about that

(99)

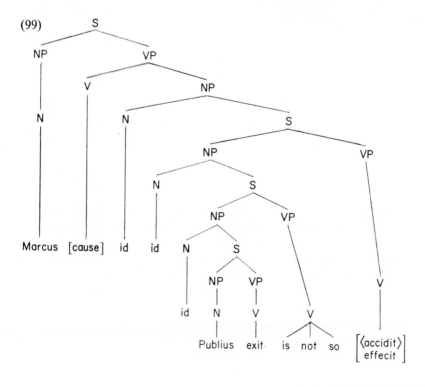

Publius did not leave.' Negative-lowering applies, and, after that, *ut*-subjunctive is attached to both sentences. It appears likely that, if this derivation is correct, *ne*-formation applies before plugging-in; we have no evidence to the contrary. Hence, *ut* + negative is the lower sentence, since it is the subject of *happen*, does not change to *ne*, and the rule cannot apply to this sentence again. Plugging-in applies next, and the structure of the sentence at this point in the derivation is illustrated in diagram (100). *It*-deletion applies, removing both *id*'s, and one of

(100)

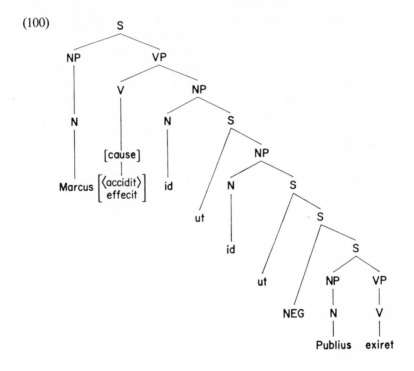

the *ut*'s is deleted as well; it is not certain which. The negative changes to *non* and moves to a position before the lower verb. The superficial structure of the sentence is as shown in (101). If this derivation, or something approximately like it, is correct, there are no known exceptions to our generalization about *ut non* and *ne*. It is true that *facio* and its compounds sometimes appear in sentences followed by *ne*, but sentences of this sort are not the result of *facio* itself introducing the complement. They are, rather, ordinary purpose clauses, which may be introduced by *facio* or any other verb. The structure of the purpose clause will be discussed in the next chapter.

(101)

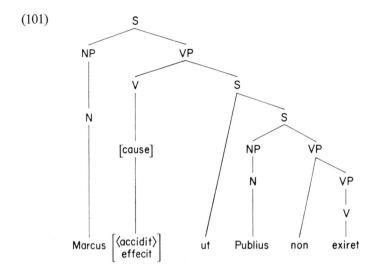

4.12 Conclusions

In this chapter we have discussed the rules producing negated sentences in Latin—in particular, those that were involved with complementation as well. We have suggested derivations for a number of different types of negation and have proposed a syntactic means of distinguishing between sentences that take *ne* and those that take *non*, when *ut*-subjunctive is the complementizer. We reserve until the next chapter discussion of two of the most frequent sentence types with *ne* and with *non*, the purpose, or final, clause and the result, or consecutive, clause. We hope to demonstrate, on the basis of evidence yet to be presented, that the negations found in sentences of these types can be accounted for by the *ne*-formation rule that was stated before. We have also presented some suggestions about the formation of *quin* and *quominus*, although we did not by any means account for all occurrences of these complementizers. We showed that, although some of these rules (such as *ne*-formation and *quin*-formation) were found only in Latin, and not even in Romance, a number of the other negation rules were common to Latin and English. For example, negative-movement, negative-attachment, and negative-transportation appear to work in both languages in essentially the same way, though with minor differences. The deep structure that must be assumed for *prevent*, for which there are syntactic justifications in English, must also be assumed for verbs of the same meaning in Latin, in which we find other, independent, ·syntactic justifications. The conclusion we reach is, once again, that

Latin and English are very similar in their deep structures and their transformational rules—more similar, indeed, than has been assumed by any philologist.

Notes

1. Sentences such as (15a) are produced by a very early rule that deletes the S of the complement in the right-hand sentence under identity with a sentence on the left. Thus, the deep structure of (15a) is really something like the following very tentative approximation:

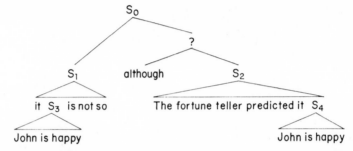

John is happy in S_4 can be deleted by this early sentence-deletion rule only if it is identical with some other sentence, under specific (and not completely understood) conditions. In the preceding sentence, *John is happy* of S_4 is identical to *John is happy* dominated by S_3, and deletion of the right-hand sentence can take place.

2. This can be shown to be true in Latin as well. There are no sentences of the form *Non non scio quis sit Caesar*, '*I don't not know who Caesar is.' But sentences like *Non nescio quis sit Caesar*, *Non ignoro quis sit Caesar*, 'I'm not ignorant of who Caesar is,' are quite frequent, like their English counterparts.

3. In Stephen R. Anderson, "Why *Do So* Does So," unpublished paper, M.I.T., 1967.

4. Real sentences exist in Latin corresponding to all of these. They were not given in the text because we wished to keep the parallelism with sentences we had been using. The type of (35a) is so frequent as to need no illustration. Examples of the others follow:

　　1. Corresponding to (35b): Di sciunt culpam istanc non esse ullam. (Pl. Merc· 3, 4, 41) 'The gods know that isn't any crime.'
　　2. Corresponding to (35c): Nec ulla deformior species est civitatis quam illa. (Cic. Rep. 1, 34, 51) 'Nor is there any kind of state more degenerate than that.'
　　3. Corresponding to (35d): Non ullam rem aliam extimescens, quam . . . (Plancus ap. Cic. Fam. 10, 18, 2) 'Fearing nothing other than . . .'
　　4. Corresponding to (35e): Virus haud ullum magis noxium est. (Curtius 9, 1, 12) 'No poison is more harmful.'

5. This analysis of *prevent* was suggested first by Lakoff (1965).

6. The nature and theoretical significance of abstract verbs will be discussed in the fifth chapter.

5. Abstract Structures

5.1 The Need for Abstract Verbs

There exist in Latin a number of independent subjunctives, with very different meanings from one another. It is generally supposed, or at least hoped, by Latin grammarians that all these diverse subjunctives can be traced to a common origin, a single meaning, to account for the single morphological ending. Since this is patently impossible, a second choice is to explain that one is derived from an optative, another from a potential, a third from the true subjunctive, and then to invent specialized meanings for each of these. Dependent subjunctives, namely those we have discussed and shown to be produced by complementizer-change, are assumed by these writers to be the products of embedding of independent subjunctives within other sentences. But, apparently, there must be rules stating that subjunctives may be embedded only inside specific classes of verbs—in verbs of wishing, for example, but not verbs of thinking. Sometimes infinitives can be embedded inside these, too, with no difference in meaning from the subjunctive. Sometimes it is *quod* plus the finite verb that can be substituted for the subjunctive; sometimes *quod*-finite and the infinitive are substitutable for each other. All these possibilities have been accounted for by postulating complementizer-placement and complementizer-changing rules, governed by the main verb of the sentence and having no influence on the meaning of the sentence. If the philologist is to adhere to his definition of the subjunctive ending as a carrier of meaning, then he must explain both how the infinitive is a carrier of the same meaning (in *volo*), but of indicative-type meaning (as in *dico*); and why *quod*-finite carries "subjunctive" meaning in subject complements (when it is parallel to *ut*-subjunctive).[1] If the subjunctive is truly independent in certain uses, the philologist must also give semantic motivations for the distinction between *non* and *ne*, a distinction strictly observed by all writers of Latin. The philologists have been unable to find any satisfactory semantic justification for this distinction. Their semantic explanation of the subjunctive, then, fails: it fails to tell why subjunctives often are identical in meaning to infinitives, in embedded structures, and even, as we shall show later, in independent sentences; it fails as well to account for the use of *non* in some subjunctives and the use of *ne* in others. It also fails to account for numbers of other important facts, which will be brought out in the discussion to follow.

As an example of the independent subjunctive, let us examine this sentence:

(1)   Venias.

It is agreed by all Latinists that this sentence is at least three ways ambiguous. It may be translated in any of the following three ways:

a. It may be an imperative form: 'Come; you should come.'
b. It may express a wish: 'May you come! If only you were to come!'
c. It may express a possibility: 'You may come; perhaps you are coming.'

The philologist distinguishes between these by assuming the first is a kind of true subjunctive, the second an optative, the third a potential. This is, of course, begging the question. It tells us nothing about why all these forms have the same ending, and it does not really give any insight into their relationship. The philologist never points out, nor does his theory enable him to point out, that there are various means by which these sentences may be disambiguated in Latin. For example, if we negate (1), we shall find either of the following:

(2a)   Ne venias.

(2b)   Non venias.

The first of these is still ambiguous, but only between the first and second meanings given: 'Don't come!' and 'May you not come!' The second is always, and only, the negation of the third meaning, 'You may (perhaps) not come.' If, as is usually assumed by philologists, the first and the second are of different origins, then why are they negated identically? Why is the third different?

In the preceding chapter it was pointed out that the distinction between *non* and *ne* was attributable to the type of complement that the main verb took, whether subject or object. But in these sentences no main verb is apparent. We shall either have to say that, in cases like these independent subjunctives, there is another reason for the *non/ne* distinction, or we shall have to assume that there is something present in the deep structure of these sentences that is not present at the superficial level. We shall, in fact, eventually make this latter claim. But first we snall present more evidence that such a claim is warranted.

When it has the meaning of an imperative, the subjunctive is not found in the first person singular. This is a well-known phenomenon: no language has a first-person singular imperative.[2] Thus, *ne veniam* is not ambiguous, but *ne venias* is. The former has only the optative meaning. This fact can, of course, be expressed as a special fact about the independent subjunctive with the imperative meaning, that it cannot occur in the first person singular. Thus stated, it is an *ad hoc* formulation, unrelated to anything we know about subjunctives. The nonoccurrence of a specific person of a verb in a sentence has been noted before, in earlier chapters: this occurred in certain classes of verbs, in which the subject of the lower verb could not be identical to the subject of the higher verb (as in verbs of ordering) or had to be identical (as in verbs of trying). This is typically a subject-subject constraint. Only here is it, apparently, due to purely semantic factors. This recalls the problem brought up in an earlier paragraph of this chapter about negation: only with independent subjunctives was the choice of negative found to be based on purely semantic factors. Elsewhere it has been shown to be syntactic.

Moreover, only one of the three independent subjunctives can be questioned, either in a yes-no question or with an interrogative pronoun or adverb. Thus, *veniasne*, if it exists at all (I have found no examples), could mean only, 'Is it possible that you are coming?' Even in translation the other two meanings are inconceivable. *Quis veniat* can mean only 'Who may come?' or 'Who would come?' This is very frequent. But it is never found to mean anything like 'Who do I wish would come?' or 'Whom do I order to come?' Hence, when negated, it is always *Quis non veniat*, 'Who wouldn't come?' and never *Quis ne veniat*.

There is another means, too, of disambiguating these subjunctive types. For example, suppose the verb in question is a stative verb:

Altus sis. This can mean either 'May you be tall!' or 'You may (perhaps) be tall,' but it is never a command, ' Be tall!'

As was pointed out before, certain types of independent subjunctives can be replaced by independent infinitives, with accusative subject, with the same meaning. A kind of subjunctive close in meaning to the potential is one of these types. This subjunctive has the meaning " It is likely (that)" and generally occurs in questions. It is sometimes found in the subjunctive, *Tune venias?* 'Can it be that you are coming?' and sometimes with accusative-infinitive, *Tene venire?*, with the same meaning. There are other types of accusative-infinitive independent constructions, which will be discussed later, at least one of which also alternates with a subjunctive. It should be pointed out that this alternation closely resembles the alternation governed by choice of complementizer-changing rules. Moreover, the presence of the accusative in sentences of this kind cannot be accounted for if the deep structure of the sentence contains no verb of which the accusative can be a direct object and no verb that can take *for-to* as a complementizer. These constructions are usually considered semantically motivated, occurring in expressions of emotion. But it is hard to understand the connection between emotion, a purely semantic concept, and accusative case marking, which is purely syntactic.

If we are not to consider these phenomena as semantic, what is the alternative? If they are syntactic, they are governed by a verb in a higher sentence; but in the surface structure of these sentences there is no higher sentence, and there is no verb. Our suggestion is that there is a verb in the deep structure that governs these subjunctives or infinitives. The meaning-class of this verb will give the meaning of the subjunctive, govern whether it is negated by *ne* or *non*, and account for whether or not it can be questioned; where independent infinitives are found, this higher verb will dictate whether the subject of the infinitive is accusative, as in the examples already given, or nominative, as in other cases.

In this way, all the properties of these independent constructions, which must be treated separately by the philologist, are accounted for by postulating verbs present in the deep structure but absent in the surface structure, verbs whose syntactic properties correspond to those of real verbs of the same meaning-class.

Lest it seem that philologists alone are at fault in their analyses of mood, it should be pointed out that until recently transformationalists had no more satisfactory way of dealing with the issue. For most transformationalists, mood was considered simply as an auxiliary verb, generated along with, and parallel to, tense, modal, etc., as an optional expansion of VP. The transformational grammarian operating under such a theory has the following phrase structure rules in his grammar:

S → NP VP

VP → V NP

V → Aux Main Verb

Aux. → (Mood) (Modal) (Have) (Be) Tense

Mood → $\begin{cases} \text{Indic.} \\ \text{Subj.} \\ \text{Imper.} \end{cases}$

For anyone using these rules, then, subjunctive was part of the deep structure and was therefore a meaning-bearing element, like tense. Essentially, then, the treatment of the subjunctive by classical philologists and Indo-Europeanists and its treatment by such transformationalists as Klima (class lectures, 1964–1965) and Chomsky (1965a) have the same effect and are equivalent. The main difference between the two is that the philologists recognize the existence of a problem in dealing with the subjunctive, and they are at least worried about the inconsistencies of their position; the transformationalists who deal with mood in this way have never thought deeply about the question at all.[3]

Our treatment is very different. We are suggesting that no indicators of mood per se can be present in the deep structure. The markers of mood—subjunctive in Latin, subjunctive and optative in Greek—are all complementizers and, as such, are always devoid of meaning of their own and are transformationally introduced. What is present in the deep structure is a verb with semantic and syntactic properties similar to those found in real verbs but with no phonological form; such verbs govern the application of complementizer-placement, complementizer-change, and sometimes other rules as well.

5.2 Justification for Abstract Verbs

Such verbs are called "abstract verbs." We can compare a theory containing abstract verbs with the traditional transformational view given previously, in which arbitrary symbols like Indicative, Subjunctive, Optative, Potential, and Imperative can appear in the deep structure, and are assumed to carry meaning.

The best theory is one that can most completely express the generalizations that the speaker of a language knows exist in his language. In the present case, the linguist must discover which rules are independently motivated and which rules are needed for describing dependent sub-junctives and infinitives in any theory anyway. He must also see whether these rules alone can be used to give us the sentences of the language, in a theory using abstract verbs, without extending the grammar by a large number of special rules to handle the "independent" cases. If a theory containing abstract verbs can make use of independently motivated rules and thus avoid setting up special rules, while a theory without abstract verbs must set up special rules and thus lose the ability to make this significant generalization, the former will naturally be preferred.

If a theory uses abstract verbs, there must be a semantic theory connected with the syntactic theory to assign meanings to these verbs and assign them to meaning-classes: There must be rules of semantic interpretation. But such rules are, of course, needed for real verbs of these classes; no new rules of semantic interpretation need be postulated for abstract verbs, because, semantically, they behave precisely like real verbs.

In a theory containing abstract verbs there must be a way of express-ing deep-structure constraints on these verbs. Just as the real verb of ordering, *impero*, is under the constraint that its subject cannot be identical to the subject of a lower verb, this is true of the abstract verb with the meaning of 'order.' But this is a constraint on the whole meaning-class of verbs of ordering. The supposition of the existence of an abstract verb of ordering does not have any effect at all on these constraints.

We have assumed that the complementizers appearing in the surface structure are assigned, in the case of abstract verbs, exactly as they are assigned in the case of real verbs. For each meaning-class, certain com-plementizer-changing rules are marked, certain unmarked. This marking, as explained in the second chapter, is done by a redundancy rule, and the redundancy rule affects the whole meaning-class and is unaffected by the number of verbs in the meaning-class. The same redundancy rule that covers the real verbs of ordering (*impero*, *mando*, *iubeo*, etc.) will automatically cover the abstract verb. No additional rules are needed.

Besides complementizer-placement and change, there are other rules that apply to complement constructions. For example, there is a rule discussed in the fourth chapter which changes the negative to *ne* under certain conditions. These conditions require the presence of a main verb on which the complement is dependent as a subject or an object. In independent subjunctives the negative *ne* is also found. If we assume that the subjunctive is, in fact, independent, we shall have no way of motivating the change from a negative to *ne* by the rule that operates for dependent subjunctives. But this rule will have to be stated in a grammar of Latin for independent as well as dependent subjunctives. Then how will the linguist who does not have recourse to a theory making use of abstract verbs account for the presence of *ne* in some independent subjunctives, *non* in others? How does he manage to get the correct meanings?

In order for such a linguist to arrive at the correct syntax and the correct semantics, he would have to deny that there exists a relationship between any independent subjunctive and any dependent subjunctive, no matter how close the meaning might be, and to allow for three separate expansions of mood in his phrase structure rules to carry the appropriate meaning for the three sentences *venias* that we have been discussing, as follows:

$$\text{Mood} \rightarrow \begin{cases} \text{Imperative} \\ \text{Optative} \\ \text{Potential} \\ \text{etc.} \end{cases}$$

The subjunctive ending in *venias* is added by a rule that was triggered by the occurrence of one of the arbitrary symbols Imperative, Optative, or Potential. This rule is entirely different from the normal rule of adding subjunctives as complementizers in dependent sentences. The claim is that one process had nothing to do with the other. Similarly, the *non/ne* distinction with independent subjunctives must be made by a rule of the form

$$\text{Neg} \rightarrow \text{ne}/ \begin{cases} \text{Optative} \\ \text{Imperative} \end{cases}$$

This rule is completely independent of the *ne*-formation rule found in dependent subjunctives. The presence of *ne* in the optative *ne venias* is assumed to be completely unrelated to the presence of *ne* in *volo ne venias*.

We claim that in a theory containing abstract verbs, to explain the properties mentioned in the foregoing paragraphs, we can use the same rules that were used to explain these properties in dependent clauses. The only additional apparatus needed are late rules deleting abstract verbs. But all the relationships that the speaker of a language senses between certain dependent uses of the subjunctive and certain independent uses are expressed in this theory through the sharing of rules by the apparently independent and the overtly dependent types.

However, in a theory that uses arbitrary symbols such as are found in the phrase structure rules given earlier, none of these generalizations could be captured. Because the subjunctives, etc., were generated in the deep structure, separate semantic interpretation rules would be needed in order to assign meanings to them; the rules assigning optative meaning to a subjunctive, for example, would have nothing whatever to do with the rules that assign meanings to verbs of wishing.

These deep-structure constraints could not be stated as ordinary constraints between sentences. The restriction on the subject of the imperative, preventing a first-person singular imperative, would have to be expressed in a rule that applied specially to the imperative marker. It would be unrelated to the property that we observed in verbs of ordering.

Complementizer-placement and complementizer-change can apply only when the sentence that is to undergo these rules is dependent on a verb in a higher sentence. But if subjunctives and imperatives were independent and were generated in phrase structure rules, there would be no sentence above them. The presence of *ut*, with an independent subjunctive, or an accusative with an independent infinitive, would require special separate rules, unrelated to complementizer-placement and complementizer-change. The fact that *ut* in *Ut venias* behaves like the *ut* in *Volo ut venias* could only be described as coincidental. Likewise, the presence of an accusative case marker on the subject noun of an independent accusative must be interpreted as a fact unrelated to the fact that one of the complementizer-changing rules attaches an accusative ending to the noun along with an infinitive ending on the verb.

Finally, a rule such as *ne*-formation could not be applied to both independent and dependent subjunctives. The way that the general rule for dependent subjunctives is stated requires the presence of a higher verb. Another rule would have to be formulated to account for the independent cases.

We have shown that a theory containing abstract verbs can express a great many relevant generalizations, without adding much extra apparatus to the grammar. A theory without abstract verbs misses all these generalizations and is forced to contain a great many more rules than the other theory. Therefore it appears that, if one believes that it is the task of the linguist to capture significant generalizations in grammar —and if one does not believe that the linguist's task ends with merely providing derivations, *ad hoc* or not, for all the possible sentences of a language—one would appear forced to adopt a theory that allowed abstract elements such as the ones we have been discussing. Such a theory is much more abstract than other transformational theories that have been proposed and assumed by other generative grammarians. Their claim is that a theory allowing these abstract devices is too strong and that a linguist using abstract verbs operates relatively free of all constraints—in other words, that a linguist whose theory included abstract verbs could use an abstract verb of some class or other to eliminate, in an *ad hoc* way, all syntactic problems. This linguist, they say, could postulate an indefinitely large number of abstract verbs with any properties he desires. We claim, on the contrary, that our theory of abstract verbs specifically prevents *ad hoc* treatment and severely restricts the number and possible syntactic properties of these verbs.

5.3 The Nature of Abstract Verbs

We have defined abstract verbs (Section 5.1) as being verbs that have semantic and syntactic properties similar to those of real verbs. But, clearly, every possible combination of semantic and syntactic properties cannot be used to define an abstract verb. For some classes of verbs, abstract verbs cannot exist. An abstract verb will be found for a given class of verbs only if that class comprises what we call a "meaning-class." We shall consider this as a technical term, the definition of which here is stricter than that assumed by traditional grammarians. For them any class of verbs that shared some vague general meaning—such as verbs of ordering or verbs of eating—comprised a meaning-class. For us this is not so. We define a meaning-class in terms of both syntax and semantics, as a set of semantic markers that can function in syntactic rules. Not all semantic markers function in syntactic rules. For example, the semantic markers that define verbs of ordering will function syntactically in a redundancy rule specifying that, for this semantic class, one or more of the complementizer-changing rules must apply. On the other hand, for verbs of eating there is no semantic marker that functions syntactically or that distinguishes a rule that applies to verbs of eating from one that can apply only to verbs of drinking or verbs of digesting.

Since we can have syntactic rules referring to the semantic class of verbs of requesting, there is the possibility in a language that there will be an abstract verb [*request*]. But there will never be an abstract verb [*eat*] in any language. Further, a language might contain a morphological affix that would have the meaning of "request." But it would never have an affix that, attached to a verb *x*, would give the meaning "perform the action *x* while eating." This theory also severely delimits the potential number of abstract verbs in a language, since there can be only one per meaning-class (in our sense of the term); there can be, in theory, an indefinitely large number of real verbs in a meaning-class. By our definition there will never be two abstract verbs with the same meaning and syntactic properties. Thus we see that the postulation of abstract verbs is constrained in our theory, and the hypothesizing of an abstract verb cannot be *ad hoc.* There are further reasons, too, why a theory such as we are outlining actually prevents, rather than encourages, irresponsible and *ad hoc* derivations.

An abstract verb behaves like a real verb in one way that may be unexpected: it can be irregular with respect to the redundancy rules of its meaning-class. Thus in Latin, verbs of ordering regularly take the complementizer *ut*-subjunctive: *Impero ut venias.* But a verb of ordering may be marked in the lexicon as undergoing *for-to* complementizer-change instead, as is *iubeo: Iubeo te venire.* It is conceivable that a verb of ordering in Latin might be able to undergo either of these rules; this was true for some speakers of Latin in the case of *impero*, for others with *iubeo.* It is equally conceivable that the abstract verb of ordering, which underlies the imperative, might function this way and that we might find alternative forms of the imperative, *Venias* and *Te venire.* That only the first of these appears in Latin is not altogether accidental but rather the result of the fact that a language will generally choose the unmarked complementizer for a class in an abstract verb, though it will not invariably do so. It may choose a marked possibility, but it will never choose one that is impossible for the meaning-class; thus, it is predicted that **Quod venit* and **Venit* are impossible as imperative forms in Latin, as of course they are.

In the hypothetical case that both *Venias* and *Te venire* existed side by side as imperative forms in Latin, we should have several possible ways to interpret the situation. We could assume there was only one abstract verb of ordering, marked as optionally undergoing either of the two complementizer-changing rules, or we could assume there were actually two abstract verbs, belonging to two different meaning-classes. Our choice of hypothesis would depend on whether the meanings of the two were identical and the two were completely interchangeable— in which case we should pick the former interpretation—or whether there was some difference of meaning or use, perhaps very slight, in which case we should have to pick the latter interpretation in order to account for the facts. In this case the two verbs would be members of two different, but closely related, meaning-classes and would share many semantic and syntactic properties, but not all.

What we are attempting to do, then, in our postulation of abstract verbs is to express formally an intuitive notion: that often in language a verbal concept can be expressed without the superficial presence of a verb. A suffix, or a marker of mood, can carry verbal meaning. The theory we are proposing describes how such suffixes and markers function in the grammar: how they are introduced and how they function in rules.

In his thesis Lakoff (1965) discussed the theory of abstract verbs, but his theory differs in fundamental ways from the one set forth here. In his theory an abstract verb consisted of a minimally specified semantic matrix, in a sense the lowest common denominator of a meaning-class, containing all the features shared by all the verbs in a meaning-class, and no other features. There was thus no opportunity for an abstract verb in this system to behave idiosyncratically, as we have found numbers of them do. Lakoff's abstract verb was generally much less like a real verb in its properties than ours is. There was no internal necessity for any of his abstract verbs to undergo any syntactic rules, other than plugging-in and *it*-substitution, while a large part of our justification for abstract verbs is that they must undergo a large number of syntactic rules that real verbs undergo and that traces of their having undergone such rules remain in the surface structure, providing syntactic motivation for postulating these verbs, which would otherwise be lacking. We shall illustrate this claim in later sections. Briefly, abstract verbs must undergo the following rules, though, of course, no one abstract verb undergoes them all:

1. Complementizer-placement
2. Complementizer-change
3. Negative-movement and negative-attachment
4. *Ne*-formation
5. *It*-substitution
6. *Ut*-deletion
7. Flip (perhaps)
8. Sequence-of-tenses rules

Thus, if there is in Latin an abstract verb that means "wish," it will share the syntactically relevant semantic features of the whole class of verbs of wishing. It will theoretically be able to undergo either *for-to* or *ut*-subjunctive complementizer-change. It must undergo one or the other, like the real verbs of its class. Actually, in Latin, the abstract verb of wishing may undergo only *ut*-subjunctive complementizer-change; in this way, it is irregular. Sequence-of-tenses rules must operate on sentences dependent on abstract verbs. If the dependent verb is negated and it occurs in an object complement dependent on an abstract verb, it will undergo *ne*-formation just like a real verb in that position. We shall show in later sections of this chapter that most of the different types of subjunctives that occur in Latin can be derived from sentences dependent on different abstract verbs and that the syntactic behavior, as well as the meaning, of these independent subjunctives follows naturally from the syntactic constraints on, and the meaning of, the abstract verb on which the lower sentence is dependent. Thus abstract verbs can be distinguished from one another by the different syntactic reflexes each leaves in the surface structure; these verbs lack only specification in their phonological and morphological matrices. For example, the real verb *impero* must be marked as being a first conjugation verb; this is a morphological fact with no syntactic implications. But the abstract verb of ordering carries no marking of this sort.

5.4 Implications for Transformational Theory

With this interpretation, the concept of the abstract verb has considerable implications for the theory of transformational grammar. Without it, deep structures are not very abstract: the phrase-structure rules given before, necessary in a transformational theory that does not make use of abstract verbs, generate a deep structure that is very close to the surface structure. All that distinguishes the product of these rules from surface-structure verb phrases is a difference in the order of words and the later addition of some morphological elements, such as participial endings. It is also true that this sort of deep structure is valid only for English: the way it is formulated makes it unusable in other languages, where *have* and *be* are not represented as morphologically independent entities and where different combinations of auxiliaries exist. Conservative transformational grammar is unwilling to accept the position, now held by some of the more radical transformationalists, that the deep structure is the same in all the Indo-European languages and may possibly be language-universal.[4] A theory of which abstract verbs were not a part cannot make this assumption. A theory that uses the concept of the abstract verb may easily make this assumption, although, of course, the presence of abstract verbs does not necessitate the adoption of such a belief.

The proponent of a theory using abstract verbs believes deep structure is far more abstract than does someone whose theory does not contain these mechanisms. The theory of the former assumes a grammar with a set of phrase structure rules, a deep structure, and a transformational component very different from that assumed in a more conservative theory. The phrase structure rules will be much simpler. The last three of the phrase structure rules given earlier will not be present, nor will further rules expanding the various optional elements of the last two rules. The grammar that contains these rules will naturally have a very complex phrase structure component, generating a complex deep structure with many different relationships between words possible in the deep structure itself. By contrast, a theory allowing abstract verbs will have an extremely simple phrase structure component:[5]

S → NP VP

VP → V NP

NP → NP S

NP → N (S)

These rules will generate all possible deep structures. Deep structures will, then, contain only subject noun phrases, verbs, and direct object noun phrases. Some adverbials, moods, tenses, auxiliaries, and all other elements found in the surface structure will be transformationally introduced through the use of abstract verbs. In this chapter we shall illustrate some of the ways these abstract verbs are found in the base and how surface structures containing certain adverbials and moods are produced transformationally. It will be clear that the transformational component of the grammar will be rather more complicated than it would be in the more conservative theory. But this is not, in itself, a drawback, any more than the greater complexity of the deep structure in the other theory is a drawback for it. The criterion of simplicity is irrelevant in deciding between these two theories. What is relevant is the amount of generalization about the grammar each theory allows to be expressed, and it would seem that a theory using abstract verbs is preferable for this reason. We have already given some cases in which the assumption of an abstract verb in the deep structure allows us to account for the behavior of embedded sentences using, except for abstract-verb deletion, no more rules than were necessary for sentences containing real verbs. The presence of *ne* in the environment of abstract verbs that take object complements and of *non* in the environment of those that take subject complements is an example of such a generalization. A theory lacking abstract verbs must have separate rules telling where *ne* and *non* occur in dependent and independent subjunctives. But it is evident that there is a correlation in meaning between independent subjunctives with *ne* and dependent subjunctives with *ne* and between independent subjunctives with *non* and dependent subjunctives with *non*. A grammar should express the fact that such a relationship exists, or it is not expressing something the native speaker uses in speaking his language. With abstract verbs we can express this generalization.

For some of the abstract verbs we shall be discussing, the abstract verb is limited in its person or tense. In other cases, it may occur in any person or in any tense. The restriction on person is of two sorts: either the person is always third singular, the verb is impersonal, and its subject is always *it*—this is, of course, true with all verbs taking subject complements—or the verb is one of a number of abstract verbs that are performatives. This term, " performative," was first introduced by the philosopher J. L. Austin (*How to Do Things with Words*, 1962), to describe verbs whose subject must perform the action of the verb when he uses it. For example, if I say "I promise to give you ten dollars," I am making the promise by saying "I promise." Necessarily, then, a performative verb is always first person singular. Lying is impossible with a performative. A speaker can say "I am not hungry" when he is hungry, but he cannot say "I am not ordering you to leave" at the same time as he is ordering someone to leave. They cannot be embedded in verbs expressing opinion: "I think I am hungry" is grammatical, but "I think I am making a wish that I were king" is not possible. Hence, if we have an abstract verb that is a performative, it cannot be embedded in a verb of opinion. It also cannot be embedded in another performative. " *I wish that I were ordering . . ." is not possible with the meaning that the speaker is ordering as he speaks; only the nonperformative is possible here. But it may be embedded in other kinds of sentences, and examples will be discussed later in which performative abstract verbs in Latin are embedded in other verbs, real or abstract. On the other hand, nonperformative abstract verbs are under no restriction as to being embedded in performatives. It has been suggested (Ross, 1967) that questions are formed by the presence, in the deep structure, of a sentence *I [question] whether S*, or the like, dominating the questioned sentence. This abstract verb, [*question*], is a performative. For this reason, and because a sentence containing a performative cannot be dominated by a performative, *veniat* in *Quis veniat?* is never either an imperative or an optative subjunctive, since the abstract verb of ordering and the abstract verb of wishing are both performatives. Performatives are always present tense. (The case of the optative *Venires* and *Venisses*, 'Would that you were coming' and 'Would that you had come!' respectively, will be dealt with later in the discussion of the optative abstract verb.)

The fact that the imperative abstract verb is a performative, and therefore always first person singular, explains why there is never a first person imperative. (There is, of course, a first plural hortatory subjunctive, where a different verb is involved.) The reason is that verbs of ordering operate under the constraint that the subject of the higher sentence can never be identical to the subject of the lower sentence. This is true for the whole class and therefore need not be stated specially for the abstract verb. The performative is always first person; hence, the lower verb can never be first person. In this way, the concept of the abstract verb can be used to account naturally, and with no increase in the number of rules, for a linguistic universal.

Earlier (Section 5.1) it was noted that, if a stative verb appeared in the subjunctive, the imperative meaning was automatically ruled out. In a theory using abstract verbs, this is accounted for naturally. All verbs of ordering are constrained so that they cannot dominate stative verbs. Thus we cannot have *I order you to be tall*. The fact that *Be tall!* is not found is, under the theory proposed here, only a natural extension of the first fact, requiring no additional rules.

A number of abstract verbs will be discussed in detail later, but the list of abstract verbs in Latin is by no means exhausted. There are many cases that we do not understand and that therefore have not been dealt with at all. Among these are: subjunctives connected with contrary-to-fact conditional sentences (*Si venires, irem*); subjunctives connected with expressions of time and cause (*cum*); subjunctives introduced in indirect questions; subjunctives in causal clauses (*quod*) in which the speaker does not take responsibility for the truth of the assertion of the cause; subjunctives in indirect statement; and a number of others. Whatever is happening here, it does not appear as if doubt or uncertainty were reflected in the use of the subjunctive in most of these cases. They have never been satisfactorily explained, nor will they be here.[6]

There are, too, a great many more conceivable abstract verbs in Latin (as in any language) which remain undiscovered. For example, it is known that there are many varieties of imperatives: some stronger, some more peremptory, some gentler. The relations among them in English have been discussed by Bolinger (1967). Bolinger's points about English are equally relevant to Latin. The conclusion to be drawn is, apparently, that there is not only one imperative abstract verb but several, with varying meanings (*I suggest, I insist, I urge*) and varying syntactic properties. We shall discuss this point briefly later, in the section on the imperative abstract verb, but we cannot really be sure exactly how many abstract verbs of ordering there are. If this is true, there may well be several abstract verbs underlying each of our categories listed. But we cannot make delicate distinctions, as we can for English.

In the remainder of this chapter we shall be discussing a number of the clearest cases of abstract verbs in Latin. They will be considered in this order:

The imperative abstract verbs: [*imper*], [*hort*]
The optative abstract verb: [*vel*]
The jussive abstract verb: [*oport*]
The concessive abstract verb: [*lic*]
The deliberative abstract verb: [*aequum*]
The potential abstract verb: [*poss*]
The abstract verb of the purpose clause: [*vol*]
The verb of the relative purpose clause: [*designate*]

We shall also discuss briefly the result clause in Latin, although its deep structure is at present unclear.

5.5 The Imperative Abstract Verbs [*Imper*] and [*Hort*]

In Latin, sentences containing a verb of ordering (such as *impero*) followed by a subjunctive with *ut* (negative *ne*) are frequent.

(1a)   His uti conquirerent et reducerent imperavit. (Caes. B. G. 1, 28, 1) 'He ordered them to search and bring back.'

(1b)   Suis imperavit ne quod omnino telum reicerent. (Caes. B. G.1, 46) 'He ordered them not to throw back any weapon.'

In sentences such as this, ordinary sequence-of-tenses rules are in operation: in essence, since the lower verb must always refer to the future in a verb of ordering, the perfect and pluperfect subjunctives are never found. As has been pointed out earlier, the persons of the two verbs cannot be identical for verbs of ordering. Even if the number is different, a verb of ordering cannot have a subject that is included in the subject of the lower sentence. Thus, *Eis imperat ut veniant*, 'He orders them to come,' is grammatical only if the subject of *veniant*, *ei*, 'they,' does not include the person giving orders as one of them. For this reason, **Impero ut veniamus* is always ungrammatical, since the first person plural must include the speaker. But in Latin, as in English, verbs of related meaning, such as 'urge, advise, suggest' (Lat., *hortor*, *moneo*), are slightly less restricted. For them, the persons cannot be identical, but the person advising can include himself in the group to which he is giving advice.

(2a)   *I suggest that I go.

(2b)   I suggest that we go.

(2c)   *Hortor ut eam.

(2d)   Hortor ut eamus.

Therefore, we can distinguish at least two of the abstract verbs of ordering: one is of the class of *impero*, and this is the verb ordinarily found in imperatives. The other, a milder form of ordering, is in the same class as *hortor*. Verbs dependent on [*imper*] usually undergo a further rule transforming them to imperatives. Verbs dependent on [*hort*] sometimes undergo this rule. Even if the sentence depends on [*imper*], the lower verb need not become an imperative; it may remain a subjunctive. This is most often the case when the verb is negative and is in the perfect subjunctive in the surface structure. In Latin prose of the classical period, the third person usually remained subjunctive, with only the second person taking imperative endings. But in archaic Latin, there are many examples of third person imperatives. The verbs [*imper*] and [*hort*] underlie a number of different surface-structure types. They can underlie a sentence that has a verb in the present subjunctive, either positive or negative.

(3a)   Isto bono utare dum adsit, cum absit ne requiras. (Cic. Sen. 33)
         'Use this advantage while you have it, do not miss it when it is
         no longer there.'

(3b)   Naviget, haec summa est, hic nostri nuntius esto. (Verg. Aen. 4,
         237) 'Let him sail, this is the point, let this be our message.'

In (3a) the writer is giving advice, and the abstract verb is undoubtedly [*hort*]. In (3b) Jupiter is clearly ordering rather than suggesting, and the verb is [*imper*]. These verbs can underlie sentences where the verb is a perfect subjunctive, but only if this subjunctive is negated. The verb here may be [*imper*] or [*hort*].

(4a)   Ne sis admiratus. (Cic. Fam. 7, 18, 3) 'Don't be surprised.'

(4b)   Ne necesse habueris. (Cic. Att. 16, 2, 5) 'Don't consider it
         necessary.'

Admiratus sis and *Necesse habueris* are probably ungrammatical. There appears to be, in verbs of this class, a rule that switches aspect in certain conditions.[7] This rule will be discussed later. It must have operated here, since *Admiratus sis* and *habueris* refer to the future.

Most frequently with [*imper*], the true imperative is found. In classical prose, instead of the expected negation with *ne*, a circumlocution is used, with the imperative of *nolo*, 'be willing,' and the infinitive, as in

Noli hoc facere, 'Don't do this.'[8] But the imperative with *ne* is found fairly often as well.

(5a)   Consulite vobis, prospicite patriae, conservate vos. (Cic. Cat. 4, 3) 'Take care for yourselves, look out for your country, preserve yourselves.'

(5b)   Equo ne credite, Teucri! (Verg. Aen. 2, 48) 'Do not trust the horse, Trojans!'

(5c)   Te ipsum concute. (Hor. Sat. 1, 3, 35) 'Examine yourself!'

In the first sentence the verb of ordering may be [*imper*], or it may be [*hort*]. In the second it is almost certainly [*hort*]; *credo,* 'trust,' is a verb that cannot occur in a sentence depending on a verb of ordering, though it may depend on a verb of advising. **I order you to trust John* is ungrammatical; *I advise you to trust John,* however, is acceptable. The verb in (5c) is probably [*imper*].

We also find sentences with the so-called "future" imperative, both positive and negative. This imperative is actually parallel to the perfect subjunctive and is therefore more properly considered a perfect imperative than a future imperative. All imperatives refer to the future, and the claim that this form of the imperative is used when there is a reference to future time is therefore meaningless. The other definition of this form, that it is used to refer to an event taking place after some other specified event, is false, as will be shown by sentence (6b), in which the action of the imperative is going on at the same time as the action in the rest of the sentence. In legal texts, where this form is most frequent, it seems to be used to express forceful commands: it appears to substitute for the perfect subjunctive in affirmatives, where, as we showed before, the perfect subjunctive is not found. Later we shall give a few examples of sentences in which imperative forms and subjunctive forms are used side by side. In such cases, the present imperative usually is found with the present subjunctive, and the perfect (or future) imperative with the perfect subjunctive (negated). This is further evidence that this subjunctive is simply a form derived from the perfect subjunctive by the same rule by which the present imperative is derived from the present subjunctive. Examples follow of the perfect imperative used alone:

(6a)   Cum testem produxero, refellito, si poteris. (Cic. Verr. 5, 154) 'When I have produced my witness, refute him if you can.'

(6b)   Hoc flante, ne arato, semen ne iacito. (Plin. H. N. 18, 334) 'When this wind is blowing, do not plow, do not plant seed.'

Finally, there are cases where imperative forms are mixed with subjunctives. As we said earlier, usually perfect subjunctives are matched with perfect imperatives, present subjunctives with present imperatives.

(7a)   Primum ignosce patrio dolore, deinde sinas [me] nutricem percontari. (Livy 3, 48, 4) 'First, pardon a father's grief; then, let me question the nurse.'

(7b)   Hoc facito, hoc ne feceris. (Cic. Div. 2, 127) 'Do this, don't do this.'

There are a number of rules associated with this abstract verb. First, *ut* is deleted obligatorily if imperativization takes place: *Ut veni is never found. It is probably obligatory even if imperativization does not take place, as there seem to be no examples of the imperative-type subjunctive preceded by *ut*. Another rule switches aspect. That this rule is restricted to abstract verbs is shown by the fact that **Impero ut veneris* is ungrammatical. The presence of the perfect tense does not mean that the imperative refers to the past—an imperative cannot refer to the past. If there is any difference between the perfect subjunctive (and imperative) and the present tense forms, it is that the former seem to indicate a stronger order and hence are the forms used in legal writing; they appear always to be at least [*imper*], never [*hort*]. But it is not certain whether these forms are derived from sentences with [*imper*] or from sentences with a stronger verb, with the meaning of 'insist, adjure.' If there really is this slight difference in meaning, then there probably are two different verbs: [*imper*] cannot undergo aspect-switch, but [*insist*], or whatever this other verb is, either may or must. It is not clear whether some present imperatives also may have this meaning. If they do, then the rule is only optional for [*insist*].

After aspect-switch, imperativization occurs. This rule operates on a verb that is dependent on [*imper*], [*insist*], or [*hort*]—perhaps others of this class as well—to remove the subjunctive marker (this has not yet been converted to the subjunctive endings, which are added in the morphological component) and substitute in its place an imperative marker. In the morphological component this imperative marker will be converted to one of a number of endings, depending on aspect, person, and number. Imperativization must take place if aspect-switch has occurred and the verb is not negated. In the grammar of most writers of classical Latin, it apparently could not take place if the verb were third person. *Ut* is deleted regularly after an abstract verb. There are exceptions to this rule in the case of some of the other abstract verbs, but there appears to be none in this case. This *ut*-deletion rule, therefore, is governed, operating optionally if certain abstract verbs are present, obligatorily in other verbs. The occasions where *ut* is deleted after an abstract verb do not correspond to occasions where it may be deleted after a real verb. For example, after real verbs of ordering in Latin, *ut* is only very occasionally deleted. But it is obligatorily deleted after the abstract verbs of ordering. The rule deleting the abstract verb itself is later.

It is well known that there are other ways of expressing the imperative in Latin. Both in Latin and in English the future tense may have the force of an imperative:

(8)   Si quid acciderit novi, facies ut sciam. (Cic. Fam. 14, 8) 'If any thing new happens, you'll let me know.'

It is not clear how this is to be interpreted. It is true that the future tense is present in the deep structure of every verb dependent on a verb of ordering. (See Chapter 3, note 3.) Perhaps in some circumstances future is not deleted. This would be true only in case there were an abstract verb on which the lower verb depended. If future is not deleted, perhaps then complementation cannot take place in these verbs. Either of two possibilities exist as to the nature of this imperative form: either the nondeletion of future takes place only when a special verb of ordering is present, or it optionally takes place with any of them. The choice rests on the question of whether there is a difference in meaning, for example, between a sentence, such as (8), containing a future tense verb and one in which *fac* replaced *facies*. In any case, all of this is highly speculative.[9] These problems are discussed at greater length in Bolinger (1967).

Aside from these problematic cases, most of the more frequent types of imperatives can be accounted for by postulating abstract verbs of ordering. In this way, the correct meanings are assigned and the correct syntactic properties found in imperatives, without having to have special rules for them, except perhaps for aspect-switch, with which any formulation of the imperative would have to deal specially in some way.

5.6 The Optative Abstract Verb [*Vel*]

Real verbs of wishing in Latin (*volo, cupio, opto,* etc.) can be followed by either *for-to* or *ut*-subjunctive. In the latter case, the negative is *ne*. Frequently the verb of wishing (particularly *volo*) is found in the subjunctive, like English "I'd like." This appears to represent a conditional sentence, the protasis of which is omitted: "I'd wish for *X*" (if such a wish were reasonable). This type of sentence, with *vellem* and an imperfect subjunctive complement, is the only means available in Latin for expressing (with a real verb) a wish referring to the present. *Volo* (or *velim*) could take only present subjunctives, which refer to the future. All the following are found:

(9a)   Volo ut quod iubebo facias. (Pl. Bacch. 4, 8, 65) 'I wish that you would do what I will order you to.'

(9b)   At ne videas velim. (Pl. Rud. 4, 4, 23) 'But I wish you wouldn't see.'

(9c)   Quid nunc vis? Ut opperiare hos sex dies saltem modo, ne illam vendas, neu me perdas. (Pl. Ps. 1, 3, 102) 'What do you wish now?' 'That you wait just these six days, at least, that you not sell her, and that you not ruin me.'

(9d)   Maxime vellem, iudices, ut P. Sulla . . . modestiae fructum aliquem percipere potuisset. (Cic. Sull. 1, 1) 'I would especially like it, gentlemen of the jury, for P. Sulla to have been able to reap some reward for his good conduct.'

(9e)   Equidem vellem uti pedes haberent. (Cic. Fam. 7, 33, 2) 'Myself, I would like it for them to have feet.'

Corresponding to these closely in meaning is the optative subjunctive. These subjunctives have the meaning "Would that! If only!" and the like. The negative is always *ne*, with a very few exceptions of the type discussed in Section 4.11. The positive occurs in any of various forms: either without any complementizer introducing it; with *ut*; with *utinam*; or rarely, in archaic Latin, with *qui*. (*Utinam ne* is also possible.) Examples of all these types of optative expressions are as follows:

(10a)   With no complementizer introducing the sentence: Valeant cives mei! Sint incolumes, sint florentes, sint beati! (Cic. Mil. 93) 'May my citizens be well! May they be unharmed, may they be flourishing, may they be happy!'

(10b)   With *ut*: Ut illum di perduint. (Pl. Aul. 785) 'May the gods destroy him!'

(10c)   With *utinam*: Utinam me mortuum vidisses. (Cic. Q. Fr. 1, 2, 3, 1) 'Would that you had seen me dead!'

(10d)   With *qui*: Qui illum di perdant. (Pl. Cas. 279) 'May the gods destroy him!'

(10e)   With *ne*: Ne vivam si scio. (Cic. Att. 4, 16, 8) 'May I not live, if I know.'

(10f)   With *utinam ne*: Utinam ne vere scriberem. (Cic. Fam. 5, 17, 3) 'Would that I were not writing the truth!'

(10g)   With *utinam non*: Utinam susceptus non fuissem. (Cic. Att. 11, 9, 3) 'Would that I had not been reared!'

The *non* in (10g) may be accounted for by the principle given in the fourth chapter which allowed *ne*-formation not to operate under certain conditions, one of them being the presence of an abstract, rather than a real, verb on which the subjunctive was dependent. The examples given in that chapter were all derived from sentences dependent on one of the verbs of ordering, but it is true as well for verbs of wishing. Notice that the substitution of *non* for *ne*, both with [*imper*] and with [*vel*], is very rare. It never occurs in any specific syntactic environment. This distinguishes these cases from others to be discussed later (in Section 5.7), where an abstract verb that takes *ne* and an object complement appears to be very close in meaning to another that takes *non*, and a subject complement.

Some of these complementizers do not occur with real verbs of wishing. *Utinam*, in particular, occurs nowhere except after the abstract [*vel*]. But *utinam* is not unrelated to the other complementizers. It is formed from *ut*, in its longer form *uti*, combined with the emphatic particle *nam*, found frequently reinforcing interrogative pronouns, adverbs, and adjectives—for example, *Ubinam gentium sumus?* (Cic. Cat. 1, 9): 'Where *in the world* are we?' Since *ut* is, in origin, an interrogative adverb ('how?'), it is one of the class to which -*nam* may be added. *Qui* has been discussed before but only in connection with its use in negation. When it is used following a real verb, it apparently cannot be used except under the conditions stated in Section 4.10. In archaic Latin, *qui* could also be used following the abstract verb [*vel*]. This seems to have been restricted to expressions analogous to (10d), where the wish is that something bad may happen to someone else; it is, thus, restricted to curses even in the archaic period, and after that is not found at all in this use.

It is also noteworthy that one of the possibilities for complementizers found with real verbs of wishing is never found at all with the abstract verb. This is the accusative-infinitive: *Te venire volo*, 'I wish that you would come.' As was said before in the general discussion of abstract verbs, there is no reason why *Te venire* could not have been used in

Latin as an expression of wish. Compare, in English, "Oh, to be in England, now that April's here!" where *for-to* is used to express wishes. But in the Latin case, the abstract verb does not completely mirror the properties of the real verbs of the class. A verb of wishing might do any of three things: it might take only *for-to*, it might take only *ut*-subjunctive, or it might optionally take either. Each of these possibilities would be expressed by different markings on the separate verbs in the lexicon. The redundancy rule for the class states that a verb of wishing that takes either *for-to* or *ut*-subjunctive is unmarked for both of these and that a verb which could take only *for-to* would be marked for *for-to*. Such a verb would not need to be given any marking for *ut*-subjunctive if we assume there is an ordering of the complementizer-changing rules: Rule (2a) would, under this system, be given a chance to apply or not apply, optionally or obligatorily, before Rule (2b) was reached at all. This is an *ad hoc* solution, since there is no indication at all that these rules are ordered with respect to each other; this would be merely a device to simplify a complicated situation. If we do not impose this device, it is difficult to see how we could handle the problem of verbs of wishing at all, for there must be provision for the existence of the second kind of exception, a verb of this class taking only *ut*-subjunctive. A verb of this type would be unmarked for *for-to* but marked for *ut*-subjunctive. The redundancy rule states that, if a verb is marked for one of the rules, it undergoes it obligatorily. Therefore, even though the nonmarkedness of *for-to* complementizer-change in a verb of this kind might enable it to take *for-to*, when the next marking is reached, it becomes clear that the verb cannot do anything but take *ut*-subjunctive. This is a rather awkward way of dealing with the situation, but there appears to be no other way. A verb of this type, taking only *ut*-subjunctive, is [*vel*]. This abstract verb, therefore, does not act like any of the real verbs of its class (though, of course, an abstract verb easily could, as [*imper*] does), but it acts as a verb of its class might act if specially marked. It is, then, acting like an irregular verb of wishing.

Another way in which [*vel*] appears to act differently from real verbs of wishing is in the tenses of the verbs that are found in complements of [*vel*]. All of the tenses of the subjunctive may be found with optative meaning, though some are rare or archaic. In a few cases, one tense form may be equivalent to either of two tenses in translation.

(11a)   With present subjunctive referring to the future: Utinam reviviscat frater aliamque classem in Siciliam ducat! (Gellius 10, 6, 2) 'Would that my brother might return to life, and lead another fleet against Sicily!'

(11b)   With present subjunctive referring to the present—rare and archaic: Utinam nunc stimulus in manu mihi sit. (Pl. Asin. 418) 'Would that there were now a goad in my hand!'

(11c)   With perfect subjunctive referring to the future—rare, archaic, and restricted to the -s- perfect: Di te servassint semper! (Pl. Asin 654) 'May the gods preserve you always!'

(11d)   With perfect subjunctive referring to an action in the past, from the vantage point of the future—rare: Utinam vere auguraverim. (Cic. Rep. 4, 8) 'I hope that it may be that I have been a true augur.'

(11e)   With imperfect subjunctive referring to the present: Homo hic ebrius est, ut opinor. Utinam ita essem! (Pl. Amph. 575) 'This man is drunk, I think.' 'I wish I were!'

(11f)   With imperfect subjunctive referring to the past—rare: Utinam te di prius perderent quam periisti e patria tua. (Pl. Capt. 537) 'Would that the gods had destroyed you before you were lost from your country!'

(11g)   With pluperfect subjunctive referring to the past: Utinam me mortuum vidisses. (Cic. Q. Fr. 1, 3, 1) 'I would that you had seen me dead.'

There are two main problems connected with the tenses found in these optative subjunctives. The first problem is that, in addition to the meanings expected for each of the tenses, all but the pluperfect can have other meanings as well: the perfect subjunctive can have present (that is, future) meaning; the imperfect subjunctive can have past meaning; the present subjunctive can have present meaning. The second problem is that of the imperfect and pluperfect subjunctives. According to the sequence-of-tenses rules, they should not exist at all. We pointed out before that the abstract verb [vel] occurred only in the first person singular of the present tense. According to the sequence-of-tenses rules, only two tenses of the subjunctive can ever follow a present tense verb (excluding historical presents, which may break the rules): the present and the perfect. The imperfect and pluperfect can only follow secondary tenses: imperfect, perfect, pluperfect. The second problem has been mentioned already, and its solution is easier than that of the first.

The sentences that contain an imperfect or pluperfect subjunctive appear to be derived from a sentence containing [vel], with [vel] itself embedded in a conditional. It is thus just like *vellem*, which was mentioned at the beginning of this section. In this way, we can see how

Utinam id faceret! 'I wish he were doing that!' gets its meaning. It is derived from a set of sentences like the following, with this deep structure:

(If it were a reasonable wish), I would wish it $\quad$ S

he do it.

The sentence implies that it is not a wish that could possibly be granted, since the action cannot take place at the same time as the speaker is wishing for it. In the same way, the pluperfect depends on an equally "unreasonable" wish: the speaker is wishing something had happened, when it did not happen. Therefore, [*vel*] is itself in the subjunctive. As is normal in contrary-to-fact conditions in the present time, the verb is in the imperfect subjunctive. Hence, any verb embedded in it will go into secondary sequence. Therefore, the imperfect and pluperfect subjunctive are grammatical with [*vel*].

In the present subjunctive, however, the wish is one that may yet be realized, and therefore, the wish is a "reasonable" wish. It need not be embedded in a condition. (A future less vivid construction is possible here, however, producing *velim* of (9b) in real verbs but having no effect on the tense of embedded verbs.)

The first question remains: How can we account for the different meanings of the tenses? There is no clear answer to this question. Where the perfect subjunctive is used as a future, as in (11c), the aspect-switching rule is involved. But it is not clear why this rule works only on the special sigmatic-aorist derived subjunctive. In (11c), the verb *servassint* is a special form of the perfect, plus *i*-subjunctive endings, also found in forms like *faxim*, for *fecerim*. The normal perfect subjunctive of *servo* is *servaverint*; but this form would probably be ungrammatical in (11c). Another thing not well understood about the perfect is what it means when it does not refer to the future, as it is not purely past. The definition given with (11d) is as close as the speaker of English can get to it. But it is not clear whether there must be an additional verb in the structure of (11d) (*it will be so that*, conceivably). Likewise, it is not clear why both the present subjunctive and the imperfect subjunctive, in early Latin, can refer to either of two tenses. The whole question of sequence of tenses and the relationships among the tenses of verbs in complex sentences is one that has been studied too little and dismissed with overly simple answers too often.[10]

In this section we have presented arguments for the existence of a second abstract verb, [*vel*], which produces optative subjunctives. This verb works similarly to [*imper*] but, of course, is under different constraints and obeys different rules. The subject of [*vel*] (always first person singular) may be identical to the subject of the lower verb; hence, a sentence like (10e) or (10f) is possible. Also, [*vel*] may be embedded in a conditional sentence, and therefore more tenses may occur with [*vel*] than with [*imper*]. Besides, [*vel*] may take as a complement a verb referring to the past, as [*imper*] could not. Both this last difference and the subject-constraint difference are properties that are present for all verbs of these classes. They need not be specified for the abstract verb alone.

5.7 The Jussive Abstract Verb [*Oport*]

In the third chapter the verb *oportet*, 'it is an obligation, one ought,' was discussed at some length. It was suggested that this verb was a flip, although no unassailable evidence could be found to support this claim. The suggestion was based on the almost complete synonymy of this verb with *debeo*, 'I ought,' obviously a verb taking an object complement, and the belief (against which no exceptions are known) that if two verbs are synonymous, their complements will both be of the same class, either subject or object. It was pointed out that *debeo* always occurred with *for-to*; that *oportet*, too, most frequently took a *for-to* complementizer but was sometimes found with *ut*-subjunctive. In the latter case, until late Latin, *ut*-deletion obligatorily applied. There are no cases attested of *oportet* itself negated with *ne*; if there were, it would be extremely strong evidence, in view of what was said in the fourth chapter, that *oportet* was a flip. Instead, what seems to happen in the case of this verb (as well as *licet*, to be discussed later) is that, if it is negated, *for-to* must be the complementizer chosen. We do find *oportet* used with a positive subjunctive:

(12a)   Me ipsum ames oportet, non mea. (Cic. Fin. 2, 26)[11] 'You should love me myself, not my possessions.'

(12b)   Valeat possessor oportet. (Hor. Ep. 1, 2, 49) 'The possessor should be well.'

It should be noted that this verb *oportet* can be found in any tense. Thus we have *Me ipsum amares oportebat, non mea*, 'You should have loved me, not my possessions.' Sequence-of-tenses rules of course apply, as the example illustrates.

We find in addition to these methods of expressing obligation the use of another type of independent subjunctive with the same meaning, called the jussive subjunctive. The negative of this subjunctive is always *ne*. The supposed synonyms of this subjunctive, negated by *non*, will be discussed in Section 5.10. The jussive subjunctive is found in environments in which subjunctives dependent on [*imper*] and [*vel*] were not: all persons and all tenses except the perfect are possible. It can be embedded in questions and in expressions of thinking and of saying:

(13a)   Vilicus ne sit ambulator, sobrius sit semper. (Cato R. R. 5, 1) 'A bailiff should not be an idler, he should always be sober.'

(13b)   Sed maneam, opinor. (Ter. H. T. 273) 'But I should stay, I think.'

(13c)   At tu dictis, Albane, maneres! (Verg. Aen. 8, 643) 'But you, man of Alba, should have abided by your words.'

(13d)   Moreretur, inquies. (Cic. Rab. Post. 29) 'He should have died, you will say.'

(13e)   Tu ne faceres tale. (Pl. Ps. 437) 'You shouldn't have done such a thing.'

(13f)   Quid facere debuisti? Pecuniam rettulisses, frumentum ne emisses. (Cic. Verr. 3, 195) 'What should you have done? You should have returned the money, you should not have bought the grain.'

A performative cannot be questioned, nor is it open to opinion. Hence, (13a) could not be interpreted as an optative. If it were second person (*Maneas, opinor*), it could not be interpreted as an imperative. In this respect [*oport*] is different from the first two abstract verbs discussed.

When the subjunctive is present tense, it is easy to see that the abstract verb is in the same tense, because of the sequence-of-tenses rules as well as the meaning of the sentence. For the same reasons, when the verb is in the imperfect or pluperfect subjunctive, the abstract verb [*oport*] is in the past tense—either imperfect or perfect, depending on the nature of the obligation, whether it occurred at one discrete point in time, or whether it was continuous. In the first case, the abstract verb would be equivalent to *oportuit*, perfect tense, in the second, to *oportebat*, imperfect. Thus, the abstract verb underlying (13d) must be equivalent to *oportuit*, rather than *oportebat*—one person's death cannot be repeated, continuous, or habitual. But the abstract verb underlying (13c) is very likely equivalent to *oportebat*, representing an obligation that continued for a period of time. The difference between the imperfect and pluperfect subjunctive is not clear. There appears to the non-native speaker to be no difference in meaning between them. The situation is thus much like that we found with [*vel*], and it is equally inexplicable.

In (13f), notice the fact that the subjunctive ending of the verbs *rettulisses* and *emisses* is being used as a synonym of *debuisti*, as an echoic answer to a question. The only way to account for Cicero's use of an "independent" subjunctive in a sentence parallel to a sentence containing the real verb *debeo* is to say that there is an abstract verb underlying each of the subjunctives in the answer to the question. It is as if Cicero had used *debuisti* in the first part of the sentence and *oportuit* in the second: the constructions are grammatically parallel, the verbs synonyms. The only difference is that *debeo* is a real verb but [*oport*] is abstract, and the only trace of its underlying presence is a subjunctive in the surface structure, with the meaning of "ought" and the negation *ne*. Here, too, the abstract verb does not behave like either of the real verbs in its meaning-class. [*Oport*] can take only *ut*-subjunctive; *debeo*, only *for-to*; and *oportet*, both. This is precisely analogous to the situation we hypothesized in the last section, where a possible verb of wishing might take *for-to* alone, while [*vel*] took only *ut*-subjunctive, and the other verbs of the class could take either. The markings and redundancy rules will look the same for the verbs of obligation as they did for verbs of wishing. Thus, by postulating an abstract verb, we can account for the presence of *ne*, the fact that the subjunctive can be followed by parenthetical words of opinion, and can be questioned, and we can account for the use of this subjunctive parallel to a verb of obligation in a speech of Cicero's. None of these can be done in a non–*ad hoc* way in any other theory, and in our theory all these facts follow naturally from rules we must have independently.

5.8 The Concessive Abstract Verb [*Lic*]

In the third chapter, the verb *licet*, 'it is permitted, it is allowed,' was discussed. The suggestion was made that it was a verb that obligatorily underwent flip. The reason was in part semantic (*licet* conforms in meaning to other verbs of the flip class) and in part syntactic. *Licet Marcus eat*, 'It is permitted (allowed) that Marcus go,' was derived in the third chapter from the deep structure

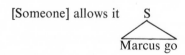

[Someone] allows it   S

Marcus go

This verb, *licet*, appears to operate under a constraint similar to the one that was noted earlier for *oportet*: if the lower sentence is negated, *for-to* must be the complementizer chosen. Hence, there are no examples of the expected *Licet ne Marcus eat*, nor, of course, of *Licet Marcus non eat*, but only of *Licet Marcum non ire*.

The verb *licet* has an additional meaning, besides the ones given: 'it is granted.' This is, of course, derived in turn from 'someone (unspecified) grants,' which undergoes flip. Sentences using *licet* in this meaning are fairly frequent. The best translation for *licet* used in this way is frequently 'though,' or 'granted that.'

(14a)   Licet omnes fremant, dicam quod sentio. (Cic. de Or. 1, 195) 'Though everyone grumbles, I shall say what I feel.'

(14b)   Sed omnia licet concurrant, Idus Martiae consolantur. (Cic. Att. 14, 4, 2) 'But though everything clashes together, the Ides of March consoles me.'

(14c)   Sim licet extremum, sicut sum, missus in orbem. (Ov. Trist. 4, 9, 9) 'Granted that I have been—as I have—sent to the ends of the earth.'

Licet in this use appears to be restricted to the present tense. Hence, the verb of the lower sentence is either present subjunctive, referring to the present, or perfect subjunctive, referring to the past.

There are also sentences found in Latin with independent subjunctives, identical in meaning to the sentences containing *licet*. These sentences are negated by *ne*, and occur with the verb in the present subjunctive referring to the present and in the perfect subjunctive referring to the past.

(15a)   Ne aequaveritis Hannibali Philippum; Pyrrho certe aequabitis. (Livy 31, 7, 8) 'Granted that you did not put Philip on a level with Hannibal; at least you will put him on a level with Pyrrhus.'

(15b)   Sit fur, sit sacrilegus, at est bonus imperator. (Cic. Verr. 5, 4) 'Though he is a thief, though he is a temple-robber, yet he is a good general.'

(15c)   Ne sit summum malum dolor, malum certe est. (Cic. Tusc. 2, 14) 'Granted that pain is not the greatest evil, yet it is an evil.'

Since this use of the independent subjunctive matches the use of *licet* with the meaning of 'granted that' so closely, both in meaning and in syntactic properties, it seems reasonable to deal with this subjunctive as the reflex of an abstract verb [*lic*], meaning 'it is granted that.' It is not clear whether this verb is to be interpreted as undergoing flip, like *licet,* and hence being negated with *ne,* or whether the abstract verb is to be considered as taking an object complement and not undergoing flip. But the fact that a verb occurs with the meaning and many of the syntactic properties of *licet* and the negation *ne* is further evidence that *licet* is itself a flip verb, according to the belief we have stated that verbs that are closely synonymous must be of the same complement type.

5.9 The Potential Abstract Verbs [*Poss*] and [*Verisimile*]

In the third chapter, we noted the distinction between subject and object complements. It is reasonable to suppose that the distribution of subject and object complements is reflected in the case of abstract verbs. There are many real verbs that take subject complements, and we may expect to find at least several abstract verbs that do the same. The subjunctive of the surface structure would, in all these cases, be negated with *non,* just as real-verb subject complements always are. It should be noted that this distinction must be syntactic, since no one has ever been successful in establishing a semantic division between *ne* and *non* independent subjunctives. In fact, the meaning of the jussive subjunctive, discussed in Section 5.4, which takes *ne* is so close to the meaning of another, which takes *non,* that most grammarians have assumed that the choice of negative is optional. We have claimed that this is never optional. Evidence will be presented later that there is another way to view these subjunctives. The choice between *non* and *ne* is determined by whether the complement is a subject or an object of the abstract verb.

One type of subject complement that has been mentioned is dependent on the phrase *Fieri potest,* or *potest* alone, 'It is possible.' This governs a subject complement, and of course the negative is *non.*

(16a)   Potest ut alii ita arbitrentur. (Pl. Ps. 2, 2, 38) 'It is possible that others think so.'

(16b)   Fieri potest ut recte quis sentiat. (Cic. Tusc. 1, 3, 6) 'It is possible that someone feels rightly.'

(16c)   Nec fieri possit, ut non statim alienatio facienda sit. (Cic. Lael. 21, 76) 'Nor would it be possible that a separation should not be made immediately.'

(16d)   Nec potest fieri homo idem duobus locis ut simul sit. (Pl. Am. 567) 'Nor is it possible for the same man to be in two places at the same time.'

Sentences like the ones just given may be paraphrased by 'Nor *could* the same man be in two places at the same time' (16d) or 'Someone *might* feel rightly' (16b). The Latin equivalent of these is the use of an independent subjunctive called the potential, as in the following sentences:

(17a)   Ego ipse cum Platone non invitus erraverim. (Cic. Tusc. 1, 40) 'I myself could err not unwillingly with Plato.'

(17b)   Nil ego contulerim iucundo sanus amico. (Hor. S. 1, 5, 44) 'In my right mind, I could prefer nothing to an agreeable friend.'

(17c)   Iam absolutos censeas, cum incedunt infectores. (Pl. Aul. 520) 'You may think they are already paid off, when in come the dyers.'

(17d)   Crederes victos. (Livy 2, 43, 9) 'You would have believed they were conquered.'

(17e)   Certum affirmare non ausim. (Livy 3, 23) 'I wouldn't dare assert for certain.'

These sentences are negated by *non*, rather than *ne*, like the abstract verbs discussed previously. The only way to account for this syntactically is to assume that the abstract verb underlying these sentences takes a subject complement. In fact, the meaning is very close to that of the sentences of (16), and *Fieri potest* takes subject complements. Thus, it seems likely that sentence (17e) has the following deep structure:

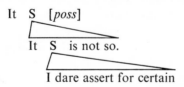

Notice that it is the lower sentence, rather than the higher sentence with [*poss*], that is being negated. The meaning of the sentence is not 'It's impossible for me to assert'; it is, instead, 'Maybe (it is possible that) I do not assert.' The effect of the potential verb is to soften the force of the assertion as a whole.

The tenses in which the potential subjunctive is found are present, perfect, and imperfect. The pluperfect is not found. When the subjunctive is present or perfect, of course, the main verb [*poss*] is also present tense: 'It is possible that.' But when the subjunctive is imperfect, then [*poss*] cannot be present. It does not seem to be embedded in a condition, or, if it is, the meaning of the conditional is not clear. What seems to be happening in sentences like (17d) is that [*poss*] is itself in the past tense, imperfect or perfect. The meaning of (17d) is then close to 'It was possible (at the time) for you to believe (at the same time) that they were conquered.' Sequence-of-tenses rules are thus perfectly regular. There is usually no distinction between the present and perfect potential subjunctive in meaning. When there is no distinction, it can be assumed that the aspect-switching rule has operated, just as it did with [*imper*] and [*vel*]. Occasionally, the perfect refers to action in the past. In this case, aspect-switch has, of course, not occurred; the verb is perfect tense in the deep structure, as in the following example:

(18)   Themistocles nihil dixerit in quo ipse Areopagum adiuverit. (Cic. Off. 1, 75) 'Themistocles couldn't have given any case in which he himself had helped the Areopagus.'

Notice that the abstract verb [*poss*] may be questioned, as it is not a performative and therefore may be embedded in a performative.

(19)   Quis umquam arbitraretur bellum ab uno confici posse? (Cic. Manil. 31) 'Who could ever have thought that the war could be settled by a single man?'

In the potential subjunctive, *ut* is always deleted.

Related in meaning to the abstract verb [*poss*] is another verb that underlies sentences which behave quite differently syntactically. These are usually rhetorical questions with the meaning 'Is it likely that . . .?' 'It is likely that' is found in Latin as *veri simile est*. This verb occurs either with accusative-infinitive (most frequently) or with *ut*-subjunctive, negated by *non*. When it is found followed by *ut*-subjunctive, *veri simile* itself is usually negated, or part of a rhetorical question, to which a negative answer is expected. But even here, *for-to* is possible. Sentences like the following are found:

(20a)   Veri simile est Marcum venisse. 'It is likely that Marcus has come.'

(20b)   Veri simile non est Marcum venisse. 'It is not likely that Marcus has come.'

(20c)   Veri simile non est ut Marcum venerit. 'It is not likely that Marcus has come.'

(20d)   Veri simile non est ut Marcus non venerit. 'It is not likely that Marcus has not come.'

(20e)   Cicerone consule, non erat veri simile ut Catilina laetus esset. 'When Cicero was consul, it wasn't likely that Catiline was happy.'

In Latin there are sentences in which there is no finite verb present in the surface structure. The main verb of such a sentence is an infinitive. In some sentences of this type the subject of this infinitive is in the nominative case. These sentences are referred to as "historical infinitives," and will be discussed in Section 5.11. In other types the subject of the infinitive is in the accusative case. We have spoken briefly of these before and have said that it is highly unlikely that case could be semantic. But this is the only interpretation of the accusative in sentences like the following if abstract verbs are not allowed in the grammar:

(21a)   Adeone hominem esse invenustum aut infelicem quemquam ut ego sum? (Ter. And. 245) 'Could there (conceivably) be any man as unhappy in love and as unfortunate as I am?'

(21b)   Te in tantas aerumnas propter me incidisse? (Cic. Fam. 14, 1) 'Is it true that you have fallen into such grief on account of me?'

In both of these sentences the question is rhetorical, and the speaker means something like 'I can't believe that . . .' or 'It's unlikely that . . . , isn't it?' Identical in meaning to these accusative constructions are sentences containing *ut*-subjunctive, usually questions. In these, *ut* is often retained, though sometimes it is not.

(22a)   Egone ut te interpellem? (Cic. Tusc. 2, 42) 'Is it likely that I would interrupt you?'

(22b)   Ego tibi irascerer? (Cic. Q. Fr. 1, 3) 'Could I have been angry with you?'

This abstract verb, [veri simile], behaves very like its real equivalent. It can take either of two complementizers. It is apparently restricted in occurrence: it occurs only in rhetorical questions. [Veri simile] may be either present tense, as in both of the sentences of (21) and in (22a), or past, as in (22b): 'Was it likely (at the time) that I was angry with you?' Notice that the enclitic -ne, the question marker, usually found attached to the first word of a yes-no question, is present in some of these sentences, though not all. (The enclitic is optional in Latin generally, though usually present in classical prose.) In the deep structure, the question performative abstract verb is in a sentence dominating the main verb; ordinarily the specifically questioned word in the sentence with the main verb receives the enclitic, raher than a word in a lower sentence. But since the main sentence here contains an abstract verb and this, along with everything else in its sentence, has been deleted before the late enclitic-attaching rule operates, the enclitic must be attached to some word in the lower sentence. The enclitic is usually attached to the word specifically being questioned. In most cases this is the main verb, and therefore *-ne* is usually attached at the right of the verb of the main sentence. Otherwise, *-ne* is attached at the right of whichever word is being questioned. But since the word specifically being questioned here has been deleted, there is no longer any word marked as undergoing *-ne* attachment. In this case, *-ne* will be attached to the first word in the lower sentence, if this word is suitable. A "suitable" word is, it appears, one that is present in the deep structure and has meaning of its own; this classification excludes, for example, prepositions and complementizers, both of which are transformationally introduced. But before this rule attaching *-ne* can operate, other rules must first apply. There is a rule that can interchange *ut* and either a subject or an object noun phrase, if *ut* is at this point in sentence-initial position. (That is, the main verb must be an abstract verb, which has been deleted earlier.) This rule is to be distinguished from ordinary scrambling; among the cases in which *ut* is not in initial position, either the subject noun is in front of it (*Egone ut te interpellem?*) or the object noun is: *Quamquam quid loquor? Te ut ulla res frangat?* (Cic. Cat. 1, 1). 'And yet, why do I speak? So that anything might sway you?' There appear to be no cases like **Interpellemne ut ego te?* or **Ego te ut inter-pellem?* If this rule does not operate and the sentence is questioned, *ut* must be dropped. This is what has happened in (22b). But *-ne* cannot be attached to *ut*, and therefore, at the point at which *-ne* attachment applies, *ut* cannot be in sentence-initial position. If it is, the ungrammatical sentence **Utne ego te interpellem?* will result. Therefore, abstract-verb deletion applies first. If the verb has been questioned, then either of two rules must apply next: either the interchanging rule applies, moving either subject or object NP in front of *ut*, or *ut* is deleted. After one of these has taken place, *-ne* is attached to the word that is now in sentence-initial position.

In this section we have given examples of two abstract verbs taking subject complements: [*poss*] and [*veri simile*]. For [*poss*], we have examples where the negation of the lower sentence is *non*. No examples of negated sentences exist for [*veri simile*]. The abstract verb [*poss*] takes *ut*-subjunctive invariably, while [*veri simile*], like the real verbs of its meaning-class, occurs with either *for-to* or *ut*-subjunctive. By postulating an abstract verb, we can account for the accusative marker on the noun, where it is found, syntactically, without resorting to obviously *ad hoc* solutions like setting up an " accusative of exclamation," as many Latinists have been forced to do.

5.10 The Deliberative Abstract Verb [*Aequum*]

In Section 5.4 the jussive abstract verb [*oport*] was discussed, and it was pointed out that this verb took an object complement, and hence was negated by *ne*. It was also mentioned that another construction was often confused with the jussive, the negative of which was *non*. This is the deliberative subjunctive.

We find sentences in Latin with the meaning *It is right that, it is right for . . . to*. These are introduced by verbs such as *aequum est, verum est, iustum est, rectum est*, all with approximately these meanings. These verbs most frequently take *for-to* complementizers, but sometimes are found with *ut*-subjunctive. The negative, in such cases, is *non*, as expected.

(23a)   Aequum est Marcum abire. 'It's right for Marcus to go away.'

(23b)   Aequum est ut Marcus abeat. 'It's right that Marcus go away.'

(23c)   Aequum est ut Marcus non abeat. 'It's right that Marcus not go away.'

Sentences like these are quite close in meaning to sentences with *oportet* or *debeo*. They both convey the idea of moral obligation. However, their meanings do differ sufficiently that one is a verb taking object complements (and a verb that requires human subjects) and the other is a verb taking subject complements (and hence a verb requiring an abstract noun subject). *It S is right* means ' It is universally right, right in general,' while *John ought to it S* or *John is obliged to it S* is used with reference to an obligation that is specifically John's. But in use, often these two meanings are indistinguishable.

The deliberative subjunctive has the meaning, "It is right that . . ." Its use is confined almost exclusively to questioned sentences in the first person and to their answers in the second. The jussive subjunctive [*oport*] is under no such constraint. The use of the deliberative subjunctive is illustrated in the following examples:

(24a)   Quid agam, iudices? (Cic. Verr. 5, 2) 'What am I to do, gentlemen of the jury?'

(24b)   Non visam uxorem Pamphili? Non visas; ne mittas quidem videndi causa quemquam. (Ter. Hec. 342) 'Shouldn't I go see Pamphilus' wife?' 'You shouldn't; you shouldn't even send anyone to see her.'

(24c)   Non illi argentum redderem? Non redderes. (Pl. Trin. 133) 'Shouldn't I have given back the money to him?' 'You shouldn't have.'

Of course, [*oport*] can be used in this environment as well as any other; hence, a positive sentence of this form is ambiguous, but a negative is disambiguated by the presence of *non* or *ne* in it. In sentence (24b), for example, the deep structure can be represented as

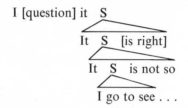

(The abstract verb here may be questioned because it is not a performative.) The literal meaning of (24b) is, then, 'Is it right for me not to visit Pamphilus' wife?' and the reply is 'It is right for you not to visit her; it is right for you not even to send someone to see her.' The effect of this sentence is that the speaker of the first part of the sentence is forbidden to see Pamphilus' wife. If the negative were *ne* instead of *non*, the effect would be the same, but the implication would be that the speaker was advised not to see Pamphilus' wife, rather than that, as here, he could rightfully refrain from seeing her (not that he ought to refrain). The difference is admittedly very subtle, and therefore *Non visam uxorem Pamphili?* is usually treated as if synonymous with *Ne visam uxorem Pamphili?* and the presence of *non* instead of *ne* treated as a random choice. But in no other abstract verb has this fluctuation been observed; the interpretation given here accounts both for the meaning and for the syntax.

A construction with accusative-infinitive also occurs with this meaning. This is indistinguishable in form from the [*veri simile*] cases, but there clearly are two possible meanings for such a sentence, and in general the context will disambiguate the sentence.

(25a)   Mene Iliacis occumbere campis non potuisse? (Verg. Aen. 1, 97–98) 'Is it right that I was unable to fall on the fields of Troy?'

(25b)   Mene incepto desistere victam? (Verg. Aen. 1, 37) 'Is it right
         for me to desist from my purpose, conquered?'

In (25a), it is evident that the speaker did *not* fall on the plains of Troy,
or he would not be speaking. Hence, [*veri simile*] could not be the
abstract verb.

The existence of sentences like (24) and (25) makes it necessary to
postulate the existence of an abstract verb, [*aequum*], with the meaning
'It is right.' When [*aequum*] takes *ut*-subjunctive, it may be either present
or past tense. The lower verb seems always to be present tense. When it
takes *for-to*, it is not clear what the tense of [*aequum*] must be. In the
previous examples [*aequum*] is certainly present tense in the second
case and probably present in the first as well. It states a general truth
about the rightness of the fact that the speaker could not fall, rather
than saying it was not right at the time when he could have fallen that
he did not. The lower verb may be past or present with *for-to*. As with
[*veri simile*], the infinitive here seems to be used with rhetorical questions
with a negative answer expected. The subjunctive is found when the
question is not rhetorical. This is probably a fact about style, rather
than a constraint on the choice of complementizers (an impossible
constraint to state).

5.11 The Historical Infinitive

In Section 2.17 we noted very briefly that certain verbs, which appear
superficially to take object complements, were in fact intransitive verbs
taking subject complements. This was true for verbs like *begin, tend,
continue, stop*. That is, in the sentence *The cat began to chase her tail*,
the deep structure is actually

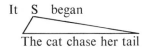

In English, *for-to* or poss.-*ing* (*The cat began chasing her tail*) complementizer-change takes place; in Latin, only *for-to* is possible for these
verbs. *It*-substitution obligatorily takes place in both languages, so that,
in the previous sentence, *The cat*, the subject of the lower sentence, is
moved into subject position of the higher sentence. To a deep structure
such as

for-to placement applies, yielding

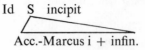

Id   S   incipit

Acc.-Marcus i + infin.

It-substitution applies. The structure now is in its superficial form:

Marcus incipit ire.

The subject of the lower verb is nominative, and the lower verb is infinitive. This is the derivation underlying all Latin sentences containing these verbs.

(26a)   Marcus currere incepit. 'Marcus began to run.'

(26b)   Marcus carmina mala recitare solet. 'Marcus tends to recite bad poems.'

(26c)   Marcus pergit negare se Caesarem interfecisse. 'Marcus continues to deny he killed Caesar.'

We find in Latin sentences with the same meaning as these sentences, but without an overt verb meaning "begin, continue, tend." The sentence has a subject in the nominative case, and the verb describing the action being begun or continued is an infinitive. This construction is called by grammarians the "historical infinitive" because of its relative frequency in the historical writers. But it is found in virtually all types of literature, as the folloing examples attest.

(27a)   Clamorem utrimque ecferunt. Imperator utrimque Iovi vota suscipere, utrimque hortari exercitum. (Pl. Am. 229) 'On either side they raise a shout. On either side the general begins to offer prayers to Jupiter, on either side he begins to encourage the army.'

(27b)   Si quando ad eam accesserat confabulatum, fugere e conspectu ilico, videre nolle. (Ter. Hec. 181) 'If she ever came to talk to her, she would immediately run away from sight, she wouldn't want to see her.'

(27c)   Postulo ut mihi respondeat qui sit is Verrucius. Clamare omnes neminem umquam in Sicilia fuisse Verrucium. Ego instare ut mihi respondeat. (Cic. Verr. 2, 2, 188) 'I demand that he answer my question, who is this Verrucius. Everyone begins to shout that there never was any Verrucius in Sicily. I keep insisting that he answer me.'

(27d)   Ego illud sedulo negare factum. Ille instat factum. (Ter.
          And. 146–147) 'I unceasingly keep on denying that I did it.
          He insists I did do it.'

(27e)   Repente omnes tristitia invasit: festinare, trepidare, neque
          loco neque homini cuiquam satis credere. (Sal. Cat. 31, 1)
          'Suddenly uneasiness comes over everyone. They begin to
          rush around, to tremble, and to have confidence neither in
          the situation nor in any man.'

These sentences have meanings as though there were a verb such as
incipio, 'begin,' *soleo*, 'tend,' or *pergo*, 'continue,' in their deep structures. They also look exactly like sentences actually containing these
verbs, except that the verbs themselves do not appear. The subject noun
has undergone *it*-substitution, and the verb has undergone *for-to* complementizer-change. These two rules are both obligatory for verbs of
beginning, tending, and continuing in Latin. These sentences cannot be
explained at all unless one assumes that there is a verb with one of
these meanings present at some point in the derivation of these sentences,
both giving the infinitives the correct meaning and accounting for the
nominative case in the noun and the infinitive ending on the verb.

Interestingly, these abstract verbs, along with the real verbs of the
same class, are the only underlying subject-complement-taking verbs in
Latin which undergo *it*-substitution at all. In the third chapter it was
noted that, while *John is right to go* is grammatical in English (and
its counterpart, incidentally, is grammatical in Greek), **Marcus aequus
est ire* is not found in Latin. *It*-substitution applies in *derived* subject
complements, with flip verbs like *videor* and with passives, to produce
the personal passive. But verbs like *begin, tend,* and *continue* are the
only verbs in Latin which take deep-structure subject complements and
undergo *it*-substitution, and these obligatorily undergo this rule. The
abstract verbs of this class also obligatorily undergo *it*-substitution.

5.12 The Abstract Verb Underlying Expressions of Purpose

In Latin, as in English, there are a number of alternative ways to
express purpose on the part of the subject of a sentence. Several of
these—the use of the gerund with *causa*, the gerundive, the infinitive,
and the supine—occur under very restricted circumstances and are,
therefore, probably not to be considered basic. The relative clause of
purpose is likewise severely constrained in its occurrence. There is
only one means of expressing purpose such that it can be used under

any circumstances. This is the use of *ut*-subjunctive, negated by *ne*, as in these examples:

(28a)   Revorti uti (= ut) me purgarem. (Pl. Am. 909) 'I returned to clear myself.'

(28b)   Ab aratro abduxerunt Cincinnatum, ut dictator esset. (Cic. Fin. 2, 12) 'They took Cincinnatus from the plow, so that he might be dictator.'

(28c)   Dionysius, ne collum tonsori committeret, tondere filias suas docuit. (Cic. Tusc. 5, 58) 'Dionysius, in order not to entrust his neck to a barber, taught his daughters how to shave.'

(28d)   Gallinae pullos pennis fovent, ne frigore laedantur. (Cic. N. D. 2, 129) 'Hens keep their chicks warm with their wings, so they may not be harmed by the cold.'

(28e)   Scalas parari iubet, ne quam facultatem dimittat. (Caes. B. G .1, 28) 'He orders ladders to be gotten ready, so as not to let any opportunity go by.'

The embedded sentences in these examples appear at first sight, perhaps, to be ordinary instances of object complements dependent on the main verb of the sentence; thus, *uti . . . purgarem* in (28a) would be the direct object of *revorti* in the deep structure. They have undergone complementizer-placement and *ut*-subjunctive complementizer-change, and in addition they are negated by *ne*. But a deeper inspection quickly shows that these cannot be considered simple complements depending on the main verbs of these sentences. In the second chapter the nature of the complement was discussed at length; the point was made there that only certain classes of verbs could receive object complements. The verb had to be transitive, of course. It had to be able to take as a direct object only an abstract noun phrase, never a concrete noun phrase. And, of course, only one direct object abstract noun phrase is possible for a single verb. If we interpret the sentences of (28) as containing object complements that are dependent on the main verbs, we shall find that in each sentence one or more of the principles we have just listed has been violated.

In (28a), *reverto* is not a transitive verb. It cannot take direct objects, either concrete or abstract. In (28b), *abduco* is transitive, but it can take concrete nouns only following it: *Abduco Marcum ab aratro*, 'I took Marcus away from the plow'; but **Abduco veritatem a Marco*, '*I removed truth from Marcus.' In (28c), *doceo* can take an abstract noun phrase object, and it therefore can take complements, but in this sentence *docuit* already has a sentence embedded in it, *Filias suas tondere.* Therefore, it cannot have another. In (28d), *foveo* in the sense of 'keep warm' requires concrete objects. In (28e), *iubet* already contains an embedded sentence, *Scalas parari;* and, besides, *iubeo* seldom takes a subjunctive complementizer. Therefore, all of these perfectly typical purpose clauses cannot be simple object complements of the main verbs of their sentence. But they must be embedded in some sentence, if our proposal is true that there are no independent subjunctives. If we investigate the behavior of subjunctives in purpose clauses and ask what their properties are and what constraints there are on expressions of purpose, perhaps we shall be able to account for these sentences, which have been discussed at great length in the literature without any substantive conclusions having been drawn.

There is some relationship, certainly, between the main verb and the subjunctive: sequence-of-tenses rules apply, with the tense of the latter dependent, apparently, on the tense of the former, just as if the subjunctive were dependent on the main verb. For example, the verb in (28a) is perfect, and secondary sequence is observed: the subjunctive is imperfect. In (28d), the main verb is also present. It should be noted, too, that in purpose clauses, the subjunctive refers to a time that is future with respect to the time of the main verb. In a very few instances this is not true.

(29a) Illud affirmare pro certo audeo, me omni vi adnisurum esse ne frustra vos hanc spem de me conceperitis. (Livy, 44, 22, 2) 'I dare to assert that as a certainty—that I will strive with all my strength so that you may not have conceived this hope in vain.'

(29b) Neve hoc impune fuisset, gorgoneum crinem turpes mutavit in hydros. (Ov. Met. 4, 800) ' So that this should not have gone unpunished, she changed the gorgon's locks to loathsome snakes.'

In these cases, the result is still to take place in the future, but the relationship among the tenses is unclear. The facts presented here may be analogous to those presented in Section 5.4, in the discussion of [*vel*], where we found examples of the perfect subjunctive referring to an act seen as accomplished at some time in the future relative to the main verb [*vel*]. Here, the act is also seen as accomplished at some time in the future: if the main verb is present, the action is described in the perfect subjunctive; if the main verb is past, the subjunctive is pluperfect, as sequence-of-tenses rules require. But it is not evident how these tense relationships can be expressed by the use of a perfect subjunctive or a pluperfect subjunctive, since future reference is clearly involved.

Let us turn to a close examination of the syntactic properties of these purpose clauses. It will be noted that they always answer the question "Why?" Of all adverbial clauses, only purpose and causal sentences (those containing *because*, not *since*) answer "why?" Sentence (30a) may be answered by (30b) or (30c), but by none of the other possibilities.

(30a)   Why did you rob the bank?

(30b)   In order to make money.

(30c)   Because the Mafia leader told me to.

(30d)   *When I saw that I could not pay tuition this semester.

(30e)   *Since all my friends are juvenile delinquents.

(30f)   *Although my mother brought me up to be poor but honest.

This fact suggests that the purpose clause *in order to*, or *ut*, contains *because*. Another reason why this may be true is that *in order to* may be used in sentences parallel to *because*. This is closely related to the fact that both answer "why": the parallel structure test (developed by Lakoff and Ross) is a means of showing deep-structure parallelism between sentence types. Sentences that are parallel in this sense can be conjoined and the verb phrase of the second reduced to *do so*. Sentences that are not parallel cannot undergo this reduction:

(31a)   John slices salami with an ax, but I do so with my trusty bowie knife.

(31b)   *John slices salami with an ax, but I do so in the yard.

(31c)   *John slices salami with an ax, but I do so with enthusiasm.

(31d)   *John slices salami with an ax, but I do so with Sally.

(31e)   John slices salami with an ax, but I use a bowie knife to do so.

Sentence (31a) is grammatical because the right-hand side of the sentence contains an instrumental adverbial, the same type of adverbial that the left-hand side of the sentence contains. The two halves of this sentence are thus parallel to each other. But in (31b) the adverbs are clearly different: *with* is an instrumental adverbial, but *in* is locational. Hence, example (31b) is ungrammatical. In (31c), although the *with* on the right appears superficially to be just like the *with* on the left, it is not: one expresses instrument, the other circumstance. Hence, they are derived from different deep structures, and (31c) is ungrammatical.

For the same reason, (31d) is ungrammatical: *with* on the right is an adverbial of accompaniment. But most interestingly, in (31e), where the surface structures of the two sides of the sentence are the most disparate of all the examples given, the sentences may be conjoined, and therefore (31a) is grammatical. This is an indication (and there are numerous other reasons for believing this is true) that sentences containing the instrumental *with* and sentences containing *use* are derived from the same deep structures. This is an indication of how parallel structure can signal relatedness between deep structures. Parallelism cannot take place unless the elements conjoined share some structure. If we attempt to apply the parallel structure test to *because* and *in order to*, we shall find results that support our claim that *in order to* contains *because*, as part of its meaning.

(32a)   I rob banks because I need money, but Igor does so in order to annoy the police.

(32b)   *I rob banks because I need money, but Igor does so when the moon is full on Fridays.

(32c)   *I rob banks because I need money, but Igor does so after he spends his allowance on Superman comics.

It should be pointed out that this parallelism is not a fact about *because* and *in order to* in English alone. It is a fact about the meaning of these words and will necessarily be true about the translations of *because* and *in order to* in every language. Hence, we can use the results of the parallel structure test for Latin and draw the same conclusions about the relationship between the *ut* of purpose and *quod*, 'because,' in Latin as we drew about their translations in English, and we are not handicapped in this case by the lack of native speakers on whom to test these sentences.

Because is not, of course, the only nonovert element in the purpose clause and by itself does not express the idea of purpose or intent. We must examine these sentences further to see if their superficial forms can be used to shed light on their deep structures.

One important fact about purpose clauses in any language is that the subject of the main verb must be animate. Thus, sentence (33a) is grammatical, and (33b) is not, in English; similar sentences and non-sentences could easily be constructed for Latin.

(33a)   The hunter shot the deer in order to kill it.

(33b)   *The gun shot the deer in order to kill it.

Notice that, in (33b), the ungrammaticality of the whole sentence does not result from an ungrammaticality of either of its surface-structure parts. Both *the gun shot the deer* and *the gun killed the deer* are grammatical. There must be some element present in the underlying structure of these sentences which renders purpose clauses ungrammatical if the subject of the main verb is inanimate. The subject of the lower verb may be different from that of the main verb and may be inanimate: *John caught the stone so that it would not hit Bill on the head.* But the fact that *the gun shot the deer* is grammatical indicates that the constraint on animacy is not to be stated as a constraint on the main verb (here, *shot*) but rather as a constraint on some verb present in the deep structure but absent in the surface structure, and that this verb is one that cannot take inanimate subjects.

Consider the following sentence:

(34)   John is leaving New York today in order to be in Chicago tomorrow.

We do not find the sentence **John is in Chicago tomorrow.* That is, future-deletion must have applied here. In earlier chapters, we noted that future-deletion was normal in a number of verb classes, among them verbs of wanting and wishing, verbs of requesting, and verbs of ordering. We are assuming that the element present in the deep structure of purpose clauses is a verb because, insofar as we know anything at all about it, it behaves like a verb. The necessity for an animate noun to be the subject of the main verb can be traced to a subject-verb constraint between the deep-structure verb not present in the surface structure and its subject, and a restriction on the subject of the main verb that it must be identical to the subject of this other verb. The fact that future-deletion occurs is likewise a verbal property. Therefore we are justified in thinking of this element as an abstract verb.

Which verb it is becomes very easy to see if one simply asks what the meaning of purpose clauses is. The *in order to*, or *ut*, part of the purpose clause expresses the intent of the subject of the main sentence that the action expressed in the remainder of the sentence take place. That is, in *I robbed the bank in order to get money*, *in order to* expresses the idea that I intended—or wanted, or meant—to get money by robbing the bank. In fact, *I robbed the bank in order to get money* is semantically equivalent to the sentence *I robbed the bank because I wanted to get money*, or *because I intended (meant) to get money*. In this way the *because* that the parallel structure test showed was necessary in the deep structure of purpose clauses is fitted into the general meaning of these sentences. But this is only semantic justification for the postulation of *want* in the deep structure of the purpose clause. If we are to make this claim seriously, we must present syntactic justification.

There is some justification within English, but the most convincing evidence lies in the behavior of purpose clauses in Latin and their development in Spanish. We shall discuss the Latin evidence in this chapter and the Spanish evidence in the next chapter.

Within English itself it is clear that some of the properties we had to assign to the abstract verb of purpose are properties of all verbs of the class of wanting. They all must refer to the future necessarily (as verbs of wishing, for example, need not), and they must all have animate subjects.

(35a)   The boy wants to shoot the deer.

(35b)   *The gun wants to shoot the deer.

In Latin the evidence is much clearer. We know that *volo* and verbs of its class may take *ut*-subjunctive. (They may also take *for-to*, but it is not necessary that the abstract verb should share all the transformational properties of the real verbs.) *Volo* takes an object complement, and its negative therefore is *ne*. The negative in purpose clauses is always *ne*. Facts like these, added to the facts that are universal about future-deletion and animateness of subject, and added to the similarity in meaning between the abstract verb of the purpose clause and verbs of wanting, lead us to believe that a verb with the general meaning of "want, mean, intend" underlies the purpose clause in every language. We can give this verb the representation [*vol*].

This verb [*vol*] is not a performative, as was the abstract verb nearest it in meaning, [*vel*]. [*Vol*] may occur in any person and any tense. If this fact were true in isolation, it would pose a serious theoretical problem: all traces of the verb itself, its subject, and its tense are of course deleted. But the deletion must be recoverable, and, in fact, it is. In any purpose clause we can easily tell what the subject and the tense of [*vol*] must be.

This is because of the constraints we mentioned before. The subject of [*vol*] that is generated in the deep structure must be identical to the subject of the main verb, and the tense of [*vol*] must be identical to the tense of the main verb. Otherwise, the rule that will ultimately delete the abstract verb [*vol*] is not able to apply and the abstract verb will appear in the surface structure, and therefore the sentence will be ungrammatical. But the subject of the verb embedded in the object of [*vol*] may be identical to that of [*vol*] or may not, and the tense may be any tense provided it refers to the future with respect to the tense of [*vol*].

In this way, we can account for the meaning and the structure of the

Latin purpose clause. The meaning is given by a combination of *because* and *want*. Syntactically, the application of future-deletion, the presence of *ut*-subjunctive as a complementizer, the fact that the negative is *ne*, the fact that the lower verb refers to the future with respect to the higher verb, and the fact that the higher verb must have an animate subject can all be accounted for using the same rules we need for the real verbs of wanting. Nothing new must be added to the grammar except an additional abstract-verb deletion rule. All these facts had to be accounted for separately in other theories of grammar—when they were accounted for at all. The generalization that all these facts were related was always missed. This treatment captures the generalization and is therefore to be preferred to other treatments.

We can illustrate by going through the derivation of a Latin sentence such as this one: *Marcus abiit Roma ne Clodium videret*, 'Marcus left Rome so as not to see Clodius.' The deep structure of this sentence is not given; its form depends on the deep structure of *because*, which is at present unknown. We shall assume that rules have already applied, producing an intermediate stage in which *because* is already in its derived form [*because*], with both a subject and an object complement. Our assumptions here are the following: The verb underlying sentences containing *because* in English and *quod* in Latin is a verb meaning "cause," but not the [*cause*] that underlies verbs like *persuade* and *prevent*. The [*cause*] in these latter verbs requires an animate noun subject and an abstract noun object, and therefore the complement is the object of this [*cause*]. The [*cause*] underlying *because* acts differently.

Unfortunately, it is not at all clear precisely how it does work, but the following is suggested purely as a speculation and as an attempt to begin the analysis of these structures. This verb takes two complements, a subject and an object, like *entail*. The subject of [*cause*] is the sentence that follows *because* in the surface structure, and the object is the sentence superficially preceding *because*. Complementizer-placement applies to this verb: the underlying subject complement sentence undergoes *quod*-finite complementizer-placement in Latin.[12] This abstract verb [*cause*] behaves very much like the other verbs already discussed in this chapter. The object complement of [*cause*] does not appear in the surface structure with any complementizer: an abstract complementizer which is later deleted must be attached. [*Cause*] cannot, in Latin, undergo any of the complementizer-changing rules, and thus *quod*-finite is the final form of *because* in Latin. Flip applies and inverts the subject and object sentences. Now the sentence containing *quod* is in object position, and we have approximately the derived form of sentences containing *because*.

In our analysis of the purpose clause, we shall assume that complementizer-placement and flip have applied already to [*cause*] for the sake of simplicity, although in reality complementizer-placement applies to the sentence dependent on [*cause*] at the same point in the derivation at which it applies to the sentence dependent on [*vol*], and flip applies after this, as in diagram (36). Negative-lowering applies in the lower

(36)   Marcus abiit Roma ne Clodium videret.

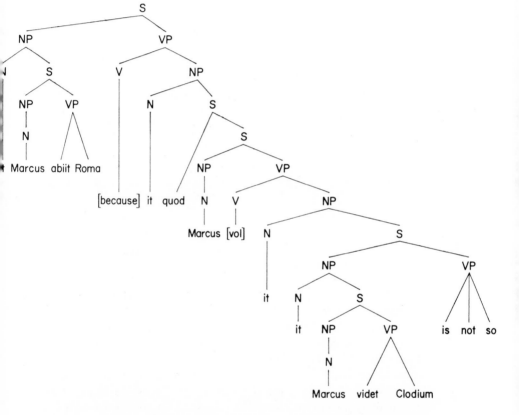

sentence, as does complementizer-placement and *ut*-subjunctive complementizer-change. On the left, *it* is deleted, as is the abstract complementizer. *Ut* plus the lowered negative dependent on [*vol*] form *ut ne*, then *ne*. The derived structure at this point is shown in (37). Pronominalization applies between the subject of [*vol*], *Marcus*, and the subject of the sentence dependent on [*vol*], if they are identical. The pronoun *is* is later deleted by the rule that deletes unemphatic subject pronouns.

(37)

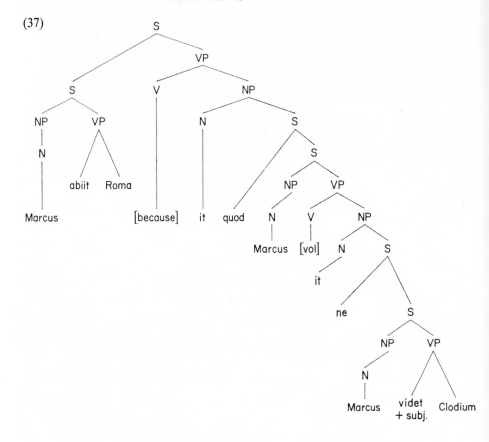

Now the subject of [*vol*] is deleted under identity with the subject of the main verb *abiit*.

It should be noted that this sort of deletion under identity is unlike other rules that delete words under identity. For one thing, the subject of [*vol*] must be identical to the subject of the main verb in order for the whole structure ultimately to emerge as a grammatical sentence of Latin. For another thing, the two subjects that must be identical are separated by an intermediate sentence. It is impossible to state the rule that deletes *Marcus*, the subject of [*vol*]; and for similar reasons it will be impossible to state the rule that is to delete the marker of tense on [*vol*], which also must be identical to that of the main verb. Sequence-of-tenses rules apply between [*vol*] and *videt*, and *videt* is thus given both a subjunctive marker by complementizer-placement and complementizer-change and an imperfect-tense marker by the sequence-of-tenses rules. Now the tense of [*vol*] is deleted. The *it* object of [*vol*] is deleted, as is usual. The abstract verbs [*vol*] and [*because*] are now deleted, and at this point the derived structure is as in diagram (38). There are now two complementizers side by side: *quod ne*. The same rule that deleted superfluous complementizers in verbs like *prevent* will delete *quod* here, and we shall be left with the correct superficial form of the sentence.

(38)

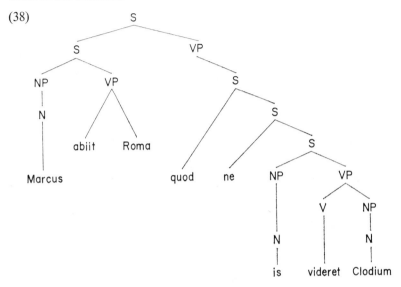

In this way, purpose clauses can be handled in Latin as well as in English. We have spoken here only about the *ut-ne* type of purpose clause, but it is well known that this is only one of many ways of expressing purpose in Latin. It is, however, the only means of expressing purpose that can always be used; the others are found only in special circumstances. One form, the relative purpose clause, is usually considered an alternative to the *ut*-purpose clause. But, as will be seen in the next section, this type is not really equivalent in meaning to the *ut*-purpose clause, and therefore it should not be assumed to have the same deep structure. There are five alternative ways of expressing purpose, all of which appear to be identical in meaning to the *ut*-subjunctive type.

The first of these is the gerundive with *ad*. This is common in classical Latin and may be used if the lower sentence contains no negative, the verb of the lower sentence is transitive, and the subject of the lowest sentence (dependent on [*vol*]) is identical to the subject of the main sentence. In form the gerundive is an adjective, and it agrees with the noun that is the direct object of the lower verb in the deep structure.

(39)   Vivis non ad deponendam sed ad confirmandam audaciam. (Cic. Cat. 1, 4) 'You live not to put off but to confirm your daring.'

Notice that the negative here is negating not the gerundive but rather the higher sentence: 'It is not so that you live to put off your boldness' rather than 'You live in order to not put off your boldness.' This sentence is a grammatical answer to the question "Cur vivis?" and behaves in other ways like a purpose clause with *ut*. Its deep structure is presumed to be the same as that of the *ut*-purpose clause, and this is assumed as well for all the other expressions of purpose to be discussed in this section.

Another means of expressing purpose is through the use of the gerund in the genitive case, followed by *causa* (sometimes *gratia*), 'for the sake of.' This is used instead of the gerundive when the lower verb is intransitive and there is therefore no direct object with which the gerundive could agree, but when the other conditions required for the gerundive are met. Occasionally the gerund may take a direct object; but when there is a noun phrase that is a direct object, the gerundive is usually found.

(40)   Pabulandi aut frumentandi causa progressi. (Caes. B. C. 1, 48) 'having gone out for the purpose of collecting fodder or supplies.'

The gerundive may also be used, modifying a noun that is a deep-structure direct object, followed by *causa*, in the genitive, with the same meaning:

(41)   Vitandae suspicionis causa. (Cic. Cat. 1, 19) 'For the purpose of avoiding suspicion.'

Another way to express purpose is with the supine. This form is the accusative of a nominal form of the verb and thus functions as a sort of accusative of limit of motion, like the accusative *Romam* in *Romam veni*. (This prepositionless accusative has, in most uses, been replaced in classical Latin by a preposition such as *ad* with the accusative, but it survives in these expressions of purpose with the supine.) These can be used only if the main verb is a verb of motion, if the lower sentence is not negated, and if the subject of the lower sentence is identical to that of the higher sentence.

(42)   Venerunt questum iniurias. (Livy 3, 25) 'They came to complain about wrongs.'

There is another expression of purpose that is found under the same conditions as the supine. This is the use of the infinitive, rare in classical

Latin but found in poetry and in older Latin. This, too, cannot be negated.

(43)   Filius intro iit videre quid agat. (Ter. Hec. 345) 'Your son has gone inside to see what's going on.'

Finally, in later writers the future active participle is sometimes found to express purpose, probably under the influence of the Greek construction.

(44)   Egreditur castris Romanus vallum invasurus. (Livy 3, 60, 8) 'The Roman leaves the camp to attack the rampart.'

All of these alternative expressions of purpose are derived from the same deep structure that underlies the *ut*-subjunctive purpose clause. If the derived structure of the sentence is one that may undergo any of the further rules, it optionally undergoes any of them that it is able to. What these rules are and how they operate are not known.

5.13 The Relative Purpose Clause

In English we find sentences like "John is the one to see about that," "Caesar sent soldiers who were to seize the town." These sentences express purpose, but they are not equivalent to purpose clauses: they are not answers to the question, "Why?" The second example given is not an answer to "Why did Caesar send soldiers?" whereas the sentence "Caesar sent soldiers to seize the town" is an answer to that question. Since these sentences are not answers to "why?" there is no reason to claim that they contain *because* in their structures. This is undoubtedly true for Latin sentences of this type as well: *Caesar praemisit equites qui cuniculum Paschalem interficerent* does not answer the question *Cur Caesar praemisit equites?* which is answered by *Caesar praemisit equites ut cuniculum Paschalem interficerent.*

Sentences of this type are very frequent in Latin. The relative may be a pronoun, the subject or object of the lower sentence, or an adverbial phrase. The relativized word must always have an antecedent in the higher sentence, while in an ordinary purpose clause neither the subject nor the object of the lower sentence needs to be identical to anything in the main sentence. The same facts are true for this type of sentence in English.

It is also significant that both in English and in Latin the lower sentence of a relative purpose clause may not contain a negative: for example, *John is the man not to see about that*; *Caesar praemisit equites qui oppidum non caperent*. But [vol], the abstract verb of the ordinary purpose clause, can dominate negatives. This fact suggests that [*vol*] is not the verb we are looking for here. Besides this, *want, intend* does not really express the meaning of the subjunctive in these sentences. If we try to arrive at a suitable meaning, with a verb that cannot take a negated inner sentence but which takes a subjunctive complementizer, the verb will have to be of the class of *appoint, select, designate*: for example, **They appointed Arthur not to shoot the Easter bunny; *Penelope was chosen not to run the errand.* Then it seems likely that such a verb is the abstract verb underlying sentences containing relative purpose clauses in Latin, like the ones following:

(45a)   Mittitur L. Decidius Saxa qui loci naturam perspiciat. (Caes. B. C. 1, 66) 'L. Decidius Saxa is sent to inspect the ground.'

(45b)   Faenum condito quod edint boves. (Cato. R. R. 53) 'Store up hay for the oxen to eat.'

(45c)   Scribebat Aelius orationes quas alii dicerent. (Cic. Brut. 56) 'Aelius would write speeches for other men to deliver.'

(45d)   Locum petit unde hostem invadat. (Livy 4, 2, 7) 'He looks for a place from which to attack the enemy.'

(45e)   Huic ne ubi consisteret quidem contra te locum reliquisti. (Cic. Quinct. 73) 'You have left him not even a place to stand against you.'

(45f)   Habebam quo confugerem. (Cic. Fam. 4, 6, 2) 'I had somewhere to escape to.'

The sentences containing adverbials (*unde, qua, quo, ubi*) are beyond the grasp of this analysis: the nature of even simple adverbials is not completely understood at present, and these are comparatively complex. But insights are possible into sentences in which the relative word is a subject or direct object noun phrase, as in (45a), (45b), and (45c). In all of these, the person who is doing the designating in the lower sentence is the subject of the main sentence. Since [*designate*] requires a human subject, the subject of the main verb must always be human. In (45a) the subject of both the main sentence and of [*designate*] is the unspecified "someone" since there is no agentive specified. In (45b), the subject of [*designate*] is *tu*, the subject of *condito*. In (45c), the subject of [*designate*] is *Aelius*, the subject of *scribebat*. As an example of how this construction is derived, we can illustrate (45c), which is probably the least complicated case, by diagram (46). If the subject of the lowest verb, rather than its direct object (here, *orationes*), were the relativized word, the structure would be very similar except that the subject NP of the lowest sentence would contain the word identical to the word in the highest sentence that was being relativized, rather than the object NP. This is the case, for example, in a sentence like *Caesar misit exploratores qui loci naturam perspicerent*, 'Caesar sent scouts to inspect the ground.'

(46)

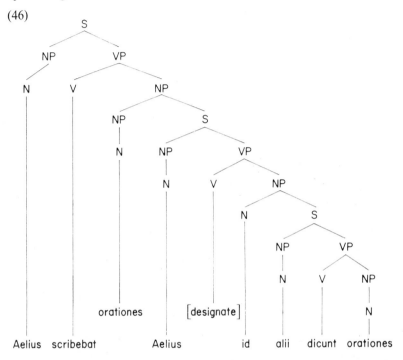

In all languages relativization can take place over indefinitely many sentences: *I hoped that John would see the boy who Alice felt John believed nobody understood.* In (46), relativization takes place over three sentences. Complementizer-placement operates in the sentence dependent on [*designate*] as does *ut*-subjunctive complementizer-change. Sequence-of-tenses rules must apply. [*Designate*] in this construction, like [*vol*] in purpose clauses, must agree in tense with the main verb. In this sentence, then, it is a secondary tense, and the verb in the lowest sentence, originally future like any verb dependent on a verb of the class of *designate*, becomes imperfect subjunctive by the application of future-deletion, subjunctivization, and sequence-of-tenses agreement. *Orationes*, the object of *dicerent*, undergoes relativization. This process is described in Lakoff and Ross (in preparation); its effect is to move *orationes* out of its position in the lower sentence and

Chomsky-adjoin it to the sentence that is dominated by the same NP by which the antecedent of the relativized word is dominated.

Relativization: Z NP $[\ X$ NP $Y \ ] \ W \to 1 - 2 - 3 - \emptyset - 5$

$$\begin{array}{cccccc} 1 & 2 & & 3 & 4 & 5 & 6 \end{array}$$

if $2 = 4$

Chomsky-adjoin 4 to $3 - 4 - 5$

delete 4

This leaves the structure shown in diagram (47). Now it is evident that this is not a grammatical sentence of Latin, because the complementizer *ut* is present, and it can never be present in a sentence of this kind.

(47)

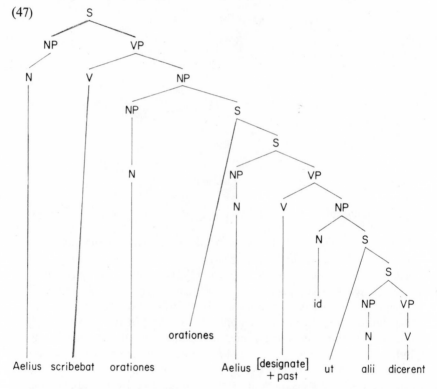

This is analogous to a fact known about English; thus the first of the two following sentences is grammatical, and the second is not.

(48a)   I saw the boy who I knew was right.

(48b)   *I saw the boy who I knew that was right.

In Section 2.12 we discussed a rule that deletes *that* from sentences like *I knew that the boy was right.* This rule is always optional, however. But in these relativized sentences the relative and *that* cannot both be present. Since *that*-deletion is optional, this must be handled by saying that, if *that*-deletion has not taken place, neither can relativization take place, or the sentence is ungrammatical. The same constraint holds in these Latin sentences. *Ut*-deletion (cf. Section 3.11) and relativization are related in the same way in these relative purpose clauses as relativization and *that*-deletion are in ordinary English relative clauses. Therefore, *that*-deletion takes place, *id* is deleted as usual, [*designate*] is deleted by ordinary abstract-verb deletion, and the sentence is now in its superficial form, that of (45b).

This suggested derivation of the relative purpose clause is probably not completely correct. The abstract verb is probably close in meaning to [*designate*], but it is not clear exactly what its meaning is. The relative purpose clause with adverbial relatives is even more resistant to analysis. A great deal of work must be done before these constructions are properly understood.

5.14 Remarks on the Result (Consecutive) Clause

Much less can be said about clauses of result than would be ideal. Their structure is by no means well understood. What little can be stated with any confidence will be. Examples of typical result clauses follow:

(49a)   John is so stupid that he thinks the world is round.

(49b)   His language was such that women ran away when they heard it.

(49c)   You are not the sort of person who I would have thought would do a thing like that.

The same sorts of sentences occur frequently in Latin. The complementizer is always *ut*-subjunctive; the negative is *non*.

(50a)   In Lucullo tanta prudentia fuit ut hodie stet Asia Luculli institutis servandis. (Cic. Ac. 2, 3) 'There was so much wisdom in Lucullus that today Asia stands by preserving the ordinances of Lucullus.'

(50b)   Patriae tanta est vis ut Ithacam vir sapientissimus immortalitati anteponeret. (Cic. de Or. 1, 196) 'So great is the power of one's native land that the wisest of men chose Ithaca over immortalit.'

(50c)   Tanta vis probitas est ut eam in hoste diligamus. (Cic. Lael. 29) 'So great is the strength of honesty that we cherish it even in an enemy.'

(50d)   Multa rumor adfingebat, ut paene bellum confectum videretur. (Caes. B. C. 53) 'Rumor invented many tales, so that the war seemed almost over.'

(50e)   Multi ita sunt imbecilli senes ut nullum offici munus exsequi possint. (Cic. Sen. 35) 'Many old men are so weak that they cannot perform any public office.'

(50f)   Multis gravibus volneribus confectus, ut iam se sustinere non posset. (Caes. B. G. 2, 25) 'Exhausted by many serious wounds, so that he could no longer keep himself up.'

(50g)   Ita te ornatum amittam ut te non noveris. (Pl. Rud. 730) 'I will send you away so ornamented that you won't recognize yourself.'

Sentence (50a) illustrates a fact about result clauses that distinguishes them from most other subjunctives: the sequence-of-tenses rules do not always apply. *Fuit* is a historical tense, but *stet* is present subjunctive. This indicates that, whatever the verb is that is present in the deep structure but not present in the surface structure, on which *stet* depends, it need not agree in tense with the main verb of the sentence. On the other hand, usually the sequence-of-tenses rules do apply, as in (50d). The only other assertion that can be made with any degree of certainty is that, whatever the verb is that the lower sentence is dependent on, it takes a subject complement. Otherwise, the negative would not be *non*. Beyond that, there is nothing to be said about the structure of these sentences. It is perhaps worth remarking that the name "result clause" is an accurate description of the meaning of the abstract verb present in it, [*vol*]; perhaps the verb here is [*result*], an abstract equivalent of *consequitur* or the like. This verb takes two complements: *It S results from it S*. Pursuing this speculation a little further, we can set up a conceivable deep structure for (50b):

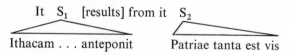

It S_1 [results] from it S_2
Ithacam . . . anteponit   Patriae tanta est vis

Sentence S1, which will receive the complement *ut*-subjunctive, is, in this analysis, the subject of *result*. We should expect *ut non* rather than *ne*, and *ut non* is what we find. *Result* must then undergo flip, perhaps to something analogous to *result in*. But this is far from a complete derivation. The sentence *Tanta est vis patriae* is not basic. If the two complements were parallel types of sentences, as they usually tend to be in structures of this kind, we should expect *tanta . . . patriae* to be derived from *That the influence of the fatherland is so great.* But there is absolutely no syntactic evidence for such a derivation. Part of the problem, therefore, is that the separate sentences which compose these larger structures are themselves poorly understood, much more so than are the components of expressions of purpose.

5.15 Conclusions

In this chapter we have stated the tentative hypothesis that mood is not a deep-structure characteristic. The marker of mood itself does not carry meaning. This assumption can be supported by pointing out the contradictions that one is led into by assuming that subjunctive endings do carry meaning: each of the various uses of the subjunctive represents a separate meaning, although the ending is the same. It has been suggested that, instead, the subjunctive is to be treated as a marker of complementation, like the infinitive, wherever it occurs. Its use in a sentence where it is not dependent on a verb present in the surface structure is essentially the same as its use in a sentence where it is dependent on a verb that is superficially present. The meaning of each type of subjunctive is supplied by an abstract verb, present in the deep structure, which governs complementizer-placement and change as well as other rules and is deleted obligatorily by a late rule. The abstract verb is not an arbitrary element that might optionally be present in a language, like the marker that previous transformational treatments of mood have inserted in the phrase structure rules. We base our theory of abstract verbs on the notion of semantically oriented meaning-classes, which delimit and define the possible abstract verbs in a language. Traditional grammarians assume that certain grammatical rules depend on meaning-classes: for example, whether or not a given verb can take *ut*-subjunctive as a complementizer will depend on whether the verb belongs to a meaning-class that can take this complementizer. We have refined the notion of meaning-class to make it more rigorous. We define a meaning-class as a set of semantic markers that function in syntactic rules (cf. Sections 5.2 and 5.3). These are the syntactically relevant semantic markers, and these alone can occur in rules of grammar. We have defined an abstract verb as a verb with the property that *all* of its semantic markers are syntactically relevant. Theoretically, each meaning-class in a language might define one abstract verb. But often the possibility is not realized. Each language probably picks only a certain number of abstract verbs, and different languages will express them in different ways—one through the use of complementizers and mood endings, another through suffixes and plugging-in. Except for the abstract-verb deletion rule, there is no added complication to the grammar in a theory that makes use of abstract verbs: on the contrary, many significant generalizations can be stated in such a theory that other theories could not handle. Without abstract verbs, treatment of many of the rules discussed in this and earlier chapters must be *ad hoc* and must overlook relationships among facts that are obviously related. Some of these relationships are co-occurrence restrictions among subjects, tense restrictions, and the choice of *non* or *ne* in negation, all easily accounted for, with the correct meanings assigned, if it is assumed that the subjunctives are not independent. This has been shown for so many of the seemingly most clearly independent subjunctives that it seems very likely that eventually it will be found that other subjunctives not dependent on verbs in the surface structure are dependent on verbs in the deep structure. These types will become clearer when such phenomena as conditional sentences and temporal and causal clauses become better understood. We have also discussed "independent" infinitives and have shown that in a theory which makes use of abstract verbs these forms can be accounted for, and correct meanings assigned, at no cost in complexity to the transformational component except for one or two abstract-verb deletion rules.

Notes

1. The claim that *quod*-indicative states a fact, while *ut*-subjunctive states an unrealized possibility, is false; cf. *Est ut Marcus veniat*, 'It's a fact that Marcus is coming.'

2. It is true that in some languages a form exists which is called by grammarians the "first-person singular imperative." Upon closer examination, however, these forms will be found perhaps to share morphological similarities with the true imperatives but to differ from them distinctly in usage and meaning.

3. An exception to this statement may be found in Katz and Postal (1964), pp. 74–78 and in particular, note 9, p. 149. On p. 149 the authors suggest speculatively that perhaps the imperative is derived from something like *I request that S*. They point out that this would account for some of the constraints on imperatives that are known to exist. They carry their hypothesis no further, however, and it has generally been ignored by other transformational grammarians.

4. There is at present no empirical evidence to support such an assertion. The choice of deep structure cannot be determined in any definitive way even for English, much less for other less-studied languages. The choice of deep structure will affect the rest of the grammar, of course, but in no case at present has the

nature of the transformational component forced on us a specific choice of deep structure. Hence, since the nature of the base in any language cannot be determined conclusively, the decision as to whether the base is language-specific, Indo-European, or language-universal must rest on other factors. Thus, the linguist will work on each language individually, assuming no universality of the phrase structure rules. The appearance of similarities between unrelated languages would, of course, support the hypothesis of a universal base, but not prove it—not until all known languages have been shown, on independent grounds, to share the same deep structure will the hypothesis be proved empirically. This will probably never be done.

One reason why the linguist might wish to assume, at least tentatively, a theory in which the base is universal, is that such a theory is far more powerful and exercises far more control over the form of phrase structure rules than a theory in which the base is language-specific. It is not, of course, claimed that the stronger theory is necessarily the preferable one; rather, if we follow this stronger theory as far as we can, making the necessary assumptions, we shall learn more about the nature of language and about what is universal about language than if we assign arbitrary deep structures to individual languages. If the stronger theory is proved wrong, we can always return to a weaker one; but since there is no way to disprove the weaker sort of theory, if we use it, we may never discover much that we should like to know about linguistic universals.

5. This will be true only insofar as this theory enables its proponents to account for other complex-sentence types in terms of deep-structure sentences containing abstract elements. For example, if it cannot be proved that all adverbials are derived from extra sentences, then an adverbial node must be postulated in the base in any event. For this reason, more conservative transformational linguists (such as Chomsky) prefer to keep the base complicated and the transformational component simpler, on the grounds that, since little is known about complex sentences, such a theory will be able to handle the facts in a generally simpler way.

6. It has been suggested by Ross (oral communication) that in some of these cases, there is an abstract verb with the meaning 'I allege' above the sentence containing *because* in sentences of Latin in which *quod* appears and that the subjunctive is the result of the presence of *allege*. This is an interesting suggestion, but no details have been worked out. It does not explain some very strange phenomena, such as the fact that in subordinate clauses in indirect statement the verb is subjunctive when it is an integral part of the embedded sentence, and indicative otherwise (as, for example, when it is a statement on the part of the speaker himself). This kind of fact seems altogether unrelated to the use of the subjunctive with *quod*, where the presence of the subjunctive indicates that the speaker himself is not taking responsibility for the truth of the assertion. Clearly, there is much that is still imperfectly understood about subjunctives, and we are at best shedding a single ray of light into the darkness.

7. We use the term "aspect" for lack of any other, rather than to imply that the perfect suffix of Latin operates in a way comparable to the perfective prefixes in Russian, for instance. In nonfinite and subjunctive forms, the perfect suffix does indeed seem to have elements of perfective aspect; thus the use of the perfect infinitive indicates that the action was already completed at the time of the main verb of the sentence. But in the indicative, and sometimes in the subjunctive too, there is no aspectual significance evident in the perfect system.

8. The preference for the complex form of negation is not easily explained. It should perhaps be noted, in partial explanation, that the usual negative in Latin is derived from a stative verb, discussed in Chapter 4. It is generally true that verbs of ordering cannot immediately dominate statives, as discussed earlier (Section 5.4). Usually, when we find a negative imperative, the interpretation of the sentence is that the negative has the meaning 'refrain from,' a non-stative verb, rather than 'It is not so.' Thus, *Don't do that!* is interpreted as meaning 'I order you to refrain from doing that,' rather than 'I order that it not be so that you do that,' which is meaningless. But in some langauges there is no simple negative imperative at all. This is the case in the Australian language, Walbiri, according to K. Hale (oral communication). The interpretation of this fact would appear to be that in such languages the abstract verb *[refrain from]* does not exist and that, therefore, since only the stative negative exists, it is never found directly dominated by the imperative abstract verb. In Walbiri, as in Latin, negative commands are expressed by circumlocution: *Sit there not doing that = Don't do that*. This latter structure is grammatical with a stative: *I order you to sit there while it is not so that you do that* (whatever the structure of the latter part of the sentence really is). We may speculate that something of the sort is true for Latin. In Latin the abstract verb *[refrain]* exists. It must be present underlying sentences containing negative commands: *Impero ne veniat*, for example. But if it appears dominated by the abstract verb *[imper]*, the resulting surface structure acquires an archaic or poetic flavor, though it can be understood. It is interesting to note that in the modern Romance languages *[refrain]* has come into ordinary use: *No venga*.

9. In English, one of the strong reasons for assuming the presence of a future tense verb dominated by *[imper]* is the existence of tag questions on imperatives in the future tense. Thus, parallel to

> John came, didn't he?
> Mary is here, isn't she?
> Selma will scrub the floor, won't she?

we find

> Come, won't you!

And, just as we do not find

> *John will come, didn't he?

we do not find

> *Do that, did you!

In Latin, there are no tag questions, so the presence of the future tense in imperatives is not as strongly proved. It should be noted that we have no idea how tags are formed or how they interact with abstract verbs.

10. For an example of overly simple answers to this difficult question, see Woodcock (1958), whose discussion (p. 88) is fairly typical of that of philologists:

> As the present subjunctive normally refers to the future, it does not necessarily imply the impossibility of fulfilment. A wish that things were different from what they are in the present does imply unfulfilment. Early Latin does not yet clearly distinguish between wishes that are still capable of fulfilment and those that are not. . . . But already in Plautus a tense-shift is taking

place whereby the imperfect subjunctive is used to express unfulfilled wishes in the present, and the pluperfect to express past unfulfilled wishes.

The mechanism of the "tense-shift" that is taking place in Plautus is the interesting question here, and one that is completely ignored. It is also a very difficult question, which we cannot attempt to solve.

11. The observant reader will note the presence of *non* in the second half of this sentence and will wonder whether it is an exception to our rule that the negative becomes *ne* in object complements or whether it refutes our claim that *oportet* is a flip. The answer is that it probably does neither. The verb *oportet* and the subordinate subject and object *Tu amas* have been deleted on the right, leaving only the direct object and the negative. Therefore, it is impossible to tell from the surface structure alone what is being negated; theoretically, it could be either *oportet* or the deleted *ames*. The presence of *non* suggests that the first possibility is the more likely: 'You ought to love me, you ought not to love my possessions,' rather than 'You ought to love me, you ought to not love my possessions.' In the second sentence, the parallelism seems to be destroyed, and the structure is not fully grammatical in English. The speaker does not wish to say that it is the obligation of the hearer that he not love the speaker's possessions. What he is saying is that it is not the obligation of the hearer to love those possessions; his obligation is, on the other hand, to love the speaker. Thus, the only logical interpretation of this sentence is in accordance with the claim about *non* and *ne*.

12. In connection with this, it should be pointed out that, in archaic English, *that*-finite was the complementizer found with *because*. In archaic English this verb was followed by the preposition *for*, so that the final form of *because* was *for that*. In modern English this has been replaced by *because*, a form containing the verb itself. In older English and Spanish, the treatment of [cause] was exactly parallel to its treatment in Latin. Thus, in Spanish, *porqué* is derived from the preposition *por*, equivalent to *for* in English, and *que*, 'that.' Preposition-deletion never applies in Spanish. This treatment of *quod* in Latin, then, also can be used to account for the forms taken by *because* in related modern languages and can help to explain the nature of the change in the means of expressing this concept between older and modern English.

6. Diachronic Change in the Complement System

A comparison of the superficial syntax of the complement systems of Latin and Spanish might surprise the linguist who expects that two closely related languages will look alike in all respects. He is already aware from comparing lexical entries in the two languages that there is a very high correlation between words found in Latin and words found, with the almost same form and the same or virtually the same meaning, in Spanish. If he were to inspect the phonology of the two languages, he would find that Spanish shared a great many of the rules of Latin, though perhaps differently ordered, and that the superficial form of the phonological component of Spanish is easily identified as derived from Latin. Even in the morphology, where more change is discernible, the relationship is apparent: each of the tense-endings in Spanish can be shown to be derived from a readily identifiable Latin form.[1] Even though the classical Latin grammar did not, for example, make use of *habeo* to form auxiliaries, as Spanish uses *haber*, still *habeo* exists in Latin, and is occasionally found as a sort of auxiliary even in the classical language.[2] But when one comes to inspect the syntax of Spanish, one finds that, on the surface, it resembles that of Latin very little. The complement system is a case in point.

218

6.1 Previous Work on Syntactic Change

A cursory inspection of complement sentences in Spanish will convince the examiner that the grammar of Spanish has little to do with the grammar of Latin. The distribution of the various complementizers in Spanish is very different from that of Latin, and the complementizers themselves are different in form. Complement rules, such as equi-NP-deletion and *it*-substitution, occur in Spanish where they do not in Latin, and vice versa. For these and other reasons, it is easy to understand why most traditional grammarians who have dealt with the subject have concluded that there is a drastic change between Latin and Spanish and that there is little relationship between Latin constructions and most of their equivalents in Spanish. If this is true, then syntactic change is different from phonological change, where there is no wholesale changing of rules.

Historical linguists tracing the changes in syntax between Latin and Spanish have had surprisingly little to say of substantive value. All that is usually done is to document changes in constructions, note when the first indications of each change were observed, and give subjective explanations of how each change might have been induced. The changes in one construction—for example, in the purpose clause—were felt not to be related to the changes in any other construction—for example, in the types of complementizers that could follow verbs of wanting—because there was no mechanism at the disposal of Romance philologists to account for any relationship between superficially different constructions.

In the preceding chapters, we have proposed and discussed a theory in which the superficial forms of sentences may be very different from their underlying forms. The idea that the same abstract representation might produce very different superficial representations, with different sets of rules, enables serious work in syntactic change to begin. The first serious and detailed study of syntactic change in a generative grammar was done by Klima. He showed that, for English, changes in the syntax could be produced by changes in the ordering of rules, rather than by the rules themselves.[3] In this chapter, we shall consider changes of a different sort.

We shall restrict ourselves to an examination of a few of the rules that have been discussed in the second and third chapters in order to see whether and how each occurs in the grammar of modern Spanish and, if there are changes from Latin, how these changes may be described and whether the resultant complement system of Spanish differs from that of

Latin. Where it differs, we shall attempt to pinpoint the location of the difference and see in what part of the grammar these differences occur.

6.2 The Location in the Grammar of Governed-Rule Change

In our inspection of the changes in the complement system between Latin and Spanish, we shall be dealing almost exclusively with governed rules. Some of the changes that will be examined are the following:

1. The complementizers that occur with various classes of verbs in Latin are usually different from the ones that occur with corresponding words in Spanish. In some cases we shall find a situation that occurs nowhere in Latin: that the choice of complementizer in certain classes of words is dependent on whether the noun of the lower sentence is identical to that of the higher sentence.
2. The complementizers themselves look different from their Latin counterparts, even when they appear to be performing identical functions in the grammar. Thus, *que*-subjunctive does not look like *ut*-subjunctive, but it is used in much the same way.
3. Equi-NP-deletion applies in more classes of verbs in Spanish than it does in Latin. It is also obligatory in Spanish: in Latin the rule is frequently optional (as in verbs of wishing) or nonapplicable (as in verbs of saying and thinking).
4. *It*-substitution occurs in Spanish optionally in subject complements where it does not occur in Latin. (In Latin it occurs in underlying subject complements only if it obligatorily applies in a given class of verbs; it is never optional. In Spanish it is optional for some classes of subject complements.)
5. Sentence types that in the last chapter we suggested were produced through the presence of abstract verbs sometimes behave differently in Spanish. We shall ask whether the change follows any pattern.

Upon inspection of the types of changes just summarized, it will be seen that there is no need to change any of the transformational rules that have been given in order to describe the changes from Latin to Spanish. The changes all come about because of changes in the properties of the verbs themselves. In the second chapter the operation of redundancy rules in the grammar of English was discussed, and in the third chapter their operation in the grammar of Latin. These redundancy rules specified which of the governed rules each meaning-class of verbs underwent. For example, a redundancy rule states that in Latin *for-to* complementizer-change is obligatory for verbs of saying and thinking, and *ut*-subjunctive complementizer-change for verbs of ordering. For a verb of saying or thinking, if it takes *for-to*, it is unmarked, and if it takes anything else, it is marked. But a verb of ordering taking *for-to* is marked, while such a verb taking *ut*-subjunctive is unmarked. For verbs of wanting and wishing, the choice is optional between *for-to* and *ut*-subjunctive. It is stated nowhere in the transformational component that *impero* undergoes *ut*-subjunctive complementizer-change and that *iubeo* undergoes *for-to*. Nor is it stated in any way in any of the transformational rules that *impero* is regular and *iubeo* irregular. The fact that *impero* takes *ut*-subjunctive and *iubeo* takes *for-to* is indicated in the representation of each verb in the lexicon, along with its phonological specifications. This is true for every verb in the language and for every governed rule. Thus, the redundancy rule for verbs of saying in classical Latin states that equi-NP-deletion is nonapplicable even if the structural description for that rule is met. For verbs of wishing, the redundancy rule will state that equi-NP-deletion is optional. For verbs of trying or of being able, on the other hand, equi-NP-deletion will be obligatory. All of these facts are represented in the lexicon and the redundancy rules; hence, if any of them change in time, the change will take place, not in the transformational component, but in the lexicon and in the redundancy rules; the latter will state what is regular and what is not for a given meaning-class, as well as what rules can apply at all. Hence, although complementizer-placement and change, equi-NP-deletion, and *it*-substitution, all governed, act in Spanish to produce very different structures superficially from their counterparts in Latin, this is not to be ascribed to a difference or change in these rules themselves; it is a change in the redundancy rules instead. Since these define regularities in the lexicon, it is not surprising that they change readily, since the lexicon is the most flexible part of a grammar.

What we have found and shall document in succeeding sections of this chapter is that redundancy rules can change in the following ways: they can extend to new classes of verbs rules that formerly did not apply to them; they can make rules that did apply to a class cease to apply, thus restricting the domain of a rule; and they can make rules optional in a class that were obligatory, and make obligatory rules that were optional.

Can anything be said about what causes the redundancy rules to change? In some cases, yes. Several of the cases we are about to discuss changed in a way to make the superficial structure of Latin more closely resemble that of Greek. These "borrowings" from Greek appear, in many cases, to have remained in Latin and to be at present part of the synchronic grammar of Spanish. Other changes appear to have arisen spontaneously within Latin itself, and were not influenced by Greek. (It is, of course, conceivable that the Latin spoken in Spain was influenced by the indigenous languages of Iberia and that these encouraged the apparently spontaneous changes. But there is no reason to believe this, and it is easier merely to assume these changes occurred spontaneously.) We shall discuss the changes that are found in the complement rules under two categories: first, changes influenced by Greek models, or Hellenisms; second, changes that arose spontaneously in Latin.

6.3 Hellenisms

It is well known that there are found in some Latin writings departures from the norm of Latin influenced by Greek constructions that resemble the aberrant Latin forms; these departures are usually called "Hellenisms" or "Grecisms." Two different types of borrowings are illustrated in the outline in the next paragraph. Brenous and other writers have discussed these borrowings at length. Their intuitive conclusions do not differ materially from ours; we are attempting here to explain formally, and within the framework of transformational grammar, why certain changes, and not others, are found and how these changes may be accounted for in terms of the synchronic grammar of Latin.

In dealing with this topic, one must be careful to distinguish between two types of aberrant sentences, both of which might be called "Hellenisms."

Type 1. Found in the writings of non-native speakers of Latin:

    A. Use of rules that are found in Greek, but not found at all in Latin. Example (*Bellum Hispaniense* 14, 1): *Eius praeteriti temporis*, for *Eo praeterito tempore*, 'That time being past,' where genitive absolute (Greek construction) is substituted for the ablative absolute. This should be distinguished from B.

    B. Nonapplication of a rule that ought to apply in Latin without any discernible influence on the writer of the grammar of Greek. Example (same work): *Quod factum licet necopinantibus nostris esset gestum*, 'A deed which it was allowed to our unfortunate men to do.' Violation of sequence-of-tenses rules, which apply in Greek as well as Latin.

Type 2. Found in the writings of native speakers of Latin, for literary effect:

    Example: *Phasellus ille quem videtis, hospites, ait fuisse navium celerrimus.* (Cat. 4, 1) 'The vessel that you see, guests, says that it was the swiftest of ships.'

Type 1 is not considered true Hellenism. Type 2 is what we are speaking of, and what most grammarians restrict themselves to, when they discuss Hellenism.

In the example given for Type 2, the writer was conscious that he was adapting a Greek rule of grammar into Latin, and was doing it for literary effect. In Example A of Type 1, the writer may well have been Hellenizing unconsciously. The writer is a native speaker of Latin and knows the language well enough to be aware that he is deviating from the norm. It must be remembered that Greek was a prestige language in Rome, and imitating it consciously was an indication that the imitator was a cultured and highly educated man. Type 1 is probably due more to ignorance of Latin than to a desire to transfer a Greek rule into Latin grammar. It was not used by any native speaker of Latin, as Type 2 would have been.

Keeping to this definition of Hellenism, we find that not every rule in Greek was borrowed, or could have been borrowed, into Latin. For example, there is an equivalent in Greek to the *for-to* complementizer: it appears as accusative-infinitive, just as in Latin. A Roman wishing to Hellenize might borrow this complementizer-changing rule by using it in a class of verbs where it was not normally used in Latin, but where it was normal in Greek. He could do this because the rule itself existed in Latin and was not altogether foreign to it. But there is another complementizer in Greek (which makes use of a larger number of complementizers than Latin), *hos*-indicative. *Hos* is roughly equivalent to *ut* in Latin, but *ut* never occurs with the indicative. Therefore, it is evident that there is no rule corresponding to the Greek *hos*-indicative complementizer-changing rule in Latin. For this reason, this rule was never borrowed, and one never sees examples of *ut*-indicative anywhere in Latin. It appears that a language does not borrow rules outright: it is merely able to borrow the constraints on their applicability.[4]

6.4 Hellenisms and Synchronic Spanish

As an example of the influence of Greek models on Latin grammar, let us examine an instance where Greek may well have influenced Latin, and where the effect is present in Spanish: the operation of the rules of complementizer-change and equi-NP-deletion, in the verbs of saying and thinking.

In Latin these verbs had to undergo *for-to* complementizer-change, but although the sentence might then meet the structural description of equi-NP-deletion, it could not undergo it. Thus, *Dico me venire*,

'I say that I am coming,' is grammatical in Latin, but *Dico venire* was not. But a similar situation does not exist in Spanish.

In Spanish the most common complementizer for the class of verbs of saying and thinking is *que*-indicative, the descendant of *quod*-indicative in Latin. Later in the chapter the change from *for-to* to *quod*-indicative in these verbs will be discussed. *Que*-indicative is always grammatical in this class of verbs.

(1a)   Yo digo que Juan ha venido. 'I say that John has come.'

(1b)   Yo digo que yo he venido. 'I say that I have come.'

Thus far, the situation is easily described: there has been a curtailment in the applicability of *for-to* complementizer-change. It does not apply to verbs of saying and thinking in Spanish. But this is not true. It does apply, but only if the structural description of equi-NP-deletion is met: the subjects of the higher and lower sentences must be identical. Otherwise, *for-to* complementizer-change cannot occur. Even where it can occur, it is optional (cf. sentence (1b)).

(2a)   Yo digo haber venido. 'I say that I have come.'

(2b)   *Yo digo (a) Juan haber venido. 'I say that John has come.'

The relationship between the Latin sentences and the Spanish ones is not immediately obvious. On inspection, it appears that two significant changes have taken place: (1) there are two possible complements (*for-to* and *que*-indicative) rather than only one (*for-to*) for verbs of this class; and (2) if *for-to* applies, equi-NP-deletion must apply, while in Latin, equi-NP-deletion could not apply. For the second to occur in Spanish, the first must also have taken place; there must be a means in the language for expressing sentences like (1a). If *for-to* were the only complementizer possible for this class, and *for-to* complementizer-change could occur only if the SD for equi-NP-deletion had been met, it would be impossible to express sentence (1a) in Spanish. Therefore, the two changes are in some way connected, although this connection cannot be described formally.

The first change is probably not the result of Greek influence on Latin but rather a spontaneous development in Vulgar Latin. It would be rather tempting to think that this is not the case and that the use of *hoti*-indicative with verbs like *lego*, 'say,' in Greek influenced verbs of saying in Latin. But if this were really the way it happened, *quod*-indicative undoubtedly would not be found with verbs of thinking and perceiving, which in Greek occur with accusative-infinitive or with poss.-*ing* (accusative plus supplementary participle, in Greek, where *it*-substitution applies to the subject of the lower sentence regularly in these verbs), never *hoti*-indicative. In Latin, verbs of saying and verbs of thinking act alike with respect to complementizer-change. We find in Petronius (45, 10) sentences like *Sed subolfacio, quia nobis epulum daturus est Mammea*, 'I have a feeling that Mammea is going to throw a party for us.' Here the verb is a verb of perception, and if the use of *quod* (*quia*) were a Hellenism, it could not be used with a verb of this class. The use of *quod* in object complements is probably a spontaneous change on the part of Latin.

The second change, however, appears definitely to have occurred under the influence of Greek. In Greek, there is a division between verbs of saying and verbs of thinking, with respect to which complementizer-changing rules they undergo. Most verbs of thinking must undergo accusative-infinitive complementizer-change. But most verbs of saying do not normally undergo any of the rules of complementizer-change; they take *hoti*-indicative as a complementizer, which is equivalent to *quod*-indicative in Latin. There is one notable exception: a common verb of saying in Greek, *phemi*, always takes accusative-infinitive. When it does this, it will undergo equi-NP-deletion if the structural description of this rule is met, otherwise not. Therefore, if one wants to say in Greek, *I say that Cyrus is good*, one has the option of using *lego* (or another verb of its class) with *hoti* and the indicative, or *phemi*, with the accusative-infinitive.

(3a)   Lego hoti Kuros agathos estin.

(3b)   Phemi Kuron agathon einai.

If one wants to say, *Cyrus says that he is good* (where *he* refers to Cyrus) he also has two choices. He can use *lego*, just as in (3a), or he can use *phemi*, with an infinitive alone. In this case, *agathos*, 'good,' will be in the nominative, because the subject of the lower sentence will have been deleted (and its accusative case marking with it) before agreement across copula takes place.

(4a)   Kuros legei hoti agathos estin.⎫
⎬ 'Cyrus says that he is good.'
(4b)   Kuros phesi agathos einai.   ⎭

We find numerous examples of Latin writers adopting the Greek *phemi*-construction in Latin and allowing sentences embedded in verbs of saying and thinking to undergo equi-NP-deletion. The sentence given under Type 2 of the outline in Section 6.3, *Phasellus ille quem videtis, hospites, ait fuisse navium celerrimus*, is identical in construction to a sentence like (4b). In this way, a rule is borrowed by a native speaker of Latin into a meaning-class in which it usually does not apply. But equi-NP-deletion applies elsewhere in Latin, of course. This borrowing eventually became a part of the grammar of Vulgar Latin: sentences analogous to (2a) occur in all the Romance languages. The change between the behavior of verbs of saying and thinking, with respect to complementizer-change and equi-NP-deletion, in Latin and in Spanish may be traced through classical to Vulgar Latin and into Spanish as follows:

Redundancy Rule F

Classical Latin: $V_{saying/thinking}$
u *for-to* $\supset$ + *for-to*
Other complementizer-changing rules are not applicable; equi-NP-deletion is not applicable.

Redundancy Rule G

Vulgar Latin: $V_{saying/thinking}$
u *for-to* $\supset$ opt. *for-to*
Other complementizer-changing rules are not applicable; equi-NP-deletion is probably optional if SD is met for this class for at least some speakers.

Redundancy Rule H

Spanish: $V_{saying/thinking}$
u *for-to* $\supset$ opt. *for-to*: SD equi-NP-deletion is met.
Other complementizer-changing rules are not applicable; equi-NP-deletion is obligatory if *for-to* complementizer-change has applied, but not applicable otherwise.

These rules may be compared with the situation in Greek:

Redundancy Rule I [a]

Phemi: u *for-to* $\supset$ + *for-to*
Other complementizer-changing rules are not applicable; equi-NP-deletion is obligatory.

Redundancy Rule I [b]

Lego: *For-to* is not applicable unless passivization SD is met; u *hos*-indic. complementizer-change $\supset$ opt. *hos*-indic. complementizer-change, equi-NP-deletion is not applicable.

Neither of the possibilities in Greek corresponds exactly to the situation in Latin, nor does the Greek correspond exactly to the Spanish, but it appears that the way Latin changed was in the direction of the Greek, by borrowing part of the Greek set of redundancy rules.

There is another example of Hellenism-inspired change. In Latin, *it*-substitution applies only when it applies obligatorily, in subject complements—principally, with verbs like *begin, end, tend, continue.* Thus, **Marcus aequus est ire* and **Marcus veri similis est ire* are both ungrammatical, even when *for-to* complementizer-change has applied.

In Spanish, on the other hand, we find sentences like the following:

(5a) Hacerlo él sería imposible. 'For him to do it would be impossible.' (Lit., 'He would be impossible to do it.')

The following is also grammatical:

(5b) Hacerlo le sería imposible, 'It would be impossible for him to do it.'

In (5a), *it*-substitution has applied. The rule is optional for this verb and for many verbs of this class; native speakers are divided over which are acceptable and which are not. But it is certainly acceptable for some subject-complement-taking verbs for most speakers of Spanish. This is a clear departure from Latin. But we have shown that *it*-substitution must operate somewhere in the grammar of Latin: perhaps in object complements and certainly in flips and passives. Therefore, the rule could be extended, either spontaneously or through borrowing, into the class of subject complements where it is optional.

If we look at Greek, we notice that in this language, *it*-substitution is very frequent in these environments.

(6a) Sokrates dunatos estin ienai. 'Socrates is possible to go' = 'It is possible for Socrates to go.'

(6b) Sokrates axios estin ienai. 'Socrates is right to go.'

These occur alongside of sentences without *it*-substitution, though the latter are less frequent.

(7a) Dunaton esti Sokrate ienai. 'It is possible for Socrates to go.'

(7b) Axion esti Sokrate ienai. 'It is right for Socrates to go.'

What appears to be happening here is that through the influence of Greek the domain of applicability of *it*-substitution has been extended, so that it can apply in subject complements optionally, instead of applying only in those cases where it was obligatory.

6.5 Spontaneous Governed-Rule Change

Where change in governed rules occurs spontaneously, the same restrictions on what can change apply as in those cases where the change was influenced by the grammar of Greek. Here, too, the data we have looked at are insufficient as a source from which to draw conclusions. If it should actually turn out to be true that governed-rule change occurs only when it is an extension or restriction of rules already in the grammar of a language, and that therefore a governed rule was never added to a language, this would be a startling conclusion and one that is not anticipated in any theory of linguistic change. Obviously, the whole subject of syntactic change and, within it, the subject of governed-rule change warrant serious study.

We shall discuss here one particularly interesting case of spontaneous governed-rule change between Latin and Romance. It is interesting not only in itself but in its power to explain other facts about Spanish that have previously been treated as unrelated.

In Latin, verbs of wanting and wishing could undergo either *for-to* or *ut*-subjunctive complementizer-change. The two were about equally common. If *for-to* was chosen, equi-NP-deletion was optional. Thus, all the following were found:

(8a)   Volo ut sim consul. 'I want to be consul.'

(8b)   Volo me esse consulem. 'I want to be consul.'

(8c)   Volo esse consul. 'I want to be consul.'

If the subjects are different, both *for-to* and *ut*-subjunctive are still possible.

(9a)   Volo ut Marcus sit consul. 'I want Marcus to be consul.'

(9b)   Volo Marcum esse consulem. 'I want Marcus to be consul.'

In Spanish, not all these possibilities exist. If the SD of equi-NP-deletion is met, *for-to* is the only possibility for verbs of this class. If the SD of equi-NP-deletion is not met, *que*-subjunctive (developed from *ut*-subjunctive) is the only complementizer found.[5]

(10a)   Quiero ir a Madrid. 'I want to go to Madrid.'

(10b)   Quiero que Juan vaya a Madrid. 'I want John to go to Madrid.'

(10c)   *Quiero que vaya a Madrid. 'I want to go to Madrid.'

(10d)   *Quiero (a) Juan ir a Madrid. 'I want John to go to Madrid.'

These facts can be described in terms of changes in redundancy rules alone. There is no change in the rules themselves. Thus, verbs of wanting and wishing in Latin are described in the following redundancy rule:

Redundancy Rule J. For verbs of wanting and wishing:

Complementizer-change (must undergo one of these rules):
u R (*for-to*) ⊃ opt. R (*for-to*)
u R (*ut*-subj.) ⊃ opt. R (*ut*-subj.)
u R (...) ⊃ R (...)
u R (equi-NP-deletion) ⊃ opt. R (equi-NP-deletion)

In Spanish, the redundancy rule is more complicated:

Redundancy Rule K. For verbs of wanting and wishing.

Complementizer-change (must undergo one of these rules):
If SD of equi-NP-deletion is met:
u R (*for-to*) ⊃ + R (*for-to*)
u other complementizer-changing rules ⊃ − other complementizer-changing rules
Equi-NP-deletion is obligatory.

If SD of equi-NP-deletion is not met:
u R (*for-to*) ⊃ − R (*for-to*)
u R (*que*-subj.) ⊃ + R (*que*-subj.)
u other complementizer-changing rules ⊃ − other complementizer-changing rules

This change in the redundancy rule will give the correct structures in Spanish. Thus, in this case, where the superficial structure of sentences in Spanish appears very different from that of Latin, we can show that this is merely a change in the redundancy rule, rather than a change in the syntactic component. This is a very different claim from the one made by most Romance philologists: that the construction itself changed between Latin and Spanish. To say that the construction changed is to imply that the rule which produced the construction changed, rather than that the meaning-class itself changed its properties. In all of these cases, too, the change is one that takes place throughout a whole meaning-class, rather than in individual verbs. When *dico* becomes able to take *quod*, for example, *aio* and *puto* presumably can also do so, as can all the other verbs of this class. It is not that any verb becomes irregular but rather that the regular situation for a meaning-class shifts. Calling this a change in redundancy rule expresses this fact precisely. So, for example, when verbs of ordering change their redundancy rule between Latin and Spanish, it is changed so that both *que*-subjunctive and *for-to* are optional, rather than *ut*-subjunctive being unmarked and *for-to* being marked, as it was in classical Latin. For all verbs of ordering in Spanish this is the situation. It would be interesting, if we had cases of irregular verbs that kept their phonological shape and meaning between Latin and Spanish—if *iubeo*, for example, were retained in the grammar of Spanish—to see whether all the marked and unmarked features were erased on all verbs of ordering, when the rule changed, so that the Spanish form of *iubeo* was regular like the others of its class, taking either *for-to* or *que*-subjunctive. Alternatively, it might keep its markedness, and undergo only *for-to*. There are few cases, however, of irregular verbs being retained. They seem much more liable to be lost than do regular verbs.

6.6 Abstract Verbs and Syntactic Change

Finally, we should ask how changes in governed rules affect the abstract verbs we spoke of in the preceding chapter. If it can be shown that changes in the redundancy rules for real verbs had, in at least some cases, the same effect on abstract verbs of the same classes, it will strengthen the argument that abstract verbs exist. It is difficult to explain how an independent subjunctive changes its properties or becomes an independent infinitive in the course of time—and why it changes in a manner similar to verbs that have the same meaning as the independent construction—unless one can assume that there are real verbs in the underlying structure, governing the application of rules, and that the changes in the redundancy rules affect these verbs as well as the ones present in the superficial structure. There is some evidence for changes in the properties of several of the abstract verbs that were discussed in the preceding chapter.

In Latin, verbs of ordering, if unmarked, underwent *ut*-subjunctive complementizer-change. The abstract verb [*imper*], as well as the other abstract verbs of ordering, such as [*hort*] and [*insist*], had the same property. In Spanish, on the other hand, unmarked verbs of ordering undergo either *for-to* or *que*-subjunctive. The following sentences are both equally grammatical, and synonymous:

(11a)   Le mandé a Juan irse. 'I ordered John to go away.'

(11b)   Le mandé a Juan que se fuese. 'I ordered John to go away.'

In Spanish, there are two imperative types found. One is a form derived from [*imper*] and *que*-subjunctive. The other is derived from [*imper*] and *for-to*. They are interchangeable, although the second is much commoner, just as (11b) is commoner than (11a).

(12a)   Callarse. ' Be quiet.'

(12b)   Cállese. 'Be quiet.'

The abstract verb [*imper*] remains regular in Spanish and changes its properties along with the other verbs of its class.

Another example of this type can be seen in subject complements. In Latin, as we have said, these cannot undergo *it*-substitution in most cases. The abstract verbs of these classes sometimes take *for-to* complementizers. When they do, they cannot undergo *it*-substitution, like other members of their meaning-class.

In Spanish, verbs in which *it*-substitution is inapplicable in Latin can undergo this rule optionally (cf. sentence (5a)). Then it might be expected that abstract verbs of these classes might undergo *it*-substitution if they occurred with *for-to* complementizers. We find sentences in Spanish such as the following:

(13a)   ¿Casarme yo? 'I get married?' = 'Is it likely that I would get married?'

(13b)   ¿Ir él a Madrid? 'He go to Madrid?'

These cases are identical in meaning to sentences in Latin containing the abstract verb [*veri simile*]. In Latin, these occurred either with *ut*-subjunctive or with *for-to*. In the latter case, the superficial structure contained an accusative and an infinitive. In Spanish, *it*-substitution has taken place: the pronouns *yo* and *él* are unambiguously nominative case. This can be accounted for only if we assume that *it*-substitution has operated. Here, then, is another example of a regular abstract verb retaining its regularity with respect to a rule and changing along with its meaning-class. In these cases, it should be pointed out again, the transformational rules have not been changed at all, although the superficial constructions have changed considerably.

In Latin, the abstract verb of wishing, [*vel*], was irregular, Other verbs of its class could optionally undergo either *for-to* or *ut*-subjunctive complementizer-change, but [*vel*] could undergo only the latter. In Spanish, it retains its irregularity and behaves just as it did in Latin, although the regular verbs of its class have changed their properties.

(14a)   ¡Que vaya yo a Madrid! 'Would that I might go to Madrid!'

(14b)   ¡Que vaya Juan a Madrid! 'Would that John might go to Madrid!'

(14c)   *Ir me a Madrid! 'Oh, to go to Madrid!'

(14d)   *Ir (a) Juan a Madrid! 'Oh for John to go to Madrid!'

In Latin, [*vel*] was marked as m *for-to*, indicating that it could not undergo it. It must retain this marking in Spanish.

Finally, we have an example of an abstract verb that was irregular in Latin changing its properties to become regular in Spanish. This kind of lexical change is not unheard-of in real verbs: there is a tendency for marked forms to lose their markings—that is, for irregular verbs (or nouns) to become regular. This fact is well known in relation to morphological irregularity. So, for example, *facio* in Latin has an irregular method of forming the passive: it employs a suppletive form *fio*. But in Spanish the passive of *hacer* is regularly formed, *hacerse*. The case presented here is an example of a syntactic property of a verb becoming more regular. The case is that of the abstract verb of wanting or meaning, [*vol*], found in purpose clauses.

In Latin, [*vol*] was irregular in the same way that [*vel*] was: it could undergo only *ut*-subjunctive complementizer-change. In Spanish, on the other hand, purpose clauses behave precisely as verbs of wanting and wishing behave.

(15a)   Fui a Madrid para ver a mi amigo. 'I went to Madrid to see my friend.'

(15b)   Fui a Madrid para que Juan hablase conmigo. 'I went to Madrid so that John might speak with me.'

In (15a), the subject of [*vol*], which must be identical to that of the main verb, is identical to that of *ver*. According to Redundancy Rule 5, when there is identity between the subject of a verb of wanting and the subject of the embedded sentence, *for-to* complementizer-change is obligatory. Normally, the only way to say (15a) in Spanish is by using the infinitive, although very rare exceptions are found (and are found equally rarely after verbs of wanting), and native speakers recognize these sentences as exceptional. Likewise, (15b) is the only possibility if the subjects are not identical, again with rare exceptions. Thus, purpose clauses in Spanish behave just like verbs of wanting and wishing and unlike any other class of verbs. The only way to account for the behavior of these sentences in Spanish is to assume an abstract verb [*vol*], which behaves like a regular verb of wanting.

6.7 Changes in Other Complementation Rules

The changes occurring in the other rules that we have discussed can be considered briefly. Passivization must operate in Spanish, but we do not know whether its form has changed: we do not know what its form is in Latin, or in English, for that matter.

Flip must operate in Spanish to produce sentences like (16). In the first, only flip has operated; in the second, *it*-substitution operates as well.

(16a)   Me parece que Juan esta enfermo. 'It seems to me that John is sick.'

(16b)   Juan me parece estar enfermo. 'John seems to me to be sick.'

In Spanish, as in Latin, we have no clear evidence for extraposition, but the evidence is lacking for slightly different reasons. We commonly find sentences like the following:

(17)   Es probable que Juan fué a Madrid ayer. 'It's probable that John went to Madrid yesterday.'

If sentence (17) were *Lo es probable* ..., this sentence would be evidence for extraposition. But *lo*-deletion is apparently obligatory in Spanish except under special circumstances, and **Lo es probable que* ... is not grammatical. This sentence could still be considered evidence for extraposition on the strength of the fact that the subject noun phrase with *que* follows the verb. But Spanish, although it is not a free-word-order language and therefore has no scrambling rule, nonetheless does have an optional rule that changes the order of subject and verb. Thus we have *Yo quiero ir a Madrid* and *Quiero yo ir a Madrid*. Sentence (17) may be an example of interchange of the subject (*lo que Juan ... ayer*) and the verb (*es probable*), followed by obligatory *lo*-deletion, rather than a case of extraposition.

That-deletion, found in both Latin and English, does not operate in Spanish. Thus, **Digo Juan viene* is not grammatical; *Digo que Juan viene* is the only possibility. This appears to be true both with *que*-indicative and *que*-subjunctive.

Preposition-deletion does not operate at all in Spanish:

(18a)   Consintimos en el plan. 'We consented to the plan.'

(18b)   Consintimos en que Juan fuese. 'We consented to it that John should go.'

In these sentences, *consentir en*, 'agree to,' is like the verbs in English that take prepositions other than *of*. But even these prepositions are deleted before *that* and *for-to* in English. They are never deleted in Spanish. *It*-deletion, as we pointed out earlier, is obligatory. *For*-deletion seems also to be obligatory, since there is no evidence in Spanish of this complementizer at all: either the subject noun phrase undergoes equi-NP-deletion, or it undergoes *it*-substitution. In either of these cases, the preposition is deleted obligatorily.[6]

6.8 Conclusions

In this chapter, we have discussed at length the changes that took place between Latin and Spanish in several of the governed rules of the complement system. In these cases, the superficial syntax of Spanish appears very different from that of Latin. The first assumption one might make in these cases is that changes had taken place in the transformational component of the grammar, either adding, deleting, or reordering rules, or changing the form of these rules. But in none of the cases examined is this the way to interpret the change. What seems to have happened, instead, is that the redundancy rules governing the application of these rules in specific meaning-classes of verbs have undergone change, and these redundancy rules alone have been changed. This is not presented as a well-established theoretical position, that governed rules do not change their form, for lack of sufficient evidence. More research on this question must be done. If it turns out that we have been dealing here with special cases and that there exist in language examples of governed rules that have changed in time, this is not to be considered surprising but, rather, the expected conclusion. We know of cases where ungoverned rules change, and we know of nothing that differentiates governed from ungoverned rules in such a way as to cause them to differ with respect to their diachronic behavior. If, however, the conclusion presented here for these few cases should prove to be true, it will show that there is more difference between governed and ungoverned rules than there is now thought to be, and this will be a starting point for a great deal of crucial work on syntax and syntactic change.

Notes

1. The reader is referred for discussion to the following works: J. Foley, *Spanish Morphology*, doctoral dissertation (unpublished), Cambridge, Mass.: M.I.T., 1965. P. Kiparsky, *Phonological Change*, doctoral dissertation (unpublished), Cambridge, Mass.: M.I.T., 1965.
2. For example, as early as Plautus *habeo factum* is used with the meaning 'I have (something) done,' a meaning very close to 'I have done (something).' *Fidem quam*

habent spectatam iam et diu cognitam. (Cic. Caec. 11) 'The faith that they have already seen and long known.'

3. For example, in "Relatedness between Grammatical Systems," *Language*, Vol. 40, No. 1 (January–March 1964), pp. 1–20.

4. This idea has been expressed before, for example, by Brugmann ("Die mit dem Suffix *-to-* gebildeten Partizipia im Verbalsystem des Lateinischen und des Umbrisch-Oskischen," *Indogermanische Forschungen*, Vol. V (1894), pp. 89–152):

   Das hat man hier, sonst gewöhnlich, unter Grazismus nicht zu verstehen, dass der lateinischen Sprache etwas ihr von Haus aus völlig Fremdes aufgepfropft wurde, sondern es wurde nur ein seinem Ursprung nach echt einheimischer Anwendungstypus, weil er im Griechischen ein von den Römern empfundenes Analogon hatte, nach diesen ausländischen Muster weiter ausgebildet.

5. The beginnings of this change can be seen as early as late Vulgar Latin: *Per nos ipsos non volumus emendare, sed quod ante nos veniat* (*Formulae Salicae Merkelianae* 259, 33), 'We do not wish to change by ourselves, but [we wish] that it may come before us.' It is not clear how to interpret this example; we do not know whether the writer was familiar enough with Latin not to make mistakes in complementizer-change. If he was familiar with Latin to that degree, this sentence may reflect the fact that the Spanish redundancy rule had its origin in Vulgar Latin. If, on the other hand, he was a speaker of a proto-Romance language that contained this rule, he might merely have been applying a rule of his own language to Latin, much as the author of the *Bellum Hispaniense*, cited in the text earlier, did with Greek. This sentence and numerous others like it also indicate that the change from *ut* to *quod* occurred in Latin itself, rather than separately in the individual Romance languages. *Quod* (both the complementizer and the relative pronoun), then changed to *quid*, the interrogative form; but this was purely morphological and did not affect the meaning. *Quod* was apparently first extended into object complements, with the indicative, at least as early as Petronius, and probably earlier. After this, *ut* was replaced everywhere by *quod*, leaving the subjunctive complementizer on the verb. All cases of *quod* then changed to *quid*.

6. It is possible that there is one case of the preposition being retained, but this is very speculative. It is probable that, if the preposition were to appear, it would appear as the preposition *a*, which means 'for-to,' as well as functioning as the direct object marker with animate nouns. Because it functions as direct object marker, it appears to be the replacement in Spanish of the accusative case ending and is therefore a likely candidate for the equivalent of Accusative in the accusative-infinitive complementizer. In the infinitive of ordering described previously, we sometimes find sentences like ¡*A callar!* with the same meaning as ¡*Callar!* It is perhaps possible to hypothesize that *a* is retained here, alone in Spanish as far as I know, after the noun phrase has been deleted. (The noun is always the second person pronoun and is always deleted in this situation. Thus, this noun phrase-deletion is not like equi-NP-deletion or preposition-deletion that results from *it*-substitution but may be ordered later than preposition-deletion, and hence preposition-deletion will not apply here.) This occurrence of *a* is not to be confused with its use after certain verbs, such as *esforzarse a*, 'strive to,' in *Yo me esfuerzo a acabar este capitulo*, 'I am striving to finish this chapter,' where *a* is a preposition that is part of the verb itself, rather than one introduced as a complementizer, and is parallel to *for* in *hope for*.

Bibliography

Allen, J. H., and J. B. Greenough (1931). *New Latin Grammar*⁴. Boston: Ginn & Company.

Bennett, C. E. (1910–1914). *Syntax of Early Latin*. (2 vols.) Boston: Allyn & Bacon.

Bolinger, D. (1967). "The Imperative in English," in *To Honor Roman Jakobson*. The Hague: Mouton & Company.

Bourciez, E. (1930). *Eléménts du linguistique romane*³. Paris: Klincksieck.

Brenous, J. (1965). *Etudes sur les hellénismes dans la syntaxe latine*. Rome: "L'Erma" di Bretschneider.

Chomsky, N. (1957). *Syntactic Structures*. The Hague: Mouton & Company.

―――― (1962). "A Transformational Approach to Syntax," in A. A. Hill (ed.), *Proceedings of the 1958 Conference on Problems of Linguistic Analysis in English*, pp. 124–148. Austin, Texas.

―――― (1965a). *Aspects of the Theory of Syntax*. Cambridge, Mass.: M.I.T. Press.

―――― (1965b). "Topics in the Theory of Generative Grammar," in T. A. Sebeck (ed.), *Current Trends in Linguistics, Vol. III. Linguistic Theory*. The Hague: Mouton & Company.

―――― (1966). "The Current Scene in Linguistics," *College English*, Vol. 27, No. 8 (May), pp. 587–595.

Dahl, B. (1882). *Die Lateinischen Partikel Ut*. Prog. Kristiania: Grondahl & Son.

Ernout, A., and A. Meillet (1959). *Dictionnaire étymologique de la latine*⁴. Paris: Klincksieck.

Ernout, A., and F. Thomas (1953). *Syntaxe Latine²*. Paris: Klincksieck.

Foulet, L. (1923). *Petite syntaxe de l'ancien français²*. Paris: Champion.

Greenberg, J. H. (ed.) (1963). *Universals of Language*. Cambridge, Mass.: M.I.T. Press.

Hahn, E. A. (1966). "Verbal Nouns and Adjectives in Some Ancient Languages," *Language*, Vol. 42, No. 2 (April–June), pp. 378–398.

Handford, S. A. (1947). *The Latin Subjunctive*. London: Methuen.

Hanssen, F. (1945). *Gramatica historica de la lengua castellana*. Buenos Aires: El Ateneo.

Hirt, H. (1937). *Indogermanische Grammatik*, Vol. VII (Syntax II). Heidelberg: Carl Winters.

Humbert, J. (1954). *Syntaxe grecque²*. Paris: Klincksieck.

Jeanjaquet, J. (1894). *Recherches sur l'origine de la conjonction " que."* Neuchâtel: Attinger Frères.

Katz, J. J., and P. M. Postal (1964). *An Integrated Theory of Linguistic Descriptions*. Cambridge, Mass.: M.I.T. Press.

Klima, E. (1964). "Negation in English," in J. A. Fodor and J. J. Katz (eds.), *The Structure of Language: Readings in the Philosophy of Language*. Englewood Cliffs, N.J.: Prentice-Hall.

Lakoff, G. (1965). *On the Nature of Syntactic Irregularity*. Report No. NSF-16, Mathematical Linguistics and Automatic Translation to the National Science Foundation. Cambridge, Mass.

———, and S. Peters (1966). "Phrasal Conjunction and Symmetrical Predicates," in Report No. NSF-17, Mathematical Linguistics and Automatic Translation to the National Science Foundation. Cambridge, Mass.

———, and J. R. Ross (in preparation). *The Transformational Component*.

———, and J. R. Ross (forthcoming). *The Abstractness of Underlying Structures*.

Lindsay, W. M. (1894). *The Latin Language*. Oxford: Clarendon Press.

Meillet, A., and J. Vendryes (1960). *Traité de grammaire comparée des langues classiques³*. Paris: Champion.

Perrochat, P. (1892). *Recherches sur le valeur et l'emploi de l'infinitif subordonné en Latin*. Paris: Soc. d'Edition " Les Belles Lettres."

Postal, P. M. (1965). "Underlying and Superficial Linguistic Structure," *Harvard Educational Review*, Vol. 34, pp. 246–266.

Ramsay, M. M., and R. D. Spaulding (1965). *A Textbook of Modern Spanish*. New York: Holt, Rinehart & Winston.

Rosenbaum, P. S. (1967). *The Grammar of English Predicate Complement Constructions*. Cambridge, Mass.: M.I.T. Press.

———, and R. Jacobs (1967). *Grammar I and Grammar II*. Boston: Ginn & Company.

Ross, J. R. (1967). *Constraints on Variables in Syntax*. Doctoral dissertation (unpublished), Cambridge, Mass.: M.I.T.

Smyth, H. W. (1963). *Greek Grammar³*. Cambridge, Mass.: Harvard University Press.

Thomas, F. (1938). *Recherches sur le subjonctif latin, histoire et valeur des formes.* Paris: Klincksieck.

Vaananen, V. (1963). *Introduction au latin vulgaire.* Paris: Klincksieck.

Woodcock, E. C. (1958). *A New Latin Syntax.* Cambridge, Mass.: Harvard University Press.

Index